Unlocking Hidden Potential

Strategic Transformation and Value Creation at Mandarin Orchard Singapore and Mandarin Gallery

NUS National University of Singapore

LKY Lee Kuan Yew School of Public Policy
ASIA COMPETITIVENESS INSTITUTE

In 2019, ACI was ranked 12th globally, 2nd in Asia, and 1st in Singapore amongst 94 think tanks worldwide under the "Best University Affiliated Think Tank" category by the Think Tanks and Civil Societies Program at the University of Pennsylvania, USA.

About ACI

The Asia Competitiveness Institute (ACI) was established in August 2006 as a Research Centre at the Lee Kuan Yew School of Public Policy (LKYSPP), National University of Singapore (NUS). It aims to build the intellectual leadership and network for understanding and developing competitiveness in the Asia region. ACI seeks to contribute to the enhancement of inclusive growth, living standards, and institutional governance through competitiveness research on sub-national economies in Asia. It identifies mitigating issues and challenges for potential public policy interventions through close collaboration with regional governments, business corporations, policy think-tanks, and academics. ACI's three key research pillars include (I) Sub-national economies level competitiveness analysis and city-level liveability analysis; (II) Firm-level competitiveness analysis in 16 Asia economies; and (III) Singapore's long-term growth strategies and public policy analysis.

ACI's value propositions may be encapsulated in its acronym:
Analytical inputs to initiate policies for policy-makers and business leaders in Asia
Capacity building to enable others through improvement in productivity and efficiency
Intellectual leadership to create pragmatic models of competitiveness and inclusive growth

The institute's core research competencies can also be encapsulated in this acronym describing our evidence-based assessments conducted on public policies for **A**SEAN in the context of the rise of **C**hina and **I**ndia.

Vision and Mission

- ACI's over-arching vision is to build up its research credibility with policy impact, contributing as a professional, world-class think-tank.
- ACI's mission is to establish our niche as a leading policy think-tank by identifying competitiveness trends, opportunities, and challenges, as well as promoting competition and synergizing complementarities amongst Asian economies and business corporations.
- ACI endeavours to articulate sound recommendations, entice discourse, and shape agenda in the arena of public policy amongst Asian governments.
- ACI undertakes evidence-based analysis of public policy issues and decisions, in order to provide assessment of their effectiveness as well as economic and societal impact.

Research Initiatives and Collaborations

I. Identify trends of competitiveness and policy analysis on trade and investment of ASEAN, within the regional context of competition and complementarities with China and India.

II. Identify competitive strengths and conduct policy analysis on Singapore within the context of regional economies with international benchmarking.

III. We are regularly releasing three indices on liveability ranking including 64 Global Cities, 100 Greater China Cities, and 17 Shandong Cities.

IV. We have established an Ease of Doing Business (EDB) Index on Attractiveness to Investors, Business Friendliness, and Competitive Policies for 21 sub-national economies of India and 33 sub-national economies of Indonesia.

V. We have signed Memoranda of Understanding (MoU) with The World Bank (2015), Enterprise Singapore formally known as SPRING Singapore (2014) and European Central Bank (2014). The MoU between The World Bank and National University of Singapore, coordinated through ACI, was signed in 2016.

VI. We have signed MoUs with various institutions in Greater China economies, including Institute of Economics at Shanghai Academy of Social Sciences (2019), Institute of World Economics at Shanghai Academy of Social Sciences (2016), Shandong Academy of Social Sciences (2015), Chongqing Municipal People's Government (2015), China Institute for Reform and Development, Haikou (2015), Counsellors' Office of the People's Government of Guangdong Province (LOI, 2014), and Chung-Hua Institution for Economic Research, Taiwan (2015).

VII. We have signed MoUs with seven Chief Ministers' Offices in Uttarakhand (2019), Andhra Pradesh (2018, 2017 & 2015), Bihar (2015), Chhattisgarh (2015), Madhya Pradesh (2015), Odisha (2015), and Punjab (2015).

VIII. We have signed a MoU with Committee for Acceleration of Priority Infrastructure Delivery at Coordinating Ministry for Economic Affairs, Indonesia (2016), Indonesia Investment Coordinating Board (2014), Indonesian Agency for Agricultural Research and Development at Ministry of Agriculture (2014), Indonesian President's Delivery Unit for Developing Monitoring and Oversight (2013), and Employer's Association of Indonesia (2013).

IX. We have signed MoUs with Asian think-tanks and institutions, including Institute of Economic Growth, India (2018), Vietnam Chamber of Commerce and Industry, Vietnam (2016), Centre for Strategic and International Studies, Indonesia (2015), Institute of Strategic & International Studies, Malaysia (2015), Philippine Institute for Development Studies, the Philippines (2015), Thailand Development Research Institute, Thailand (2015), and Central Institute for Economic Management, Vietnam (2015).

About ACI's Research Pillars

ACI has consciously engaged in economic research that has significant relevance to Singapore and the Asian region. Over the years, ACI has focused on our expertise in quantitative competitiveness analysis and simulation, spinning off volumes of research output in the applications of our methodology and regional insight. At this stage, ACI has identified three core research pillars that will guide and define its research efforts moving forward. The three research pillars are as follows:

Pillar I. Sub-national Economies Competitiveness Analysis

ACI engages in systematic and methodical competitiveness analyses of the sub-national economies by using an evidence-based, empirical approach involving a comprehensive list of relevant indicators, which are categorised under multiple layers called the 'environments'. A number of our projects, including competitiveness analyses of Greater China, ASEAN-10, India, and Indonesia, as well as other thematic research projects, were conducted by adopting this common methodology, with potential variations in the specific environments and indicators. ACI's competitiveness analysis of Asian economies goes beyond the usual ranking to offer constructive policy recommendations on how individual member states can improve their rankings vis-à-vis their sub-national or regional peers through the application of the 'what-if' simulation, which provides the projected improvements of each state's ranking whereby the bottom one-fifth of its indicators are enhanced.

Pillar II. Micro-based Firm Level Competitiveness Analysis

Micro-based firm level competitiveness analysis is ACI's second research pillar that has been developed in view of the intrinsic importance of firm-level competitiveness in terms of productivity, efficiency, and governance. In the context of globalisation, mobility of economic activities, and blurring of borders, an understanding of the determinants and dynamics of firm-level competitiveness is paramount, in order for policy makers to adjust and prepare their industries for an increasingly competitive economic landscape. To this end, ACI has partnered with the European Central Bank to carry out research in this area, possessing a solid foundation in firm-level productivity research in the form of European Competitiveness Network database and methodology. ACI envisaged the expansion of Competitiveness Research Network (CompNet) into Asia, thereby pioneering the Asia's CompNet in encompassing 16 economies in Asia.

Pillar III. Singapore's Long-term Economic Growth Strategies and Public Policies Analysis

The third and imminent research pillar focuses on Singapore's long-term economic growth strategies in the context of changing circumstances, future trends, and emerging opportunities for Singapore in the decades ahead. In particular, ACI will take on the task of critically examining Singapore's public policy strengths and areas of improvement by assessing policy successes of the past, identifying new issues to address and the current policy gaps, through a systematic and evidence-based research inquiry using quantitative methodology and empirical data, leveraging on our network of policy experts.

Founding Patron and International Advisory Panel

Founding Patron

Mr George Yeo
Visiting Scholar, Lee Kuan Yew School of Public Policy, National University of Singapore & Former Minister of Foreign Affairs, Singapore

International Advisory Panel

Co-Chairs:

Professor Michael Porter (2006-2010)
Bishop William Lawrence University Professor

Ms Marjorie Yang (2006-2012)
Chairman, Esquel Group

Members:

Professor Kishore Mahbubani
Former Dean, Lee Kuan Yew School of Public Policy, National University of Singapore

Dr Kuntoro Mangkusubroto
Former Head, President's Delivery Unit for Developing Monitoring and Oversight (UKP4), Indonesia

Mr Narayana Murthy
Former Chairman, Infosys Technologies Limited

Mr Philip Yeo
Former Chairman, Enterprise Singapore

Mr Loh Khum Yean
Permanent Secretary, Ministry of Trade and Industry

Ms Yong Ying-I
Permanent Secretary, Public Service Division

Professor Chan Kam Leung Alan
Former Dean, College of Humanities, Arts and Social Sciences, Nanyang Technological University

Asia Competitiveness Institute

Co-Directors:

Associate Professor Tan Khee Giap (2011 till now)
Professor Tan Kong Yam (2011 till now)

Unlocking Hidden Potential

Strategic Transformation and Value Creation at Mandarin Orchard Singapore and Mandarin Gallery

Harminder C. Rajan
Adjunct Instructor, Asia Competitiveness Institute
Lee Kuan Yew School of Public Policy, National University of Singapore

Gareth Tan Guang Ming
Research Assistant, Asia Competitiveness Institute
Lee Kuan Yew School of Public Policy, National University of Singapore

Tan Beng Kai, Evan
Research Associate, Asia Competitiveness Institute
Lee Kuan Yew School of Public Policy, National University of Singapore

Lee Kuan Yew School of Public Policy
Asia Competitiveness Institute
NUS National University of Singapore
World Scientific

Published by

World Scientific Publishing Co. Pte. Ltd.
5 Toh Tuck Link, Singapore 596224
USA office: 27 Warren Street, Suite 401-402, Hackensack, NJ 07601
UK office: 57 Shelton Street, Covent Garden, London WC2H 9HE

British Library Cataloguing-in-Publication Data
A catalogue record for this book is available from the British Library.

UNLOCKING HIDDEN POTENTIAL
Strategic Transformation and Value Creation at Mandarin Orchard Singapore and Mandarin Gallery

ISBN 978-981-121-453-0

Desk Editor: Jiang Yulin

Typeset by Stallion Press
Email: enquiries@stallionpress.com

Printed in Singapore

CONTENTS

PREFACE

Business transformation is never an easy task, as it fundamentally requires a paradigm shift or reinvention, and experience and track records have shown that attempts to activate transformational change of a business venture or organisation have mostly ended in failure. Vision and leadership are paramount in activating transformational change which can be impeded by change burnout, constrained by unsuitable organisational structure, restricted by old corporate culture and, resisted by threat to job security and personality conflicts. Very often, one needs a firm leadership committed to change with a sense of urgency, effective communication and empowerment of ideas so as to not only consolidate wins but also sustain change.

In this Asia Competitiveness Institute Business Case Study Series, we have highlighted how the old hidden potential of the old Mandarin Singapore which was built more than four decades ago as part of a single property comprising both hotel and a shopping arcade were successfully transformed into a top hospitality project now called Mandarin Orchard Singapore and a niche shopping mall known as the Mandarin Gallery, with a combined value now estimated to be worth about $2 billion.

Such a highly entrepreneurial effort and risk-taking business venture is therefore worth an in-depth analysis which could serve as a good business case study for classroom teaching. It can also be a gainful resource for younger entrepreneurs in the fields of hospitality, food and beverages. In fact, it is also an excellent account of decision making for civil servants who were bold enough to approve a brave plan submitted by the property owners to the authorities, much to the pleasant surprise of the management team! I believe readers will find the business case study interesting and beneficial.

Tan Khee Giap, PhD
Co-Director, Asia Competitiveness Institute
Lee Kuan Yew School of Public Policy
National University of Singapore

ACKNOWLEDGEMENT

This report is the first business case undertaken under the Asia Competitiveness Institute-Business Case Study Series (ACI-BCSS) at Lee Kuan Yew School of Public Policy, National University of Singapore.

This business case study, entitled "Unlocking Hidden Potential: Strategic Transformation and Value Creation at Mandarin Orchard Singapore and Mandarin Gallery" explores the transformation of both Mandarin Orchard Singapore (MOS) and Mandarin Gallery (MG) from a financial and non-financial perspective, focusing on the physical restructuring, rebranding and repositioning, human resource initiatives, and, leadership decisions by OUE Enterprise.

This report has benefitted immensely from Associate Professor Tan Khee Giap, Co-Director, Asia Competitiveness Institute in helping to pin down the major research theme and business issues and connecting with the property owner Dr Stephen Riady, Executive Chairman, OUE Enterprise. We would also like to express our appreciation to Brian Riady, and the senior management of Mandarin Orchard Singapore, Mandarin Gallery and OUE Enterprise who were very generous in their time as we conducted multiple interview sessions with them.

The completion of this business case study would not have been possible without the support of our research and administrative colleagues. In particular, we would like to extend our sincere thanks to Professor Tan Kong Yam, Dr Zhang Xuyao, Jigyasa Sharma, Nursyahida Bin Ahmad, Yap Xin Yi, Tracy Cai, Yip Fung Yi Estelle, Nurliyana Binte Yusoff, and Dewi Jelina Ayu Binte Johari.

We place on record our appreciation to the encouragement from Dean Danny Quah.

Harminder Rajan, Gareth Tan Guang Ming and Tan Beng Kai, Evan
Asia Competitiveness Institute
Lee Kuan Yew School of Public Policy
National University of Singapore

ABOUT THE AUTHORS

Harminder Rajan was an adjunct instructor with the Lee Kuan Yew School of Public Policy (LKYSPP), National University of Singapore (NUS) from 2015 to 2017. She is currently an adjunct assistant professor at the College of Business, Embry-Riddle Aeronautical University, Worldwide (Singapore Campus) where she teaches courses related to leadership and human resource management. She is concurrently an adjunct adult educator with the Institute of Adult Learning (IAL) in Singapore. Dr Rajan has previously taught at the NUS Business School and the Singapore Management University (SMU) in the areas of management, leadership and organizational strategy. She also has extensive work experience in the private and not-for-profit sectors in the areas of leadership development, human resource management, curriculum design and training. Dr Rajan earned her doctorate from the George Washington University in the U.S. where she was the recipient of Helen Waters Endowment Fund and Vest Graduate scholarships. She also has a Masters in Human Resource Management from Rutgers University (USA), Graduate Diploma in Education from the University of Adelaide (Australia), Diploma in Human Resource Management, Singapore Institute of Human Resource Management and B.A in English Language and Literature from the National University of Singapore.

Gareth Tan Guang Ming was a Research Assistant at the Asia Competitiveness Institute (ACI), at the Lee Kuan Yew School of Public Policy (LKYSPP), National University of Singapore (NUS). Having graduated with a First Class Honours from the University of York at undergraduate level, Gareth subsequently pursued a Masters in World Literatures in English at the University of Oxford, from which he graduated with a Distinction in 2016. Gareth oversaw the completion of the institute's ACI Business Case Study project on the Mandarin Orchard Singapore. He also assisted with ACI's projects on China and liveability, which include the 2017 Annual Update of the Competitiveness Analysis for 34 Greater China Economies, the Urban Composite Index for 17 Shandong Cities, the Greater China Liveable Cities Index and the Global Liveable Cities Index. Gareth has co-authored an op-ed entitled "Forging a new consensus for the future economy", which was published in *The Straits Times*. His research interests include urban development and liveability, economic development in the Greater China Region, as well as the intersections between foreign policy and economic growth *vis-à-vis* ASEAN member states.

Tan Beng Kai, Evan was a Research Associate with the Asia Competitiveness Institute (ACI) at the Lee Kuan Yew School of Public Policy (LKYSPP), National University of Singapore (NUS). Evan was the project coordinator in charge of conducting and supporting research activities for the Asian Economic Connectivity Vision 2030 (AECV 2030) flagship project on regional integration and the OUE Business Case Study project, and also coordinated the automation of computer-based research processes in ACI. He received certification from the Massachusetts Institute of Technology (MIT) for completing an eight-week Big Data and Social Analytics online course with top marks, taught in the Python programming language. Evan holds a Master's of Management (Finance) from the Melbourne Business School and a Bachelor of Arts, Politics & International Relations (Major) from the University of Melbourne. His research interests include examining the policy challenges and connectivity issues facing the development of a more integrated ASEAN community and market.

LIST OF FIGURES AND TABLES

Chapter 2

Chapter 3

Chapter 4

Chapter 5

Appendix 2

Appendix 3

Appendix 5

Appendix 6

LIST OF ABBREVIATIONS

A&A	Additions and Alterations
ALP	Average Labour Productivity
AOR	Average Occupancy Rate
APM	Arbitrage Pricing Model
ARR	Average Room Rate
CAGR	Compound Annual Growth Rate
CAPM	Capital Asset Pricing Model
CED	Central, Enduring, and Distinctive
CMSL	Capital Market Services License
CWB	Counterproductive Work Behaviours
DBS	Development Bank of Singapore
DCF	Discounted Cash Flow
EBITDA	Earnings Before Interest, Tax, Depreciation and Amortisation
EI	Employee Involvement
F&B	Food and Beverage
GFA	Gross Floor Area
HIO	High Involvement Organisations
HPWP	High-Performance Work Practices
HR	Human Resource
HRM	Human Resource Management
IPO	Initial Public Offering
IR	Integrated Resorts
IVS	International Valuation Standards
M&A	Mergers and Acquisitions
MAS	Monetary Authority of Singapore
MBWA	Management By Walking About
MG	Mandarin Gallery
MOS	Mandarin Orchard Singapore
MTI	Ministry of Trade and Industry
NLA	Net Lettable Area
OE	Operational Efficiency
OECD	Organisation for Economic Co-operation and Development
OI	Organisational Identity
OR	Operational Revenue
OUB	Overseas Union Bank
PATA	Pacific Asia Travel Association

PRC	People's Republic of China
R&D	Research and Development
REIT	Real Estate Investment Trust
RevPAR	Revenues per Available Room
SARS	Severe Acute Respiratory Syndrome
SATO	Spread-at-Origination
SISV	Singapore Institute of Surveyors and Valuers
SME	Small and Medium Enterprises
STB	Singapore Tourism Board
STPB	Singapore Tourist Promotion Board
UOB	United Overseas Bank
UOL	United Overseas Land
URA	Urban Redevelopment Authority
VA	Value-Added
WDA	Workforce Development Agency
WSQ	Workforce Skills Qualification

EXECUTIVE SUMMARY

This report presents a case study of the factors that contributed to the turnaround of Mandarin Orchard Singapore (MOS) and Mandarin Gallery (MG), a high-profile redevelopment project undertaken by OUE Limited after its acquisition in 2006. Mandarin Singapore was built as a single property comprising both a hotel and a shopping arcade more than 40 years ago in 1971. The property was purchased by the Lippo Group in 2006 via a joint venture and underwent a significant refurbishment exercise in 2006. In 2010, it was re-launched featuring an entirely new façade and a transformed high-level shopping gallery occupying four storeys of high-end retail and hospitality.

The study focuses specifically on the business practices and decisions involved in transforming both assets from underutilised investments into profitable and contemporary developments. Utilising a case study approach, the team conducted structured interviews and correspondences with key office holders at OUE Limited and MOS, reviewed archival data and reports, and toured the hotel and gallery.

The report consists of seven main chapters. Chapter 1 will trace the evolution and change of ownership to the present day OUE Limited. Chapter 2 will present the transformational change model and accompanying literature on the key concepts of the model. Chapter 3 will discuss the role of corporate culture and identity in a family-owned business and its impact on corporate strategy. Chapter 4 will highlight the various business policies that were implemented to enhance the performance of the property. Chapter 5 will review the financial strategy and performance of the property. Chapter 6 will focus on the leadership in OUE Limited followed by a concluding chapter.

The findings of the study reiterate that achieving transformational change requires aligning the company strategy with key business components of an organisation, such as finance, human resources, branding and marketing. Along with this, a strong leadership role and corporate culture need to support and champion change efforts within an organisation. Given that the case involves a family-owned business, the report also addresses some best practices to sustain a family-owned business.

Chapter 1
INTRODUCTION

This report outlines the transformation of Mandarin Orchard Singapore (MOS) and Mandarin Gallery (MG), a high-profile redevelopment project undertaken by OUE Limited after the company was acquired in 2006. MOS forms the hotel component while MG forms the retail component of the property, which is strategically located in the heart of Singapore's shopping district, Orchard Road.[1]

The study details the turnaround of MOS and MG, focusing specifically on the business practices and decisions involved in transforming both assets from underutilised investments into profitable and contemporary developments.

The Revamped Mandarin Gallery and Mandarin Orchard Singapore

The report will present an analysis of the performance of the two assets from both financial and non-financial perspectives, focusing on the physical restructuring, rebranding and repositioning of the property, and leadership decisions by OUE Limited's Executive Chairman, Dr Stephen Riady.

This report is targeted at entrepreneurs, government officials, small and medium enterprises (SMEs), family-owned businesses and educational institutes keen on understanding and learning best practices for leading a successful family-owned conglomerate in the hospitality and retail industry.

The methodology used for data collection in the report included conducting structured interviews and correspondences with key office holders at OUE Limited and MOS, reviewing documents such as archival data and current reports, and conducting a tour of the hotel and gallery (see Appendix 1). The series of interviews were conducted with members of the leadership team from OUE Limited and MOS, who played a key role in the transformation and

[1] Mandarin Orchard Singapore and Mandarin Gallery technically form a single legal title and had previously gone by the name "Overseas Union Building". For the purpose of this report, the term "property" mostly refers to both MOS and MG collectively, while "hotel" would typically refer to MOS and "gallery" to MG exclusively.

refurbishment of the property. In addition to the interviews, secondary information from annual reports, financial reports, media releases and restructuring plans were also collected for review. As part of the research, the property tour of the hotel and gallery was conducted to understand the physical restructuring and layout of the property before and after the transformation. Contents of the interviews have been lightly edited for grammatical reasons and readability, and to protect the confidentiality of the research participants, names of interviewees have been omitted where appropriate. Formulas, data values for figures and tables used in this report can be found in the appendices, when specified. Additional relevant information that was not entirely within the scope of the report can be found in the appendices, when mentioned within the report.

1.1 THE EVOLUTION OF THE HOTEL: MANDARIN ORCHARD SINGAPORE

"Mandarin Singapore" was built more than 40 years ago in 1971, as part of a single property, comprising both a hotel and a shopping arcade, which would later go on to become the MOS and MG, respectively. The property underwent a series of ownership transfers before finally being purchased by the Lippo Group in 2006 via a joint venture. Dr Stephen Riady, a Chinese Indonesian, assumed the position of Executive Director of OUE Limited in 2006 and in the

The Original Main Tower of 'Mandarin Singapore' with the Iconic 'Top of the M' Revolving Restaurant Atop It

same year, the property underwent a significant refurbishment exercise.[2] The refurbished property was unveiled in 2009 and featured an entirely new façade, alongside a transformed retail podium, MG, which occupies four storeys of high-end retail and services.

At the time of release of this report in 2019, both MOS and MG continue to be owned and managed by OUE Hospitality Trust, a real estate investment trust (REIT) company formed in 2013.[3] As of end 2014, the combined value of both properties stood at approximately S$1.8 billion.[4]

The hotel has also received numerous accolades, with the earliest mention found to be in the 1994 annual report, when it was rated "one of the top 10 Best Individual Hotels in the world" by the Business Traveller,[5] and has since received awards such as "Best Hotel (Asia Pacific)" in the Asia Pacific Hotel Awards for 2013 to 2014 and "Best Hotel for Singapore" at the International Hotel Awards in 2012 (see Appendix 2).

As of 2016, the MOS hotel consists of two towers, housing 1,077 rooms and 25,511 square feet of meeting and function space, including a grand ballroom. The property also offers a range of high-end retail and dining options, including a multi-level carpark with 441 car parking spaces.[6] The story of MOS, as one of the most iconic hotels in Singapore, begins with its origins in the early 1970s.

Dr Lien Ying Chow (centre) and His Fellow Associates

[2] Dr Riady was appointed as an Executive Director of OUE Limited on 30 November 2006, see Overseas Union Enterprise Limited (2007, p. 3).

[3] See OUE Hospitality Trust (2014a).

[4] As reported in the 2014 annual report, see OUE Hospitality Trust (2015, pp. 37–43).

[5] See Overseas Union Enterprise Limited (1995, p. 5).

[6] See OUE Hospitality Trust (2016).

1.1.1 OVERSEAS UNION BANK BUILDS MANDARIN SINGAPORE IN 1973

"Mandarin Singapore" was one of the earliest hotels to be built in Singapore during the 1970s. The hotel was built by banker Dr Lien Ying Chow, the Founder and Chairman of Overseas Union Bank (OUB),[7] who sought to enter the hospitality industry in 1964.[8] He established a separate company, "Overseas Union Enterprise Limited"[9] in 1964 with the goal of constructing a hotel and shopping arcade housed under the property of the Overseas Union Building.[10]

In November 1971, the hotel was partially opened and featured a French restaurant, bars, a coffee house and 150 rooms opened to the public.[11] The 40-storey hotel was officially opened as "Mandarin Singapore" on 1 August 1973 by then Acting Prime Minister of Singapore, Dr Goh Keng Swee.[12] The luxury hotel included 700 rooms, a shopping arcade and commercial offices, bars such as Mezzanine, The Library and Act One, restaurants such as Chatterbox, Pine Court and the renowned revolving restaurant on the top of the hotel, "Top of the M". The building also featured the Mandarin arcade, a three-storey shopping gallery.

Standing over 40 storeys tall, "Mandarin Singapore" was a landmark hotel at the time and held the claim to being the tallest hotel in South-east Asia.[13] The grandeur of the hotel entrance was evident in its "gold, red and white marble" lobby decorated with "Chinese-inspired canopies of gold leaf", at the centre of which was a "huge hand-made Venetian crystal chandelier fountain".[14] Individual hotel rooms were decorated in a manner which brought to mind an exotically Eastern luxuriance, which was seamlessly blended with elements of state-of-the-art Western technological practicality, such as "phones in the bathroom, bedside TV control remote and individually-controlled air conditioners".[15] Through these approaches, "Mandarin Singapore" quickly became the benchmark by which existing and future luxury hotels in Singapore would measure their excellence.[16]

It was not long after the hotel opened its doors in the 1970s that it gained a reputation in the industry of providing service synonymous with authentic Asian hospitality. The reputation of "Mandarin Singapore" thus came to be tied to a unique brand of excellent customer service.

---

[7] OUB, now defunct, was founded in 1947 in Singapore by Lien Ying Chow. It began operations in February 1949 and by the 1980s had grown into one of Singapore's "Big Four" local banks.

[8] See Lien and Kraar (1992, pp. 95–100).

[9] After an official rebranding exercise in 2013, the company changed its official name used for company filings to "OUE Limited" in place of "Overseas Union Enterprise Limited". Where required, the historical name of "Overseas Union Enterprise Limited" will be used for clarity, otherwise the company is referred to as OUE Limited within this report. See OUE Limited (2013).

[10] See Overseas Union Enterprise Limited (1970, p. 3).

[11] See Overseas Union Enterprise Limited (1972, p. 3).

[12] See Overseas Union Enterprise Limited (1974, pp. 3–5).

[13] See Singapore Visitor (1971).

[14] *Ibid.*

[15] *Ibid.*

[16] See Cunningham and Gerrard (2000).

With forecasts by the Singapore Tourist Promotion Board[17] projecting a significant rise in tourism by 1979,[18] Dr Lien decided to build a second tower (the South Wing) to accommodate the projected increase in demand for hotel rooms. Accordingly, a second extension encompassing an additional 450 rooms, 343 car park lots and a large convention hall was constructed and became operational in 1979.[19]

On 14 December 1978, "Mandarin (Singapore) International Hotels Private Limited" was first incorporated as a locally developed hotel management company which would provide management expertise and training in the international hotel market.[20] This entity would be later renamed "Singapore Mandarin International Hotels Private Limited", the hotel management company of MOS.[21] Subsequently, the "Meritus" brand, whose namesake companies function as the hotel management arm of OUE Limited, was developed in 1997 as a way to increase name recognition and promote public awareness of the hotel while more tangibly linking the various hotels owned by the group (see Appendix 3).[22]

In the early 1980s, the hotel also took measures to enhance productivity, such as computerising labour-intensive operations in the hotel and installing energy-saving devices.[23] However, the sluggish economic environment and a consequent slowdown in tourism led to an oversupply of hotel rooms across the industry. In response, Dr Lien and his team continued to enhance the competitiveness of the hotel by reducing costs and further increasing productivity by upgrading services and facilities, such as the hotel's telephone system, elevators and restaurants.

The sharp but short-lived recession in Singapore in the early 1980s resulted in restructuring and layoffs in 1985,[24] but the buoyant turnaround of the economy which followed enabled the hotel to bounce back and perform well. The major source of revenue for the business during the late 1980s and early 1990s was from the hotel operations due to significant increases in tourist arrivals and higher room rates improving the profitability of "Mandarin Singapore".[25]

[17] First established on 1 January 1964, the "Singapore Tourist Promotion Board (STPB)" was a government statutory board that currently exists as the "Singapore Tourism Board (STB)". The board was renamed on 19 November 1997, as part of the "Tourism 21" plan driven by the then chief executive of the statutory board, Dr Tan Chin Nam. See Ho (2015).

[18] The then "Singapore Tourist Promotion Board" had predicted that Singapore "could become the first Asian country to attract two million tourists" in 1979, which was discussed within the chairman's statement of the 1975 annual report. See Overseas Union Enterprise Limited (1976, p. 5).

[19] See Overseas Union Enterprise Limited (1977, p. 6; 1979, p. 6).

[20] Further details of the roles and changes to the hotel management arms of the company are provided in Appendix 3, and a discussion of the function of the "Mandarin (Singapore) International Private Limited" to pursue international hotel management business opportunities was highlighted in the 1980 annual report. See Overseas Union Enterprise Limited (1981, p. 6).

[21] See OUE Hospitality Trust (2013, p. 29).

[22] See Overseas Union Enterprise Limited (1998, p. 7).

[23] See Overseas Union Enterprise Limited (1982, p. 6).

[24] See Overseas Union Enterprise Limited (1986).

[25] See Overseas Union Enterprise Limited (1991, p. 5).

Dr Lien Ying Chow (left) at a Company Event in 1995

1.1.2 UNITED OVERSEAS BANK ACQUIRES OVERSEAS UNION BANK INCLUDING MERITUS MANDARIN SINGAPORE IN 2001

Despite its rapid growth in the 1990s, Dr Lien's OUB, remained the smallest of the "Big Four" banks in Singapore. In the early 2000s, local banks in Singapore came under pressure from the government to consolidate their assets, causing the bank to become a prime target for acquisition.[26] In 2001, two bigger local banks, United Overseas Bank (UOB) and Development Bank of Singapore (DBS), competed to take over OUB from the Lien family.

A joint press conference was scheduled on 29 June 2001 to announce UOB's "friendly takeover" of OUB for a sum of S$9 billion.[27] OUB, along with "Overseas Union Enterprise Limited", "Mandarin Singapore" and its accompanying assets were correspondingly sold to UOB on 1 June 2002. Mr Wee Cho Yaw was appointed Chairman of "Overseas Union Enterprise Limited"[28] and "Mandarin Singapore" was subsequently renamed "Meritus Mandarin Singapore" in 2003.[29] By the end of 2003, OUB was fully merged with UOB and the OUB brand fell out of use.

Under the ownership of UOB, although the "Meritus Mandarin Singapore" implemented cost-cutting measures in 2002, it subsequently carried out soft refurbishment works on the South Tower in 2004, when S$6 million and S$3 million were spent on upgrading guestrooms and lifts, respectively.[30] In 2003, however, the outbreak of Severe Acute Respiratory Syndrome (SARS)

[26] See Chua (2011).

[27] See United Overseas Bank (2002, p. 4).

[28] See Overseas Union Enterprise Limited (2003, p. 4) on the appointment of Mr Wee to the position of chairman for the company. A prominent Singaporean businessman, Mr Wee was the chief executive officer of UOB from 1974 to 2007. At the time of release of this report in 2016, he holds the position of chairman emeritus of UOB.

[29] See Overseas Union Enterprise Limited (2003, p. 6).

[30] See Overseas Union Enterprise Limited (2005, p. 5).

badly affected the tourism industry in the region, forcing the hotel to implement steep cost reduction initiatives to maintain profitability.[31]

1.1.3 UNITED OVERSEAS BANK SELLS OVERSEAS UNION ENTERPRISE LIMITED IN 2006

In 2006, the "Meritus Mandarin Singapore" property again changed ownership to the current owners, when the Singapore government passed a regulation that required local banks to consolidate assets and divest their non-core business assets (see Appendix 3). Banks such as UOB were given until 17 July 2006 to divest their non-core businesses, subject to the agreement of the authorities.[32]

This new regulation provided the Lippo Group, an Indonesian-based conglomerate, with an opportunity to acquire "Overseas Union Enterprise Limited" and its noteworthy portfolio of properties (see Appendix 3).[33] The rationale for bidding for "Overseas Union Enterprise Limited" is explained as follows by a senior management staff member of the Lippo Group:

> "*...the attraction for the Lippo group in terms of OUE Limited is the property portfolio that it has. It's not just Mandarin Orchard Singapore and Mandarin Gallery, there were also at the point of time other prime properties within the portfolio.*"[34]

In the lead up to the eventual sale of "Overseas Union Enterprise Limited" in 2006, the number of substantial shareholders had reduced considerably from 2004, with shares concentrated in the hands of UOB affiliated entities. The market was still uncertain as to what the fate of "Overseas Union Enterprise Limited" would be.

In 2006, the Lippo Group teamed up with Malaysian tycoon Ananda Krishnan of Usaha Tegas Sendirian Berhad, an investment holding company to buy over "Overseas Union Enterprise Limited" for S$989.9 million, as part of a joint venture.[35] It was during the period between 2006 and 2010 that the redevelopment of MG took place, setting the stage for the hotel's turnaround. However, in 2008, the global financial downturn adversely affected the business environment, resulting in the hotel deploying electronic distribution channels, cost containment actions and more aggressive branding and marketing.[36]

---

[31] See Overseas Union Enterprise Limited (2004, p. 7).

[32] See Monetary Authority Singapore (2003).

[33] The Lippo group is a major Indonesian conglomerate founded by Indonesian businessman Mochtar Riady in the 1960s, with significant investments in real estate, retail, hospitality and healthcare. Both his sons Stephen Riady and James Riady are actively involved in the business. See Chilkoti (2016) for a discussion on the activities of Mochtar Riady and the Lippo Group.

[34] Asia Competitiveness Institute interviews of senior management staff of OUE Limited (2015).

[35] The official divestment notice was released by UOB on 26 May 2006 announcing that "Overseas Union Enterprise Limited" had been sold to Lippo Property Investment Private Limited, see United Overseas Bank (2006). Including the purchase of the controlling stake, it was estimated that the joint venture would require S$1.8 billion "to buy the whole of OUE", see AFX Asia (2006).

[36] See Overseas Union Enterprise Limited (2009, pp. 14–19).

In 2010, differences in managing the strategic direction of the company led to the end of the joint venture between Lippo and Ananda Krishnan. Lippo Group paid S$957 million to acquire Ananda Krishnan's share of OUE Limited.[37] The reason for the purchase was attributed to the different approaches and viewpoints between the two partners about managing the strategic direction of the company. The end of the alliance was described as a move to "strengthen its asset base"[38] and align the vision for the company:

> *"So rather than having two captains putting the ship on autopilot... generally, it was heading that way while building Mandarin Gallery. But when you have one (captain) completely off the boat, and one can put his hands on the tiller, you can drive much faster and in a clearer direction, and you get to a point faster."*[39]

1.2 OUE LIMITED: A NEW BEGINNING

Following the purchase, Dr Riady became Executive Chairman of OUE Limited in 2010.[40] With the consolidation of ownership in 2010, OUE Limited was able to gain enough momentum to become one of the leading property players in the Singapore market by 2015. This was possible because final decision-making power had become concentrated in the hands of Dr Riady alone after the split in 2010, which allowed the Lippo Group to freely pursue a narrow strategic vision for the company and focus its efforts on achieving its goal of prime asset transformation.

Mr S.R. Nathan (left) and Dr Stephen Riady (right)

---

[37] See *Business Times* (2010). The remainder of the company was held by retail and institutional investors.

[38] *Ibid.*

[39] Asia Competitiveness Institute interviews of senior management staff of OUE Limited (2015).

[40] Dr Riady, who had previously been an Executive Director of OUE Limited, was appointed to the position of Executive Chairman of the board, effective 9 March 2010. See Overseas Union Enterprise Limited (2010, p. 18).

The transfer of ownership of OUE Limited to the Lippo Group was a turning point for the company, as it marked the beginning of the transformation of the various properties purchased under the OUE Limited portfolio. OUE Limited would be the centrepiece of the Lippo Group's move to shift its focus in Asia away from Hong Kong and towards Singapore.[41]

Having been appointed as the company's Executive Chairman in 2010, Dr Riady's immediate focus quickly became transforming and enhancing the value of the company's acquired assets, which were underperforming.

> "*...So we didn't just buy one Mandarin Orchard Singapore. We bought a company that owned a number of prime assets. It's a very old asset, 30 years old or something, but they've not done anything with it for the last 30 or 40 years under the bank umbrella. So I thought, there's an opportunity. We acquired it, and I saw that we could enhance many of these assets, create value.*"[42]

Under Dr Riady's leadership, this strategy of transforming underperforming assets and adding value became a defining quality of the OUE Limited strategy and brand. A key decision was the renaming of the hotel from 'Meritus Mandarin Singapore' to 'Mandarin Orchard Singapore' on 28 January 2010 so as to reflect the transformed brand identity following the extensive refurbishments.[43]

1.2.1 THE OUE LIMITED BUSINESS STRATEGY: ASSET ENHANCEMENT AND VALUE CREATION

Following its acquisition in 2006, OUE Limited experienced a resurgence due to its radically transformed business model. This business model, which saw the rapid growth of total assets worth S$1.6 billion in 2006 to S$6.7 billion as of 2014, required meticulous planning and a sound financial strategy coupled with astute business timing and calculated risk-taking.[44]

The business strategy of OUE Limited is succinctly captured in its 2014 annual report titled "Transforming Potential", in which the company lays out its paradigm of transformational thinking towards real estate developments.[45] The company views itself as not just a property company, but an entity that transforms assets by adding value to "wow" its customers, focusing on providing high-end quality products and service standards:

> "*For him (Dr Riady), he doesn't want anything sub-standard, or something that you can be ashamed of, or not proud of. And he is willing to pay for the quality of the product. That is something that is very clear from him.*"[46]

---

[41] See Warden (2010).

[42] Asia Competitiveness Institute interviews of senior management staff of OUE Limited (2015).

[43] As explained by the then General Manager of MOS, "with the hotel having just completed its multi-million-dollar major refurbishment program, as well as having been awarded its ISO 9001:2008 certification, the name change serves as the icing on the cake to complete the repackaged product that is the Grand Dame of Orchard Road". See *eTurboNews* (2010).

[44] See OUE Limited (2007, p. 33; 2015a, p. 30).

[45] See OUE Limited (2015a).

[46] Asia Competitiveness Institute interviews of senior management staff of OUE Limited (2015).

This formula of creating value drives the corporate strategy of OUE Limited, which translates into the company purchasing prime existing properties and assets that are underperforming and priced competitively, but which retain the potential for redevelopment. Hence, OUE's corporate strategy focuses on identifying iconic or well-positioned assets and converting them into quality developments, evident from the previous and existing projects undertaken as of 2016 (see Table A6 in Appendix 3). As Dr Riady shares:

> *"I think I can do more. I don't just buy because it is a commercial building. I buy because I want to add fun to it. I want to bring in the hospitality crowd. This is where I add my value to it."*[47]

In 2013, OUE Limited unveiled a new corporate identity to reflect the direction and dynamism of the group. The new corporate logo represents the group's "depths of experience and knowledge and its capabilities in developing mixed-use urban real estate and luxury spaces".[48]

As of 2014, OUE Limited is a Singapore Exchange listed, fully-integrated property company with a diversified portfolio of prime assets across the retail, commercial, residential, and hospitality sectors, located primarily in Singapore. The company controls S$6.7 billion worth of assets in total, including real estate in Singapore's hospitality, retail, residential and office-space sectors worth a combined S$5.5 billion.[49] Most of OUE Limited's assets are based in Singapore, but the company also has overseas investments in China, Malaysia and the United States (see Appendix 3). As of 2016, OUE Limited's overseas assets exceeded S$1.8 billion in value.[50] The company's consistent business strategy of value creation through asset enhancement will be showcased in subsequent sections of the report, based on the case study of the transformational change of MOS and MG.

---

[47] *Ibid.*

[48] See OUE Limited (2013).

[49] See OUE Limited (2015a, p. 32).

[50] *Ibid.*

CHAPTER 2
TRANSFORMATIONAL CHANGE: SOME THEORETICAL UNDERPINNINGS

Before proceeding to examine the specific steps taken by OUE Limited in enacting transformational change, it is important that we first develop a thorough understanding of what this kind of change actually constitutes. Section 2.1 will present a literature review of the various components based on the model of transformational change, derived as part of the case study to conceptualise and analyse factors that drive transformational change within an organisation.

2.1 OVERVIEW OF TRANSFORMATIONAL CHANGE CYCLE FOR MANDARIN ORCHARD SINGAPORE AND MANDARIN GALLERY

Transformational change has been defined by some scholars as a paradigm shift from old ways of thinking to new mindsets and underlying assumptions.[1] Others describe this kind of change as a "reengineering effort" by an organisation where a new vision is translated into a set of norms and behaviours to guide employees.[2] Another particularly useful definition can be derived from Goss, Pascale and Athos, who assert that "when a company reinvents itself, it must alter the underlying assumptions and invisible premises on which its decisions and actions are based".[3] Accordingly, at its most fundamental, transformational change involves a paradigm shift or reinvention, where old assumptions and mindsets are roundly reassessed and replaced with new norms and assumptions.

The transformational change cycle model (Figure 2.1) proposes that the process of transformational change begins with the leader's vision and leadership, which influences the development of corporate culture and values within an organisation. This in turn guides the formulation of appropriate business and financial strategies to support and sustain the transformational change process.

2.1.1 TRANSFORMATIONAL CHANGE

The cycle of transformation change begins with a leader's vision or a long-term goal of what the company wants to achieve or become. Vision is defined as a leader's ability to envisage different and positive images leading to the development of company goals.[4] Articulating the big picture or strategic vision provides a clear, common goal for employees, empowering them to act with an insight into the overall objective their individual contributions are building towards. In

[1] See Kuhn (1970).

[2] See Denning (2005).

[3] See Goss, Pascale and Athos (1998, p. 86).

[4] See Ionescu (2014, p. 66), Achua and Lussier (2013, p. 316).

Figure 2.1 Transformational Change Cycle for Mandarin Orchard Singapore and Mandarin Gallery

Source: Asia Competitiveness Institute

contrast, the absence of such an overarching vision imperils the project and raises the risk that transformational change efforts "dissolve into a list of confusing and incompatible projects".[5]

The model thus suggests that the leader's vision acts as a catalyst for transformational change, as it provides a common purpose and aligns the varied efforts of employees to a single goal. The role of leaders in a cycle of transformational change is thus paramount, as they need to communicate their visions effectively and assure employees that the agenda for change can be translated into suitable, attainable processes and policies within the organisation.[6]

Based on the transformational change cycle, a leader's vision propels the process of transformational change based on three key drivers: (i) corporate culture and values, (ii) competitive business policies for asset enhancement and (iii) corporate finance strategy. These drivers constitute the actual strategies designed by the company to implement transformational change in MOS. Section 2.1.2 will discuss these three drivers of transformational change in greater detail.

2.1.2 THE THREE DRIVERS OF TRANSFORMATIONAL CHANGE

The first driver, "corporate culture and values", refers to the role of corporate culture in shaping new behaviours in the organisation. Corporate culture is defined as "the collection of beliefs,

[5] See Kotter (1995, p. 9).

[6] *Ibid.*

expectations and values learned and shared" by employees.[7] Therefore, corporate culture reinforces and espouses desired employee behaviours to deliver a company's vision and overall corporate strategy. Based on the model, corporate culture and values include components such as management ethos, branding and corporate identity, and the specific culture of a family-owned business.

The second driver in the model, "competitive business policies", refers to the formulation of a clear corporate strategy and corresponding business policies to achieve the organisation's goals. Hence, OUE Limited's corporate strategy of value enhancement is translated into a gamut of competitive business initiatives that include productivity improvement, price and even competitiveness, human resource policies and company repositioning.

The third driver, "corporate finance strategy", refers to the overall financing strategy needed to drive and support the company's corporate strategy and business policies. In the case of MOS, risk and return analyses facilitated the adoption of financing models and investment strategies which aligned appropriately with the overarching corporate strategy and company vision.

The following sections will present a thorough literature review of these three sets of drivers and their respective components in the transformational change cycle, beginning first with a discussion in Section 2.2 of transformational change and the role of leadership in facilitating such a change. Section 2.3 will proceed to examine how the first driver, corporate culture can initiate and sustain transformational change. Section 2.4 will present the literature on competitive business policies related to human resource, price and product competitiveness. Finally, Section 2.5 will analyse the financing and investment decisions that guide corporate financing in implementing transformational change.

2.2 DEFINING TRANSFORMATIONAL CHANGE

Transformational change is viewed as a broader and more fundamental cultural change involving the reengineering of processes, structures or underlying assumptions.[8] Factors that may drive transformational change include changes in company culture, organisational strategy and changes in leadership due to acquisitions or mergers.

Some researchers have attempted to explain transformational change based on specific dimensions, such as depth, scope and speed.[9] Depth refers to radical rather than superficial change, while scope consists of change executed at the organisation level. Although transformational change is focused on the long term, there is an implicit notion that short-term changes such as "sudden shifts in views" and "moments of insights" can also occur, resulting in deep-level paradigm shifts which resonate widely within the organisation.[10]

Executing transformational change is no easy task and studies show that only 70 percent of change initiatives are ultimately successful.[11] Figure 2.2 highlights some commonly cited obstacles that hinder change efforts.[12]

[7] See Wheelen et al. (2015, p. 158).

[8] See Adeniji et al. (2013).

[9] See Termeer et al. (2016, p. 5).

[10] *Ibid.*

[11] See Al-Haddad and Kotnour (2005), Beer and Nohria (2000)

[12] See Al-Haddad and Kotnour (2005), Denning (2005) and Smith (2002).

Figure 2.2 Factors That Impede Transformational Change

1.	Poor leadership
2.	Change burnout
3.	Unsuitable organisational structure
4.	Lack of change agents
5.	Lack of employee participation
6.	Competing commitments
7.	Inertia
8.	Threat to job security
9.	Lack of trust
10.	Personality conflicts
11.	Work-group break-up

Source: Adapted from Dent and Goldberg (1999)[13]

Some of the reasons commonly cited for failed change efforts include an inappropriate or deficient leader or management team, and a lack of understanding of change implementation techniques. Another factor for the high failure rate is employees' perception of change as being "disruptive" and "painful", where employees who are used to a certain way of doing things resist the implementation of new policies and processes.[14] In order to mitigate these challenges, organisations that undergo transformational change need to ensure that the change process or method is systematic and well executed.[15] Section 2.2.1 will present some models of transformational change that guide the process of change in an organisation.

2.2.1 TRANSFORMATIONAL CHANGE MODELS

Most change models assert that both leaders and employees have a critical part to play to sustain change.

Kotter's eight-step model of transformation (Figure 2.3) proposes that management first needs to instil a sense of "urgency" by examining the market and identifying threats and opportunities that exists in the environment. Following this, an employee coalition or team is established to champion the change by creating and communicating a vision that is "emotionally appealing and strategically smart" to obtain employee buy-in.[16] Managers should also empower employees by removing obstacles and motivating employees to execute the change. The final steps in the model recommend that management celebrate and recognise success and small wins, while establishing measures to consolidate change so that it is continuous and institutionalised.[17]

[13] See Dent and Goldberg (1999, p. 28).

[14] See Gilley and McMillan (2009).

[15] See Al-Haddad and Kotnour (2005), Beer and Nohria (2000).

[16] See Kotter (2012, p. 9).

[17] See Kotter (1995).

Figure 2.3 Kotter's Eight Steps to Transforming an Organisation

1.	Establishing a sense of urgency
2.	Form a strong guiding coalition
3.	Develop a vision
4.	Communicate new vision
5.	Empower and encourage ideas
6.	Plan short-term wins
7.	Consolidate wins and sustain change
8.	Institutionalise new behaviours

Source: Adapted from Kotter (1995)[18]

The term "change master" has been coined by some scholars to describe individuals and organisations who are "greatly adept at the art of anticipating the need for, and leading, productive change".[19] Such companies constantly challenge the status quo and prepare for the future by being aware of the external environment, so that change becomes a way of life. In change-adept organisations, leaders practice "kaleidoscope thinking" and are future-oriented, facilitating a higher success rate of orchestrating change.[20]

Figure 2.4 outlines another model that depicts how organisations can prepare for and manage change. Similar to Kotter's change model, Kanter's framework emphasises the need to communicate a vision and build a coalition or support group to "sponsor" or disseminate that vision. A coalition support can only be developed if a leader transfers the ownership and nurtures others in the organisation to reinforce and consolidate the change.

Another model of change that stresses the involvement of managers in disseminating change efforts is shown in Figure 2.5.[21] Consistent with the earlier models, this framework proposes that effective change requires developing a shared vision, mobilising employees to commit to change, and formalising the change process through policies and procedures. However, the process also suggests that a critical aspect of corporate renewal should involve empowering line managers to promote the change rather than push for a top-down change agenda.

Therefore, most of the change management models presented in this section emphasise three key aspects, namely articulating a vision, communicating the vision and enlisting the support of others within the organisation to disseminate and reinforce the change process.

[18] *Ibid* (p. 2).

[19] See Kanter (2000, p. 13).

[20] *Ibid*.

[21] See Beer et al. (1990).

Figure 2.4 Kanter's 10 Commandments for Executing Change

1. Analyse the organisation's need for a change
2. Lead and unite the organisation with vision
3. Isolate structures and routines from the past
4. Instil a sense of urgency
5. Motivate and compensate employees
6. Garner coalition
7. Plan a roadmap for change
8. Provide structures to support change
9. Communicate and involve employees
10. Reinforce and institutionalise change

Source: Adapted from Kanter et al. (1992)[22]

Figure 2.5 Beer's Six Steps to Effective Change

1. Mobilise commitment to change through joint problem-solving
2. Develop a shared vision of organising and managing resources and information
3. Promote consensus for the new vision, provide training and manage competencies
4. Spread revitalisation to all departments through collaboration (bottom-up approach)
5. Institutionalise revitalisation by adapting structures, policies, and systems
6. Monitor and respond by adjusting strategies to resolve challenges

Source: Adapted from Beer et al. (2000)[23]

2.2.2 ROLE OF LEADERSHIP IN TRANSFORMATIONAL CHANGE

Many studies acknowledge that a key factor of success for transformational change is the ability of leaders in the organisation to act as change agents, particularly if it is an organisation-wide change effort.[24]

---

[22] See Kanter et al. (1992, p. 383).

[23] See Beer et al. (2000, p. 181).

[24] See Kotter (1995) and Beer and Nohria (2000).

Based on the transformational change models discussed above, and as reiterated earlier in this report, a key role of a leader in transformational change is to articulate a clear vision and motivate employees to realise the vision. Some scholars compare the leader's role in steering a changing organisation as being akin to a "long march", as it requires steering the organisation to alter its priorities towards new initiatives and goals, while maintaining the flexibility and stamina to effect the change. Therefore, a leader needs to demonstrate qualities such as passion, innovation and confidence to develop and lead a new narrative.[25] Other qualities include being "persuasive" and "compelling" so that employees are encouraged to forgo the status quo and embrace a new future.[26]

Given the potential resistance to change, management needs to address the "human side of change" by focusing on specific behaviours such as motivating others and communicating effectively.[27] In order to nurture such leaders, organisations should promote a "culture of leadership", where employees with leadership potential are given opportunities to develop their leadership skills so that they can sustain and drive the vision and business strategies.

Some studies argue that it is not personality or management style, but rather internal "action logic" which determines how leaders respond to change management initiatives. Different leaders possess varied kinds of action logic, which determine their leadership profile.[28] This is further explained in Figure 2.6, which elaborates on the various action logics possessed by leaders.

According to the leadership profiles, leaders should first make an effort to examine their own action logic and then work at changing their style to be more effective in their role. In terms of change management efforts, leadership styles such as "The Strategist", "Individualists" and "Alchemist" were found to be the most effective in "transforming", "renewing" and "reinventing their organisation in historically significant ways". On the other hand, leaders who were characterised as "Opportunists", "Diplomats" and "Experts" were least likely to succeed at implementing organisational initiatives.[29] The model argues that leaders need to be self-aware of their leadership style and that only those who are able to transform their action logic to adopt new interpersonal behaviours will succeed in their role.

Other studies on leadership and change make a distinction between a participative and autocratic style of change management such as Theory E and O (Figure 2.7).[30] Theory E refers to economic value or shareholder return, where the goal is to maximise returns using a top-down approach. Leaders who follow Theory E tend to focus on the "hardware" of the organisation and rely more on external consultants. Theory O, on the other hand, advocates using a "soft" or participative approach to develop an organisation's capability. Feedback and dialogue are used widely in this approach to improve employee morale and promote commitment to new behaviours. Interestingly, Theory O or the participative approach also appears to be more common in Asian and European firms.[31]

[25] See Kanter (2000, p. 3) and Denning (2005, pp. 12–13).

[26] *Ibid.*

[27] See Gilley, Gilley and McMillan (2009).

[28] See Rooke and Torbert (2005).

[29] *Ibid* (p. 2).

[30] See Beer and Nohria (2000).

[31] *Ibid* (p. 3).

Figure 2.6 Seven Action Logics of Leaders

	Action Logic	Characteristic
1.	*Opportunists*	• Focus on personal wins • Reject feedback, externalize blame • Self-aggrandisement
2.	*Diplomat*	• Seek to please, wants to belong • Obey group norms, doesn't rock the boat • Ignore conflict
3.	*Expert*	• Seek perfect knowledge • Pursue continuous improvement, efficiency and perfection • Use hard data and logic to gain consensus and buy-in
4.	*Achiever*	• Open to feedback • Promote teamwork • Respond to market demands to achieve goals
5.	*Individualist*	• Operate in unconventional ways • Aware of conflict situations • Ignore rules he/she regards as irrelevant
6.	*Strategist*	• Highly collaborative • Able to tackle resistance to change • Able to create a shared vision that encourages organisational and personal change • Create ethical principles and practices
7.	*Alchemist*	• Able to deal with multiple situations and people • Demonstrate high moral standards • Generate social transformations • Reinvent organisations in historically significant ways

Source: Adapted from Rooke and Torbert (2005)[32]

Despite the differences in approaches, both theories can be applied together to turn around an organisation to achieve profitability, productivity and sustain competitive advantage.[33] In fact, it is recommended that both the hard and soft theories be reconciled by sequencing the process and tapping onto managers who possess either E or O styles. This combination of E and O is critical for the organisation if it is to bring about transformational change, as such radical change involves balancing shareholder value with the development of a company's capabilities.[34]

The distinction between the "soft" and "hard" approaches to leadership is also referred to by some as "Level 5 leadership", where leaders are able to transform companies based on "Yin and Yang" characteristics, namely, deep personal humility and intense professional will (Figure 2.8). "Level 5 leaders" are therefore those leaders who possess both the ability or will, and the character or humility to create the impetus for change and transform companies from good to great.

[32] See Rooke and Torbert (2005, p. 144).

[33] See Beer and Nohria (2000, p. 1).

[34] *Ibid* (p. 9).

Figure 2.7 Theory E and O Leadership

		Theory E	Theory O
1.	Purpose	Maximise shareholder value	Develop organisational capabilities
2.	Leadership	Manage change using top-down approach little inputs from employees	Use participation to identify and solve problems (bottom-up)
3.	Focus	Streamlining "hardware" e.g. structure and systems	Building "software" of company such as corporate culture, behaviour and attitudes of employees
4.	Process	Planned programs to encourage action and enforce cooperation	Change process is experimental and evolves within the organisation
5.	Reward system	Financial rewards used to motivate	Motivate through commitment as financial rewards supplement but do not push reforms
6.	Consultants	Heavy reliance on external consultants	Low reliance on consultants as management shape their own solutions

Source: Adapted from Beer and Nohria (2000)[35]

Figure 2.8 Collins's "Level 5" Hierarchy

	Leader Type	Description
Level 5	Executive	Builds greatness using personal humility and professional will
Level 4	Effective leader	Catalyst for commitment and provides clear and compelling vision for high performance standards
Level 3	Competent manager	Organizes people and resources effectively and efficiently to meet objectives
Level 2	Contributing team member	Contributes to group objectives and works effectively in a team
Level 1	Highly capable individual	Makes productive contributions of talent, knowledge, work habits and skills

Source: Adapted from Collins (1985)

Since leadership operates within different contexts and environments, there is also more focus on the global and cross-cultural aspects of leadership. Studies on culture and leadership emphasise that leadership practices which are successful in one culture may not be successful in another, as cultural differences may influence perceptions and responses to particular styles of leadership.[36] The Globe study, a cross-cultural leadership study consisting of 17,300 managers from 62 societies, was conducted to determine how culture influences leadership effectiveness (see Figure 2.9).[37] Based on the data obtained from the study, nine different cultural dimensions were delineated to reflect the common norms, values and beliefs of a particular society in order to better assess how those factors affected management styles. Countries like Singapore, Korea and Hong Kong were grouped under the dimension of Confucian Asia, characterised by an elevated

[35] *Ibid* (p. 4).

[36] See Hofstede (2001) and King and Zhang (2014).

[37] See House et al. (2004).

Figure 2.9 Country Clusters According to Globe Study

Confucian Asia
Singapore, Hong Kong, Taiwan, China, South Korea, Japan
Southern Asia
Philippines, Indonesia, Malaysia, India, Thailand, Iran
Middle East
Turkey, Kuwait, Egypt, Morocco, Qatar
Sub-Saharan Africa
Zimbabwe, Namibia, Zambia, Nigeria, South Africa (Black Sample)
Eastern Europe
Greece, Hungary, Albania, Slovenia, Poland, Russia, Georgia, Kazakhstan
Nordic Europe
Denmark, Finland ,Sweden
Germanic Europe
Austria, The Netherlands, Switzerland, Germany (East), Germany (West)
Latin Europe
Israel, Italy, Switzerland (Francophone), Spain, Portugal, France
Anglo
Canada, U.S.A., Australia, Ireland, England, South Africa (White Sample), New Zealand
Latin America
Ecuador, El Salvador, Colombia, Bolivia, Brazil, Guatemala, Argentina, Costa Rica, Venezuela, Mexico

Source: Adapted from Northouse (2010)

emphasis on performance, collectivism and loyalty to one's family.[38] Additionally, since Confucian Asian communities are more collectivist, Chinese leaders tend to focus more on the collective efforts of their employees rather than on individual accomplishments.[39]

Due to the influence of culture on leadership, change efforts adopted by Asian versus Western leaders may also differ in terms of their processes and implementation. Some studies on leadership and culture assert that Chinese business leaders tend to be more authoritative and directive in their leadership styles due to the significant power distance that distinguishes class and status in their societies, which discourages employees from challenging or questioning their superiors or being involved in decision making.[40] Studies have also found that leaders who adopt leadership practices consistent with their cultural values are more successful than those who do not,[41] while others suggest that both Western and Asian leadership models are converging.[42]

Therefore, for a change process to occur successfully, vision and leadership are necessary but insufficient as the organisation's internal and external stakeholders also need to drive and support

[38] See Northouse (2010, p. 34).

[39] See Hofstede (2001) and House et al. (2002).

[40] See Cheng et al. (2004).

[41] See Dorfman et al. (1997).

[42] See Yukl (2013) and King and Zhang (2014).

the change.[43] The following section will discuss the three key drivers of the transformational change model: (i) corporate culture, (ii) competitive business policies and (iii) corporate finance strategy.

2.3 CORPORATE CULTURE AND VALUES

The first driver, corporate culture, refers to the culture and values within the organisation that help promote a conducive climate for change efforts (Figure 2.10). Management will need to nurture and reinforce appropriate shared values and norms that employees can internalise to achieve transformational change to replace either a dysfunctional or otherwise unsuitable culture.

Furthermore, it should be noted that this case study involves a family-owned business. The corporate culture of such entities poses especially unique challenges, as the personal objectives and aspirations of the organisation's founder and the managing family can exert a comparatively profound influence. This is clearly articulated by Denison et al.,[44] who note that "beyond profitability, family members may see success in the ability to live and operate the enterprise according to a personal value system or merely to pass the founder's legacy to the next generation."

Section 2.3.1 will discuss management ethos unique to a family-owned business undergoing transformational change and the role of corporate culture in shaping the organisation's identity and external branding.

2.3.1 MANAGEMENT ETHOS

The definition and qualification of a management ethos is foundational to any attempt at undertaking transformational change.

A company's management ethos is the realisation of its ethical and ideological core. This core can arise from stimuli passed down from the ideologies of a given company's founders or even

Figure 2.10 First Driver of Change

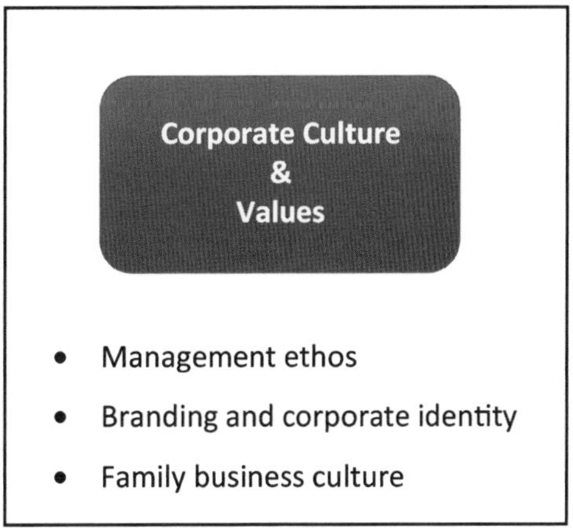

Source: Asia Competitiveness Institute

[43] See Denning (2005).

[44] See Denison et al. (2004)

from a collective agreement forged in the crucible of lively ideological discourse.[45] Regardless of the direct cause of its manifestation, however, academic sources and studies generally agree that a strong, positive ethos which reinforces the overall conceptualisation of an organisation as a distinctly ethical entity results in positive organisational outcomes from stakeholders both within and outside of the company.[46]

Particularly notable are Caza et al.'s corresponding discussions of ethos, which identify it as a vital tool in counteracting the "disorientation" which "afflicts individuals and organisations in situations where there are no referents", such as amidst the sweeping upheavals brought about by truly transformative change.[47] Serving as a "benchmark" for making sense of ambiguity, and as a source of resilience and protecting the system from harm, ethos also potentially acts as an ideological fixed point, facilitating the development of a fully realised organisational identity (OI).[48]

Due to the extensive amount of work that has been done on OI, the vocabulary associated with the topic is varied and at times contradictory. Referring to Albert and Whetten's seminal work on OI in 2006, "The concept of organisational identity is specified as the central and enduring attributes of an organisation that distinguish it from other organisations".[49] Albert and Whetten's identity definition also outlines what they call "Central, Enduring, and Distinctive (CED)" attributes which are discussed or invoked "when member agents are grappling with profound, fork-in-the-road, choices" that have the potential to impact the collective understanding of "who we are as an organisation."[50]

In other words, CED attributes both distinguish any given organisation from others, above and beyond the degree to which they are already distinguished by scale, means of production and sector. In performing this function, these unique attributes also play a key part in informing the core values of the organisation and the corresponding attitudes and actions of employees throughout the organisation when they need to make critical organisational decisions. OI is therefore not outwardly focused and serves primarily to inform the organisation's self-perception and how its employees are able to view or situate themselves relative to other organisations.

OI is also distinct as a concept from organisational or corporate culture. As Moingeon notes in comparing the two concepts, while "culture represents a group's agreement about how things ought to be done… identity refers to the consensus about 'who we are as an organisation'".[51] Correspondingly, an organisation's culture can be best delineated in accordance to Sunder's description as "the common knowledge expectation of behaviour of its members", in other words, "the expectations its members hold about the behaviour of other members".[52] To further refine the point, culture can be taken as a quality that is highly dependent on precedent, situations which a

[45] See Cornelius, Wallace and Tassabehji (2007) and Stansbury (2009).
[46] See Verbos et al. (2007) and Berrone, Surroca and Tribó (2007).
[47] See Caza, Barker and Cameron (2004, p. 171).
[48] *Ibid* (p. 172).
[49] See Whetten (2006, p. 220).
[50] *Ibid* (p. 221).
[51] See Moingeon (1999, p. 352).
[52] See Sunder (2002, pp. 182, 185).

company and its agents have encountered and resolved (or failed to resolve) before. OI, on the other hand, refers to how a company respond to a situation in which a precedent does not exist.

Several studies have been undertaken to assess the impact of OI on the efficiency of an organisation. A survey conducted on 361 employees of a large Chinese airline to determine the impact of strong organisational identity (referred to here as collective identity) on the manifestation of counterproductive work behaviours (CWB) found that "when collective identity is high, employees internalize the norms and goals of their work team, show greater commitment and loyalty to the team, and act in ways that benefit team members".[53] These findings are supported by Perez and del Bosques' findings, which note that "the transmission of the business identity to internal audiences of the organisation leads to significant benefits for the institution, especially employees' and managers' identification with the collective identity of the company".[54]

In contrast, an in-depth study of the drivers of employee discontentment conducted by Corley found that a significant source of employee discontentment arose from what he referred to as temporal identity discrepancies. The discontentment arose amongst employees "as they tried to cope with who the organisation had been versus who they knew the organisation to be currently versus expectations (both expressed and implied) for… who the organisation would be in the future".[55] In Corley's view, the problematic discrepancies arose because of the vastly differing attitudes towards identity change held by those at the upper and lower hierarchies of the organisation.

Corley observed that upper management felt that "identity was not (and could not be) rigid and unchanging, but that, in fact, it had to change to keep up with changes the organisation faced in its competitive environments", while employees lower down the hierarchy "saw organisational identity as an outgrowth of their organisation's culture and therefore as much more stable and unchanging than senior leadership saw it".[56] This led to a situation in which "different members of an organisation have different perceptions of its identity and therefore (re)act differently in regards to issues involving organisational identity", leading to systemic inefficiencies and an ideological disconnect along the company's management hierarchy.[57]

Correspondingly, Corley's findings confirm Perez and del Bosque's hypotheses, which assert that for a company to simply state "their mission, vision and values statements is not enough for an effective and successful management of identity. An adequate communication of these attributes to society and stakeholders is also necessary".[58] Establishing a clear management ethos is fundamental to maintaining clear lines of communication regarding OI and is thus key to sustaining and maintaining it over extended periods of time and across all levels of an organisation's hierarchy. In this way, a clear and operationally relevant vision of collective identity can be maintained even during a period of sweeping transformational change.

---

[53] See Yang et al. (2012, p. 191).

[54] See Perez and del Bosque (2014, p. 20).

[55] See Corley (2004, p. 1162).

[56] *Ibid* (p. 1157).

[57] *Ibid* (p. 1170).

[58] See Perez and del Bosque (2014, p. 20).

2.3.2 BRANDING AND CORPORATE IDENTITY

Management ethos thus helps to influence and shape the values and culture of the organisation, enabling members of the organisation to more effectively comprehend and internalise its organisational identity or what it is as an organisation. What becomes equally important in these considerations, however, is how this organisational identity is communicated to outsiders — how, in short, it translates into a corporate identity meant for public consumption. Corporate identity is especially critical during periods of transformational change, as during such times organisations are confronted both internally and externally with important questions and choices about who they are and what they stand for.[59] As noted, models of organisational identity argue that both the internal and external expressions of an organisation's identity have to be aligned. Specifically, what is espoused internally in terms of company values and beliefs should be congruent to what is "expressed" to the outside world in the form of branding and advertising, as a misalignment can lead to an identity crisis within the organisation.[60]

Traditionally, corporate identity has been defined simply as an external image of the organisation. However, it is now seen as an important public image that represents the values and intrinsic qualities of an organisation.[61] The role of corporate branding, defined as an external expression of an organisation's identity, is to therefore differentiate and position the organisation from its competitors.[62] Changes in corporate brands can be minor or major, with the latter encompassing a new name, symbol or design with the purpose of creating a new position for stakeholders and competitors.[63]

Studies show that rebranding is most common during mergers and acquisitions (M&As) or when a company undergoes a transformational change.[64] In these instances, a company's new corporate identity needs to be communicated to customers and external stakeholders through aggressive branding and marketing efforts so that customers continue to support and connect with the company's brand.[65] The rebranding process can be categorised into four elements: repositioning, renaming, redesign and relaunch.[66] Specifically, repositioning is a key aspect of rebranding and involves creating a new position of the product or service for the customers. Renaming communicates to the customers and external stakeholders of what the new brand stands for. Redesign represents the company logo or "visible manifestations" of the company's brand such as brochures, annual reports and print advertisements, while relaunch is the last step of officially announcing the new brand to the public and stakeholders.[67]

Leaders can promote a company's brand or brand-building behaviour by introducing initiatives within the company to motivate employees to become brand ambassadors. Such employee brand ambassadors can contribute to branding efforts of the organisation by providing positive

---

[59] See Albert and Whetten (1985) and Corley and Gioia (2004).

[60] See Hatch and Schultz (2002, p. 991).

[61] See Cornelissen et al. (2007, p. 3).

[62] See Kaufmann et al. (2012).

[63] See Muzellec and Lambkin (2006).

[64] See Muzellec et al. (2003).

[65] See Denning (2005).

[66] See Muzellec et al. (2003, p. 4).

[67] *Ibid.*

word-of-mouth about the company's products and services and participating in informal marketing efforts. Since employees play a pivotal role in corporate reputation management, they should be empowered to live the brand and "internalise, epitomise and deliver the brand values and promise".[68]

Leaders can also strengthen the company brand by engaging in "brand-oriented leadership" by communicating the company's vision and modelling behaviours which represent the desired company identity.[69] Such an approach requires the alignment of various aspects of the organisation, such as marketing, human resources and the communication of company culture.[70] Rather than assume a conservative role, these departments should become more strategic partners and align themselves to the business strategy.[71]

2.3.3 FAMILY-OWNED BUSINESS CULTURE

In the specific context of OUE Limited, these discussions of organisational and corporate identity also need to be understood with the distinctiveness of family-owned business culture in mind. As previously established, family-owned businesses often have unique and deeply entrenched cultures because the managing family's values and history can have a profound influence on the manner in which the business is run as well as the execution of succession planning within the organisation. Indeed, the culture in a family-owned business may even be stronger than a non-family firm as the leader of the organisation may draw influence both from his position in the company as well as his position in the family, thus entrenching from the outset a fairly rigid organisational hierarchy.[72] Although advocates of best practices in family businesses support the recruitment of non-family members to provide checks and balances, it is important to understand that the culture and behaviour within these firms is derived first and foremost "from a deeply ingrained, learned at-the-dinner-table sense of history and morality".[73]

Findings from some studies show that many family businesses do not have a clear vision and values to propel the company forward, which jeopardises their long-term legacy and continuity of the business.[74] According to the Family Business Institute, only 30 percent of family-owned businesses last into a second generation and only 12 percent are still viable in the third generation, while only three percent operate into the fourth generation or beyond.[75] Many studies on family-owned businesses reveal that the chance of survival after each generation diminishes drastically, with 70 percent of family-owned businesses "fail or are sold before the second generation gets a chance to take over", and a mere 10 percent remain as active privately held

[68] See Kaufmann et al. (2012, p. 193) and Gotsi and Wilson (2001).

[69] See Kaufmann et al. (2012) and Corley and Gioia (2004).

[70] See Dowling (1993, p. 101).

[71] See Kaufmann et al. (2012).

[72] See Denison et al. (2004).

[73] See Stalk and Foley (2012) and Denison et al. (2004).

[74] See Koh, Tong and Waltermann (2012).

[75] *Ibid* (p. 8).

companies for the next generation to lead.[76] Famous and ubiquitous phrases such as "shirtsleeves to shirtsleeves in three generations" or the Chinese equivalent "富不过三代" (wealth does not survive three generations) highlight the struggles that family-owned businesses have historically faced in finding suitable candidates due to a lack of governance structure and grooming of potential successors.

Therefore, the ability of the leader or patriarch to articulate a clear vision and core values is especially critical in a family-owned business, as this acts like a "power beacon" to align the different interests and goals of the various stakeholders, such as the immediate family members, extended family members and professional management.[77] In fact, successful family-owned businesses usually have a dominant family member who is at the centre of the organisation "like the sun in our solar system" or a "family gravity", that binds the organisation together through his/her vision.[78]

Family firms could potentially have a strategic advantage over non-family firms because their "founding cultures are nurtured by succeeding generations of family", therefore, "culture in family-owned firms is difficult to replicate".[79] Each generation in a family-owned business needs to understand its history or story as the "personal values and visions" are a critical part of sustaining the culture and the business for the next generation.[80] Hence, there is an emphasis by the older generation to expose the next generation to the business by storytelling and sharing the worldview of the business. Related to this is the focus on succession planning which involves preparing the next generation for a role in the business, an aspect supported by many studies that the best firms identify their potential successors early and invest in them.[81] Although entering the business with limited competencies and learning entirely on the job may be common practice, one emerging trend in family-owned businesses is for the succeeding generation to possess good educational qualifications and exposure to the business in order to contribute and take over the reins of the business more effectively.[82]

The preceding chapter has thus attempted to explain how corporate culture and organisational identity are shaped by management ethos and the unique characteristics of a family business. This is turn is communicated to outside stakeholders in the form of external branding and corporate identity. During transformational change, corporate culture and values will be challenged and ultimately even redefined, as this change will often encompass a new vision and/or leadership, thus requiring extensive modifications to the company's way of doing things and ultimately their definition of "who (they) are as an organisation".[83]

Having discussed the role and influence of the unique culture of a family-owned business, the following section will present a discussion of the literature on the second driver — the formulation of business strategies to promote transformational change (Figure 2.11).

---

[76] See Stalk and Foley (2012) and Koh, Tong and Waltermann (2012).

[77] See Koh, Tong and Waltermann (2012, pp. 10–11).

[78] See Fernández-Aráoz et al. (2015).

[79] See Denison et al. (2004, p. 69).

[80] See Schwass (2013, p. 3).

[81] See Fernández-Aráoz et al. (2015, p. 2) and Schwass (2013, p. 6).

[82] See Stalk and Foley (2012).

[83] See Hatch and Schultz (2002).

Figure 2.11 Second Driver of Change

Competitive Business Policies for Asset Enhancement

- Productivity, cost and price competitiveness
- Human resource policies
- Transformation with repositioning and differentiation

Source: Asia Competitiveness Institute

2.4 COMPETITIVE BUSINESS POLICIES FOR ASSET ENHANCEMENT

The transformational change cycle model identifies "Competitive Business Policies for Asset Enhancement" as the second driver of change. This section will discuss and examine the types of competitive business policies and initiatives that can propel transformational change. We will accordingly emphasise the designing and implementing of business policies related to human resources, productivity and price, and strategic positioning, all of which are intended to achieve the ultimate objective of successfully repositioning the organisation.

In general terms, a competitive business strategy encompasses a range of activities that allow a company to provide and sell goods and services more profitably than others. When such strategies are effectively implemented, the company is said to have a "competitive advantage" compared to its competitors. At the core of a successful competitive strategy lies the unique characteristics of a company that is to say, the qualities and competencies possessed by a company which cannot be easily imitated by its peers. To paraphrase Barney, a firm "has a competitive advantage when it utilises a strategy for value creation that is not being simultaneously deployed by other players; potential, current or otherwise".[84]

Such competitive advantages thus sometimes arise from the unique resources that a company is able to access. Based on this resources-based view, a competitive advantage can be sustained in the long term only if a company's key resources are valuable, rare, inimitable and non-substitutable.[85] Simply possessing these resources does not, however, automatically guarantee a sustainable competitive advantage. Successful incumbents also need to actively protect and maintain these resources against imitations put forward by other incumbents, as well as threats from new entrants which might add value in ways the primary incumbent's resource does not.[86]

In addition to having superior resources, companies can also gain competitive advantages through innovative alignments of their business processes with available resources. Porter argues

---

[84] See Barney (1991).

[85] See Barney (1991), Barney and Clark (2007), Conner (1991), Dierickx and Cool (1989), Mahoney and Pandian (1992) and Peteraf (1993).

[86] See Crook et al. (2008).

Figure 2.12 Categories of Competitive Strategies

Competitive Scope		Competitive Advantage: Lower Cost	Competitive Advantage: Differentiation
	Broad Target	1. Cost Leadership	2. Differentiation
	Narrow Target	3a. Cost Focus	3b. Differentiation Focus

Source: Adapted from Porter (1985)

that effective alignments of business processes result in more sustainable and defensible competitive positions, since any kind of effective imitation by competitors would require major trade-offs.[87] Simultaneous gains in both buyer value and cost positions are only possible when a company is operating below the productivity frontier. If most firms are already operating at the frontier, further gains in operational efficiency often require greater research and development (R&D) investments. However, such advantages are often temporary, and competitors are able to quickly catch up as technological innovations spread across the industry. A unique strategic positioning based on the productivity frontier, on the other hand, may not be compatible with competitors' existing business models and therefore poses a substantially more formidable barrier to entry to imitators.

In his seminal work, Porter categorises competitive strategies along two axes: competitive advantage and competitive scope (Figure 2.12).[88] Along the competitive advantage axis, a company chooses either to achieve a lower cost structure or provide differentiated products. Along the competitive scope axis, a company chooses either to cater to a broad range of market demands or to focus on a specific segment of the market. There are consequently three possible competitive strategies available: cost leadership, product differentiation, or focus on a narrow market segment. The focused strategy can be further sub-divided into the cost focus and the differentiation focus.

Subject to available corporate resources, each strategic position requires a particular set of core competencies and business process alignments. It has additionally been noted that although cost leadership and differentiation represent two different approaches to establishing a strategic position, they are not necessarily mutually exclusive.[89]

The following sections will examine the three competitive business *categories* from the transformation change cycle model that can influence the competitiveness of an organisation.

---

[87] See Porter (2008).

[88] See Porter (1985).

[89] See Hill (1988).

2.4.1 PRODUCTIVITY, COST AND PRICE COMPETITIVENESS

Productivity is defined by the Organisation for Economic Co-operation and Development (OECD) as "a ratio between the output volume and the volume of inputs".[90] Labour productivity equals value added divided by employment.[91] Furthermore, in attempting to divide productivity drives into separate constituents, the equation is multiplied by operating revenue over operating revenue. Hence, we can conclude that productivity can be improved by maximising operational revenue per worker — hard work — or increasing value added over operational revenue — smart work.[92] (see Average Labour Productivity Formula in Appendix 4 for details).

Furthermore, as a competitive strategy, having a lower cost structure is a clear advantage over competitors. In Porter's framework, cost leadership means the ability to provide products or services with qualities comparable to the competition at a lower cost.[93] In this sense, cost leadership might be best understood as productivity leadership, as the quality of a company's offerings should not be compromised in pursuit of lower cost.[94] Cost leadership, however, does not necessarily imply price leadership in market competition. Cost leaders may choose to exploit their lower cost structure by offering a lower price and thus capturing a larger market share, or retaining a higher profit margin by adopting a price on par with other competitors. Either way, productivity gains add more value for producers and consumers.[95]

In business practice, cost leadership can be derived from higher operational efficiency (OE). Improvements in OE are often driven by technological innovations, economies of scale, cumulative learning experience or better alignment of business processes.[96] While most of these factors seem to favour incumbents, new entrants with disruptive technologies may have the opportunity to drastically undercut the incumbents in cost competition.[97]

2.4.2 HUMAN RESOURCE POLICIES

Any competitive business strategy adopted by a company needs to be supported by suitable functional strategies, such as human resource, marketing and financial policies. The human resource function is particularly critical in ensuring that appropriate competencies exist within the organisation to facilitate the desired competitive strategy.

Since 70 percent of organisational change initiatives fail completely,[98] organisations undergoing change need to ensure that the company's vision is translated into suitable behaviours across the organisation. Studies argue that turnaround efforts are more successful if executed by "insiders"

---

[90] OECD (2008, p. 11).

[91] See Tan and Tan (2014).

[92] *Ibid.*

[93] See Littler (1999).

[94] See Reitsperger et al. (1993).

[95] See Stahl and Grigsby (1997).

[96] See Amit (1986).

[97] See Reid (1993).

[98] See Beer and Nohria (2000).

within the organisation, who are familiar with both the external environment and the organisation's dynamics rather than "outsiders" who are newcomers to the company.[99] This implies that change initiatives do not only require strong leaders but also "core staff" who can participate in the change by enabling its smooth integration into existing structures and processes.

One of the commonly cited human resources (HR) initiatives for successful change is employee participation or employee involvement (EI), defined as "intentional programs or practices developed by the organisation to involve multiple employees".[100] Employee involvement has been demonstrated to support change efforts, as they promote employee communication, motivation and performance. A study of over 1,000 firms found that adopting "high-performance work practices" could improve a company's financial performance, boost productivity and reduce turnover.[101] These high-performance work practices (HPWP) refer to HRM practices related to recruitment, selection, training and development, labour relations, performance appraisals, and compensation, processes and systems. For instance, it is critical to recruit and select the right candidates, as well as apply suitable performance appraisal and compensation processes, so that employees are motivated to "work harder and smarter".[102] Another study of HPWP in Asian firms contends that progressive HR practices such as delegation, empowerment, training and development, and pay-for-performance schemes can contribute to higher firm performance.[103]

The term "high involvement organisations (HIO)" has also been used to refer to employee involvement in change management initiatives. Some studies use the term "critical mass" to refer to employees who can help "design, sell, evaluate, implement and support change".[104] Other terms such as "champions of change" and "change communities" are also used to describe the involvement of as many employees as possible to drive meaningful change.[105] HIOs also tend to adopt progressive HR practices similar to the HPWPs mentioned previously, such as rewarding employee involvement, training employees in problem-solving, promoting high levels of empowerment and using team-based organisational structures.[106] The HR department can align its training, development, recruitment and reward practices to encourage the "brand citizenship behaviours" of its employees, which can promote greater customer awareness and satisfaction.[107] Such "brand citizenship behaviours" refer to employees willing to support, understand and endorse the company brand in personal as well as professional contexts.[108]

Therefore, for transformational change to be sustainable, the involvement of human resources in organisational change processes must also become "a way of life" or "momentum". This

---

[99] See Boyne and Meier (2009).
[100] See Glew et al. (1995, p. 401).
[101] See Huselid (1995, p. 637).
[102] *Ibid.*
[103] See Bae et al. (2003, p. 1308).
[104] See Sims (2002, p. 42).
[105] *Ibid.*
[106] *Ibid.*
[107] See Chang et al. (2012).
[108] *Ibid* (p. 652).

momentum needs to be driven by the company's leaders in conjunction with appropriate HR policies that can support and sustain the organisation's performance in the long run by involving and mobilising the core staff of the organisation.[109] HR strategies such as recruiting good quality core or non-managerial staff with the appropriate competencies can improve the prospects of a company turnaround. In fact, some studies even suggest that retrenchment in organisations can be a necessary evil to tackle performance problems related to "high costs and low efficiency".[110] For employees who have been with the company for extended durations, change can be an especially painful process due to their resistance to the methodological or even ideological implications of a company's changing organisational identity. This might lead to a consequent inability to "let go of the old way of doing things", impeding the achievement of meaningful change — an outcome which would necessitate their replacement with newer, more malleable individuals.[111]

2.4.3 TRANSFORMATION WITH DIFFERENTIATION AND REPOSITIONING

Another aspect of asset enhancement is the adoption of a differentiation strategy. A differentiation strategy requires a company to offer unique products or services that add more value for its customers than its competitors do. Unlike a cost leadership strategy that focuses on *process* innovation, a differentiation strategy emphasises *product* innovation.[112] Product differentiation can be tangible (such as features and technology) or intangible (such as warranty policies and customer services). Effective differentiation often depends on strong marketing and branding strategies to create and convey a perception of uniqueness among target customers.[113]

While empirical evidence suggests that the differentiation strategies often pay off in higher profit margins,[114] companies pursuing these strategies risk being imitated by competitors unless their differentiated products capitalise on unique or advantageous corporate resources, or extremely optimised alignments. Another risk that companies with highly distinct products face is adapting to often fickle customer tastes and preferences. To mitigate this risk, successful differentiators often strive to become trendsetters to preserve their competitive advantages.[115]

2.5 CORPORATE FINANCE STRATEGY

The following section will discuss the third driver of change, "corporate finance strategy", and the role it plays in achieving transformation (Figure 2.13). The section will discuss the literature on areas such as risk and return analysis, financing options and investment planning, all of which play important roles in determining the corporate finance strategy of a company.

---

[109] See Ionescu (2014, p. 69).
[110] See Boyne and Meier (2009, p. 853).
[111] See Schein (1984, p. 14).
[112] See Utterback and Abernathy (1975).
[113] See Boehe and Cruz (2010), Dickson and Ginter (1987), Gerstner, Hess and Chu (1993).
[114] See Mayhew and Wilkins (2003) and Spencer, Joiner and Salmon (2009).
[115] See Kapferer (2012).

Figure 2.13 Third Driver of Change

Corporate Finance Strategy

- Risk and return analysis
- Financing options
- Investment planning

Source: Asia Competitiveness Institute

The ACI cycle of transformation (Figure 2.1) takes into account the relationship between leadership and vision in creating both value and values, shifting the traditional focus of strategy from obtaining and sustaining competitive advantages towards a model which emphasises the search for "new, unexpected ways to create value" — drawing parallels to Zenger's formulation of "corporate theory".[116] Kraaijenbrink points out that firms are engaged in creating both value and values, where value refers to a resource-based view of generating rents and profits and also satisfying a need or providing benefits. "Values", on the other hand, refer to less objective "standards of evaluation", or a value system drawn from spheres such as the "family, religious, economic (and) aesthetic", which are adopted by people to subjectively assess the quality of goods, actions and relationships.[117]

With transformational change, both value and values as defined above are transformed. In terms of values, "when a company reinvents itself, it must alter the underlying assumptions and invisible premises on which its decisions and actions are based".[118] Furthermore, with a resource-based view of value, it has been argued that "value is created only when companies invest capital at returns that exceed the cost of that capital".[119] This is in alignment with Kaiser and Young, who explain that when it comes to creating value, "a firm must systematically invest in those projects where the expected value of cash coming in more than compensates for the cash going out, a difference commonly expressed as net present value".[120]

As a pillar of transformation, the corporate strategy focuses on enhancing the resource-based value that exists in a company. As such, it is primarily concerned with the capacity for an organisation to amass and grow the capital required to implement its vision and objectives in accordance with the overarching strategy of transformational change. Important considerations that are taken into account when planning or reassessing corporate strategy are timing, economic

[116] See Zenger (2013).
[117] See Kraaijenbrink (2011, pp. 7–9).
[118] See Goss, Pascale and Athos (1998, p. 86).
[119] See Koller (1994, p. 1).
[120] See Kaiser and Young (2009, p. 2).

conditions and market depth, as well as relationships with investors and financiers, all of which have the potential to affect the organisation's financial capabilities and capacity. A clear corporate strategy that considers available financing options and conceptualises appropriate investment strategies to maximise the value of a company's assets is thus critical for an organisation to realise its vision of achieving transformation. The following sections will accordingly explore the literature related to three key elements of corporate strategy: risk and return analysis, financing options and investment planning.

2.5.1 RISK AND RETURN ANALYSIS

In comparing hospitality risk across real estate asset types, Liu and Quan assert that while hotels behave similar to other real estate types with respect to capital appreciation, they differ greatly in terms of their income streams.[121] This is due to the lack of tenant commitment, and fluctuating rates, which cause cash flow to be more volatile (relatively speaking) over the course of a business cycle. Furthermore, these streams are dependent on the cost of wages, supplies, and financing. Hotels are consequently perceived to have a comparatively high-risk profile.

Liu and Quan also assess Spread-at-Origination (SATO) by property type over a 10-year period, with spreads defined as increments to the Treasury bond rate, and track the risk premiums for different types of real estate loans. Their findings thus reflect lenders' perceptions of the risks associated with each asset type. Liu and Quan's findings accordingly indicate that hotels were associated with the highest risk premium.[122]

This risk premium can be characterised and associated with the main phases of a given hotel's life cycle. Younes and Kett propose that a hotel's life cycle has three main phases: development, operation, and exit.[123] Development takes one to three years, following which the asset is held and operated for a further five to 25 years. After this, the property is generally sold or redeveloped. As such, hotels face risks that correspond directly to each stage of the life cycle: development risk, operating risk, and obsolescence/exit risk.

Development risk is characterised by Younes and Kett as the risk that a setback occurs during the development phase, which negatively influences either development plans or future Return on Investment.[124] Wiegelmann, and Younes and Kett concur that this phase is especially capital-intensive, requiring efficient coordination among all stakeholders involved in order to ensure the project's profitability.[125] Figure 2.14 summarises the main steps and risk elements of the development phase.

Younes and Kett define operating risks as the risk where the hotel is unable to generate sufficient levels of cash flow to justify initial investments or to catalyse an exit. In addition, as Wiegelmann notes, "the more unusual a particular type of project is for the developer, the higher the chance

---

[121] See Liu and Quan (2011).

[122] *Ibid.*

[123] See Younes and Kett (2008).

[124] *Ibid.*

[125] See Younes and Kett (2008) and Wiegelmann (2012).

Figure 2.14 Main Steps and Risk Elements in Hotel Development

- Location identification
- Zoning and planning consents
- Resort — very difficult
- Feasibility and planning — decisions on asset positioning
- Operator selection
- Capital planning and structuring
- Land acquisition
- Construction and design partner selection
- Land excavation
- Construction and design; high rise versus low rise
- Extent of facilities
- Timing and cost of capital

Source: Adapted from Liu and Quan (2011)

that the developer will misread the market and the higher the development risk".[126] As such, fluctuations in net operating income, or Earnings Before Interest, Tax, Depreciation and Amortisation (EBITDA), are the main sources of a hotel's operating risk. Consequently, given its structure, this risk can be further broken down into revenues and the fixed cost structure of the operation.

Obsolescence, as defined in Younes and Kett, is an incurable economic depreciation that has a considerable effect on the holding period returns of the hotel asset.[127] Internal obsolescence typically occurs when a hotel no longer functions the way it did when it was initially built. It is a fundamental change in the hotel's fitness for purpose, which can be either physical or operational. On the other hand, external obsolescence is the loss in income and value resulting from external factors, which can be legal, social, environmental or economic. As such, obsolescence/exit risk involves a potential decrease in a property's value at the envisaged exit period.

Younes and Kett do note as a caveat that asset classes within the hotel sector have different risk profiles throughout their cycles. For example, while full service and luxury hotels are more exposed to development and operating risks than limited service properties, they are less exposed to obsolescence/exit risk. Also, while shared ownership developments have a lower operating risk than other hotel derivatives, this asset class inherits a high exit risk.

With respect to carrying out risk and return analyses on real estate, Damodaran proposes that valuation models formulated for financial assets are appropriate, despite the differences in liquidity, cash flows, and reactions to inflation.[128] The following is thus generally agreed upon: "when evaluating a hotel investment, one would project the property's cash flow over a specific period of time, and would then apply various financing parameters to assess the value of the

[126] Wiegelmann uses the term "Development Risk" instead of "Operating Risk", see Wiegelmann (2012, p. 47).

[127] See Younes and Kett (2008).

[128] Damodaran (2002).

investment in today's prices."[129] As such, in adopting the discounted cash flow valuation to real estate, it is necessary to estimate the discount rate, expected cash flows on the real estate investment for the life of the asset, as well as the terminal value of the real estate. See Appendix 4 for the full formula.

Damodaran explains that discount rates can be estimated via conventional financial pricing models, such as the Capital Asset Pricing Model (CAPM) or the Arbitrage Pricing Model (APM). However, in doing so, we implicitly assume the following: the marginal investor in the asset is well diversified, the risk is measured in terms of the variability of returns, and only non-diversifiable risk is rewarded. Furthermore, when adopting such models, measurement issues arise with respect to risk parameters.[130] Alternatively, surveys can be carried out to estimate the discount rates.[131] In this case, the costs of equity and capital are often obtained by surveying potential investors in real estate on what rate of return they would demand for investing in different types of property investments.[132]

The following is a brief summary of Damodaran's comparison of the two methods:

Surveys are advantageous as they are not based upon abstract models of risk and return, but on what actual investors want to make. Furthermore, they allow for the estimation of discount rates without requiring a dependence upon past prices like risk and return models. However, while the survey method bypasses the issue of risk, it does not fully eliminate it. On the other hand, a well-constructed risk and return model sets reasonable bounds for expected returns. There are no such limits on survey responses. In addition, models also allow analysts to be proactive in estimating discount rates.[133] The discounted cash flow method also requires estimates of the cash flow, deducting all operational expenses, debt obligations and taxes. It can be attained by individually estimating cash inflows, cash outflows and growth rates.

Firstly, to estimate cash inflows, market rents as well as vacancy rates must be projected. According to Dreyer and Mathieson, vacancy rates are a function of the typical lease term, vacancy between leases, and the probability of renewal.[134] For formulas with respect to the computation of these variables, see Appendix 4. Additionally, Damodaran clarifies that for new buildings, the projections should factor in how long it will initially take to get occupants to rent/lease space. The longer this period is, the less the discounted cash flow value of the building.[135]

Secondly, components of cash outflow include both fixed and variable expenses. In general, real estate taxes make up a large proportion of cash outflows. They are also especially volatile, being subject to changing tax laws and external valuation. However, before they are applied to the model, growth rates of both inflows and outflows have to be estimated. Expected inflation

[129] See Younes and Kett (2008, p. 6).

[130] See Damodaran (2002).

[131] In fact, we believe this to be the method used by OUE Limited. Asia Competitiveness Institute interviews of senior management staff of OUE Limited (2015).

[132] See Damodaran (2002).

[133] *Ibid.*

[134] See Dreyer and Mathieson (1995).

[135] See Damodaran (2002).

rate is often used to proxy for this. However, the following must be noted: "In a stable real estate market, the expected growth in cash flows should be close to the expected inflation rate. In tight markets with low vacancy rates, it is possible for the expected growth rate in rents to be higher than the expected inflation rate at least until the market shortages disappear. The reverse is likely to be true in markets with high vacancy rates."[136]

The final value that needs to be estimated is terminal value. Damodaran defines the terminal value as the value of the asset at the end of the investment time horizon. Three basic approaches may be used to estimate the terminal value. Firstly, the current value of the property can be assumed to increase at the expected inflation rate to arrive at a terminal value. However, this method assumes that the current valuation is accurate. The second approach is to assume that the cash flows in the terminal year will continue to grow constantly in perpetuity. Lastly, operating income is divided by the capitalisation rate to get the value of the property.[137] Refer to Appendix 4 for detailed steps in these approaches.

2.5.2 FINANCING OPTIONS

A company typically requires financing for several undertakings, such as their business operations, funding for projects, investments and purchases. Financing options are concerned with strategies for cash management, debt management, and other customised corporate financing structures — what Finnerty terms as the branch of financial engineering which "involves creative solutions to corporate finance problems".[138] Financing typically takes the form of debt or equity, with loans and bonds considered forms of debt financing, and deciding a suitable financing mix is oftentimes a challenge (see Figure 2.15).

Depending on the composition of the asset base of an organisation, as well as their debt capacity, the mix of financing is determined by the optimal use of available resources, as well as the management of risk levels to be taken on. The difficulty of identifying the optimal capital structure for organisations is well documented in academic literature, with Modigliani and Miller in 1963 and Fama and Miller in 1972 observing that based on their theory on the cost of capital, companies should be financed nearly entirely by debt: a conclusion that they conceded to be entirely inconsistent with observed behaviour.[139] Matters of optimisation aside, the theory of financing options is also concerned with the ownership structure of a firm and hence finds relevant elements from theories of agency. Jensen and Meckling identified a potential divergence of interests between managers and owners as a "manager in a firm which has a mixed financial structure (containing both debt and outside equity claims) will choose a set of activities for the firm such that the total value of the firm is less than it would be if he were the sole owner".[140] Indeed, Jensen and Meckling drew reference from the fact that this distinction was also identified by Adam Smith, who stated that being managers "of other people's money than of their own,

[136] *Ibid* (p. 18).

[137] *Ibid.*

[138] See Finnerty (1988, p. 15).

[139] See both Modigliani and Miller (1963), as well as Fama and Miller (1972).

[140] See Jensen and Meckling (1976, p. 306).

Figure 2.15 Comparison between Equity, Loan and Bond Financing

	Equity	Bank Loan	Bond
Cost of fund	Highest in the long term as dividends	Cost of debt is tax-deductible	Depends on credit rating
Risk to fund provider	Depends on company's governance and performance	Depends on balance sheet strength (e.g. debt/equity ratio) and quality of asset as collateral	Bond default rare though possible
Control by fund raiser	Possible dilution	Subject to lender's veto power and restrictive covenants	No loss of control
Liquidity (i.e. ease of increasing/ decreasing holding)	Relatively highest	Subject to repayment terms of loan (i.e. term loan or revolving credit)	Depends on secondary market growth and call terms
Duration of use	No limit	Short term	Long term

Source: Adapted from Lam, Chiang and Chan (2011)

it cannot well be expected, that they should watch over it with the same anxious vigilance with which the partners in a private copartnery frequently watch over their own".[141] As suggested, an analysis of the trade-off of risks and returns may then suggest that alternative financing structures may be more suitable, such as finding another organisation to partner with in order to share the risks and returns as a joint venture, or the use of special purpose vehicles designated specifically for the completion of a given undertaking or project in order to limit the risks and to keep said undertakings off a company's balance sheet.

Having recognised that such decisions are often a reflection of the agency costs involved,[142] financing options available to an organisation also depend on factors such as how well capitalised a company is, the assets that it holds and the credit standing of a company. This will also affect the form of financing that a company chooses to take on in order to fulfil its objectives. Companies with limited access to credit may need to raise additional equity or to use more cash for their financing. It was even suggested that a company's financing decisions "are actually signalling *[sic]* devices, conveying information to investors about the firm's business risk and profitability".[143]

2.5.3 INVESTMENT PLANNING

When considering a company's investment strategy, it is worth noting that most firms are valued as going concerns and that "this value reflects an expectation of continued future investment by the firm".[144] Following from this, the market value of a company can be said to be composed of two parts: the market value of assets already in place and the present value of future investment opportunities.[145] Furthermore, considering that a company is composed

[141] *Ibid* (p. 305).

[142] *Ibid.*

[143] See Myers (1977, p. 148).

[144] *Ibid.*

[145] *Ibid.*

of two distinct asset types, namely, real assets which "have market values independent of the firm's investment strategy", and real options which are "opportunities to purchase real assets on possibly favourable terms", an investment strategy is effectively concerned with real options for a company.[146]

Focusing on transformation, an investment strategy that aims to help a company achieve its transformation goals can operate in several ways: through purchasing investment assets that align with a company's vision, making discretionary investments to realise returns on assets,[147] and refurbishing or repurposing underutilised assets to optimise their value. Investment decisions depend upon factors such as the prevailing interest rates, the company's capital structure and cost of capital, as well as the interests of debt holders and stockholders of the company.[148] A company's cost of capital is a combination of the company's cost of debt and cost of equity, which affect the expected returns that a company can make.

For an investment strategy, there is likewise a trade-off in terms of risks and returns, and in terms of investment goals, the returns are typically measured in terms of income and capital gains. An investment strategy looks at optimising a portfolio of investments. Decisions on when to invest and how much could "depend on net present values of opportunities as they arise in the future", and if conditions are unfavourable, a company may choose not to invest.[149] A company's decisions on whether to invest can also be affected by their current capital structure, and the levels of risky debt outstanding in the company may compel it to follow a different decision rule on making further investments.[150] Certain investments may involve several parties, usually for the purpose of sharing risks and combining resources, so as to maximise potential returns over a given period of time.

In discussing strategies for investments, it is also worth discussing company mergers and acquisitions in brief. Company mergers and acquisitions involve a target company and a bidding company developing a deal structure that fuses the two companies, with the main method for payment typically denominated in either cash, stock or a combination of the two. Regardless of the deal strategy or structure, mergers and acquisitions are typically focused on creating synergies, resulting in the value of the combined companies being greater than the sum of the parts.[151] The success of a merger or acquisition depends on whether this synergy is achieved.

Having thus presented the literature review on the various aspects of the transformational change cycle model, the following chapters will discuss the application of the model to the case of Mandarin Orchard Singapore and Mandarin Gallery. Chapter 3 will analyse the management ethos and corporate culture of OUE Limited, as well as how, being a family-owned business, it shapes its branding and corporate identity. Chapter 4 will explore the strategic business policies that were implemented to turnaround and reposition MOS and MG. Chapter 5 will provide some insights on the corporate financial strategy that was envisaged and executed to achieve the goals of asset enhancement and value creation for the property.

---

[146] *Ibid* (p. 163).

[147] *Ibid.*

[148] See Fama (1976).

[149] See Myers (1977, p. 148).

[150] *Ibid.*

[151] See Chatterjee (1986).

CHAPTER 3

UNLOCKING THE POTENTIAL OF MANDARIN ORCHARD SINGAPORE AND MANDARIN GALLERY: INTRODUCING A NEW CORPORATE CULTURE AND VALUES

Figure 3.1 First Driver of Change

Corporate Culture & Values

- Management ethos
- Branding and corporate identity
- Family business culture

Source: Asia Competitiveness Institute

3.1 MANAGEMENT ETHOS: SPIRITUALITY AND STEWARDSHIP

Based on the interviews that have been conducted with members of OUE Limited, it becomes readily apparent that every member of the organisation we speak to has a strong sense of both what is expected of them by OUE Limited and its Chairman and what they can expect in return. This is an awareness that reflects the existence of a strong and well-defined management ethos. Such a central ideological and methodological anchor would be all but necessary, especially in the context of the company's uneven early history, which in turn affected the efficiency of its operating parameters. A member of senior management recalls that period as follows:

> "*When Dr Riady took control of the company that's where you can see transformation of the whole group from that point onwards, before that, decision making was very slow and there were a lot of issues when it comes to board meetings, trying to decide on where to take, how to move the company, things like that.*"[1]

Discussions with a member of the company's top management regarding types of investors also revealed certain details about the breakneck pace OUE Limited progressively came to

[1] Asia Competitiveness Institute interviews of senior management staff of OUE Limited (2015).

operate at, after Dr Riady took control. This in turn reflected the idea that the effective investor, in the view of OUE Limited's top management, is one that seeks to identify and exploit "Momentum" — a term that in the company's lexicon encapsulates both a chronological and reputational element.[2] That is to say, for OUE Limited, it is not sufficient to grasp and exploit an initial opportunity during an appropriate timeframe, but an initial success should always be swiftly followed by a second, a third, and a fourth success, all of which build upon the prestige and expectation generated by preceding successes. As this member of management further notes:

> *"That's what I call momentum. You must know when you reach that point, because that is the best time you move things. To my board, it is the same thing, to my people, the same thing, I must know when the momentum is."*[3]

It is the case, therefore, that when OUE Limited perceives an opportunity to seek this "momentum", the company as a whole is pushed quickly into high gear to strike while the iron is hot. Because of its dedication to capturing this ever-elusive momentum, the culture of OUE Limited is thus one of constant and often unexpected upheaval, in which one could easily expect the "disorientation" described by Caza et al. to prevail.[4] However, OUE Limited is instead a streamlined and extremely effective organisation staffed by dedicated individuals, which correspondingly speaks to the strength of its management ethos and the fortitude of its collective, organisational identity.

3.1.1 ETHICS AND THE SPIRITUAL CHAIRMAN

OUE Limited and the approaches it has taken in managing individuals and assets alike have been strongly influenced by the attitudes and actions of Dr Stephen Riady, its current Chairman. As a senior manager puts it:

> *"He dares to see, he's got vision. And, he's a visionary. He's got many ideas. And if you have to put the relationship, he's the visionary, we're the executers."*[5]

Any assessment of OUE Limited's management ethos and the organisational identity which has developed from it must therefore begin with Dr Riady himself. As an individual with deeply held convictions and an unabashed willingness to share his views on morality in speeches which maintain an inoffensive and pleasantly wide religious appeal, Dr Riady's views on morality and religion are not difficult to piece together. When asked at the annual ACI conference in 2014 about what he felt could be done to make Singapore a more liveable city, Dr Riady referred to Abraham Maslow's Hierarchy of Needs, and responded thus:

---

[2] *Ibid.*

[3] *Ibid.*

[4] See Caza, Barker and Cameron (2004, p. 170).

[5] Asia Competitiveness Institute interviews of senior management staff of OUE Limited (2015).

"Then you go further up [the hierarchy of needs] after that is what? It's the need to pursue the truth. Justice. Righteousness. So what this... all this from another angle to look at it is, number one, we see that the basic institution in our society is the family unit. So if we don't have, we are not strong in that, I think people generally still will not be, or cannot be, fulfilled or satisfied. So that's why I think we need a society that has a strong family sense of home. So I think this is a belief system that we must have, to promote or to give a proper understanding of what is a family."[6]

Dr Riady is thus someone who wears his values on his sleeve, being very forthcoming in expressing his perspectives, even in public forums. His values appear traditionally conservative in nature but are notably inflected by a Christian religious rhetoric, which he himself alludes to in mentioning his church later on in his speech. As is appropriate for a businessperson operating in multicultural Singapore, however, Dr Riady is quick to also express his hope that the nation remains "a place to worship according to everyone's respective faith" towards the end of his speech.[7] It should also be stressed that our interviews with OUE Limited's employees do not reveal the Chairman's management style to be anywhere as inflected by religion as to be oppressive or coercive — indeed, he is described as displaying exactly the kind of respectful tolerance with which his speech at the ACI conference concludes.

It would thus be misguided to bluntly term Dr Riady's influence on his company "religious" or to say that his religion informs his company's decisions. Instead, it would perhaps be more accurate to say that Dr Riady's spirituality informs OUE Limited's general ethos and has functioned to define its organisational identity. As has been mentioned in the overview chapter, substantial work has been done to attempt to identify links between ethical business practices and spirituality.

A survey of attitudes amongst business students towards business ethics conducted by Conroy and Emerson (2004), for example, found a strong correlation between ethical behaviour and spirituality, with the survey's findings suggesting that "the best way to improve ethical attitudes of college students would be to promote active participation in their religion of choice".[8] In contrast, however, Worden's (2005) analysis of religion as it is specifically applied to business strategy came to a less charitable conclusion, with Worden pointedly noting that in organisations where spiritual or religious doctrines achieve dogmatic status, "managerial rigidity can result as changeless truisms of revelation are maintained even in the face of changes in the organisation or the business environment".[9] Worden thus advises that, at best "the benefits of strategic leadership from the application of religion must be measured against the costs in order to determine the optimal degree of application".[10]

In OUE Limited's case, however, it seems that Dr Riady's influence on his organisation's ethos essentially boils down to one central aspect, revealed in the interview with a senior member of Dr Riady's management team:

[6] Asia Competitiveness Institute Transcript of ACI Conference (2014).

[7] *Ibid.*

[8] Conroy and Emerson (2004, p. 391).

[9] Worden (2005, p. 233).

[10] *Ibid* (p. 234).

"The chairman always says "people appreciate", and that it is all right if people fail us, but that we should not fail people."[11]

In reinforcing this point, this senior manager related a particular incident which revolved around an elderly American migrant waiter, who had worked at Mandarin hotel for a year:

"He went to see a doctor and was diagnosed with cancer. We did not know about chemotherapy treatment and things like that, but the doctor recommended chemotherapy. Immediately when chairman heard about it, an issue came to me — the limit coverage was $15,000 but the doctor told us it was expected to exceed at least a hundred thousand. At this point he had already clocked in $30,000, so what were we to do? ... We paid for everything and in fact we footed the bill without questioning. He recovered after about six months of treatment."[12]

This was evidently a profoundly uneconomical decision to take, costing the organisation an enormous sum of money for little reward, especially since the waiter in question subsequently returned to America after requesting severance pay. However, as the manager notes, this was a decision that was made in light of OUE Limited's prevailing commitment to doing right by all its stakeholders, in accordance with the values and principles held by Dr Riady and similarly inclined individuals in upper management. This, and incidents like this, fundamentally serve to inform an organisational identity based on a personal and ideological loyalty to the company's Chairman and the moral, spiritually informed principles he represents. As our interviewee proudly concludes:

"I do not know if this is the case for other people, but this is the story I always tell my son to show him what kind of management, and what kind of Chairman we have."[13]

3.1.2 A CULTURE OF STEWARDSHIP

This element of OUE Limited's organisational identity thus informs what employees up and down the corporate hierarchy can expect of OUE Limited and Dr Riady. It enables them to function in accordance to a kind of tacit social contract and encourages them to integrate into their lives the precepts Dr Riady has set down for his organisation. However, the question of what is expected of them as employees is a separate consideration, which, while informed by similarly ideological principles, nevertheless requires separate analysis unto itself. What became obvious in our interviews with OUE Limited's employees, however, was that there was no confusion in what they perceived the organisation as a whole to expect from them. As a senior executive in Developments and Projects relates, when asked about what they felt OUE Limited represented as an organisation:

---

[11] Asia Competitiveness Institute interviews of senior management staff of OUE Limited (2015).

[12] *Ibid.*

[13] *Ibid.*

> *"Quality, I think. Something you can be proud of. I have worked for different organisations, and sometimes different things drive the company, but for us I think we are driven by Dr Riady's vision, which is always to get a quality product. He really drives quality product — for him, he does not want anything sub-standard, or something that you can be ashamed of, or even just not proud of."*[14]

This executive's response is significant not only in that it reinforces the degree to which Dr Riady's aspirations trickle down OUE Limited's corporate hierarchy, but also in its reflection of the degree to which they themselves had internalized this search for "quality". This executive, along with many others like him, are made to feel empowered in their positions and in that way are also encouraged to align their visions and objectives to those of their Chairman and organisation. This is what Covey terms as "Stewardship" or "a trust in the sense that you represent someone or something else".[15] Covey expands on this concept accordingly:

> *"The stewardship is what is given back to you once there is a common value system, common vision, and common commitment. The stakeholders basically assign people differing stewardships to assist them in fulfilling their win–win performance agreements in a system of shared vision and values. In this "mission state", moral authority begins to build in the culture. Soon, everyone is accountable to the same set of principles. No one is exempt from these principles, which are built into the value system."*[16]

At the core of stewardship as a concept is thus the need for a fundamental trust on the part of a leader in the capabilities and capacities of their subordinates. This results in the creation of a shared responsibility and accountability that relies not on the traditional structured hierarchy of a corporate entity for enforcement, but on individual personal investments in the success and well-being of the collective whole. What this also makes possible is the maintenance of corporate structures that are less traditional in configuration. In the context of OUE Limited and the Mandarin Orchard Singapore, this manifests in an organisational structure which is much flatter than those of similar organisations. As one of the aforementioned senior executives puts it:

> *"It is quite a pleasant working environment, and I think the overall tone in these organisations is shaped from the top down. I worked in an organisation where the top guy is really unapproachable. You never even go near him — it is as if you are going near the Prime Minister. You never get to speak to him, and when you do it is very tense. So, when he is tense, the next guy is tense and the next and so on. It cascades down and everybody is very tense."*[17]

OUE Limited's strong organisational identity empowers and enables its employees across the managerial spectrum. It is couched in precepts of spiritual morality that have been laid down by its Chairman, which correspondingly enable it to retain a compassionate core, enervating employees and cultivating loyalty. In also permeating the company's culture at such a

---

[14] *Ibid.*

[15] Covey (1997, p. 3).

[16] *Ibid.*

[17] Asia Competitiveness Institute interviews of senior management staff of OUE Limited (2015).

fundamental level, OUE Limited's organisational identity acts to sustain a flat managerial structure which empowers its stakeholders and encourages them to develop personal investments in the well-being of the company. And finally, as has been indicated, OUE Limited's organisational identity, which has been founded upon its strong management ethos, has allowed it to flourish, despite the trying circumstances which surrounded its birth.

3.2 BRANDING AND CORPORATE IDENTITY: RAISING THE PROFILE OF OUE LIMITED

Another element of OUE Limited's operating strategy which shone through strongly during our interviews with staff was the importance the company ascribed to its branding, its corporate or organisational image, and its overall recognisability as an organisation. This plays strongly into OUE Limited's aforementioned dedication to the concept of "momentum". As our interviewee from top management explains:

> "*I feel that if my talent is graded at 100, you may think that it is only worth a grade of 10. But one day you may find that I am doing something great, then your estimation of my talent rises to 50. Perhaps then after the third transaction and so on, you will grade me an 80. Then, this may reach the stage where a lot of people are talking about it and saying good things about me — until I am even in the papers. So at this point you even start to break the 100 mark — actually my capacity is only 100, then it breaks to 150, becomes 200...*"[18]

Aside from being reliant on success and good judgment, "momentum", as it is perceived by OUE Limited's top management, is therefore also strongly predicated on managing expectations and perceptions through outreach and engagement with the public. This is where the public-facing flipside to organisational identity — corporate identity — comes into play. We have previously discussed the degree to which this particular mechanism can be useful in initiating an organisational relaunch or reprioritisation. When Dr Riady first took over OUE Limited, it was clear that members of the organisation were well aware that they suffered from deficiencies in terms of brand recognition. To quote a senior executive:

> "*If you say you are from CDL, everybody knows what that is. But when I first joined [OUE Limited], it was around the time Dr Riady first took over — he had just bought the company. What happened at the time was that they would ask me where I was from, and I would tell them I was from OUE. They would then ask if I meant OUB or UOB or UOL and I would have to say No, none of the above — OUE! Then they would ask what OUE stood for.*"[19]

A situation like this, where the company was as unrecognisable as to be an almost completely unknown quantity, naturally meant that investor enthusiasm was initially muted at best. Indeed,

---

[18] *Ibid.*

[19] *Ibid.*

having to constantly identify itself to investors and thus reinforce the perception of its own obscurity meant that OUE Limited was itself consistently surrounded by an air of uncertainty — a quality which is understandably anathema to financiers and investors. This in turn led to the company's options initially being extremely limited and even attempting to secure a substantial line of credit became a challenge, with a member of top management noting:

> *"If I wanted 100 million, then the bank would often tell me that they were uncertain, and that I could only have 10 million instead."*[20]

Because of this, branding became a priority for the organisation as a whole, as was evinced by the fact that every single member of senior management we interviewed registered a consistent recognition of its importance to OUE Limited's continuing success, as well as the progress that had been made in that regard since the earliest days of the company's inception.

3.2.1 MAKING OUE LIMITED A HOUSEHOLD NAME

The decision to prioritise branding was evident in the fact that Dr Riady himself consistently played an enormous part in shaping OUE Limited's organisational image, acting as its public face and strongest advocate. Recalling OUE's earliest days, a senior manager recounts Dr Riady's experiences approaching potential investors in Hong Kong:

> *"He kept promoting and kept going on. I think this the kind of perseverance and determination to build up the OUE name which he valued a great deal. I think the break came when we continued to raise funds and our profile increased. From being the subject of zero analyst reports, we went to at one point having about 25 analysts covering us."*[21]

To quote another senior executive at OUE Limited, who was commenting on Dr Riady's role:

> *"He used himself — he gave himself to OUE — and made himself a tool for people to recognise OUE. I think that is very powerful, and because he is such a pleasant sort of guy, it adds to the positive image of the company."*[22]

OUE Limited's attempts to entrench itself in the public consciousness have extended substantially further than just the personal exertions of its Chairman, however. Throughout its lifetime as an independent company, OUE Limited has also endeavoured to acquire either extremely well-known or well-situated assets, with the company banking on the intrinsic recognisability of

---

[20] *Ibid.*

[21] *Ibid.*

[22] *Ibid.*

these assets, along with OUE Limited's own talent for asset renewal, to ultimately augment its standing. To date, nearly all of OUE Limited's acquisitions, from what is now Mandarin Orchard Singapore to OUE Downtown and OUE Bayfront, have followed this trend, being notable buildings which have either through their venerable histories or their prime locations been consistently well positioned to call attention to OUE Limited itself (see Tables A2 and A3 of Appendix 3 for brief summaries of these distinguishing qualities). As a senior manager at the company confidently asserts:

> *"Every one of our assets is iconic and we acquire them expeditiously. We then work to transform them and bring value to the group, and from there it loops back in on itself to continue adding value to the group."*[23]

3.3 FAMILY-OWNED BUSINESS: SUCCESSION THROUGH RENEWAL

Since a key aspect of OUE Limited's identity is that of a family-owned business, there is a great emphasis and investment in succession planning. The Lippo group was founded by Dr Riady's father, Mochtar Riady, who ensured his two sons Stephen and James gained experience in running the family business. Now in a position to do the same for his own children, Dr Riady firmly believes that he has an important role to play in honing the entrepreneurial skills of the next generation so that the family business can survive beyond the third generation.

Studies of best practices in family-owned businesses state that successful businesses identify their potential successors early on and invest in them.[24] Undoubtedly aware of the struggles that family-owned businesses can face in finding suitable candidates, and the resulting low chance of survival for these businesses across each successive generations, the Riady family has dedicated significant attention to the grooming and nurturing of talent from a young age. For example, succession planning involves firstly providing the next generation with strong first-hand experience and on-the-job training. This commitment to succession planning is evident from the approach of Mochtar Riady, Dr Riady's father, who groomed the latter to learn the ropes of the business. From a young age of 15, Dr Riady would return to Jakarta during the school holidays and job-shadow his father in different areas of the business. He recounts:

> *"Every holiday, I would go back to Jakarta and sit in the bank's foreign exchange department for one or two months. The next holiday, it would be the import department. After that, the export department. Then, the account opening, checking accounts, all these different departments, and after that international trade, letters of credit. So in actuality I did not really have holidays, every time I went back."*[25]

Dr Riady's first job was for an electronics company in Los Angeles where he worked under the guidance of his father as a financial controller for a company that was going bankrupt and

---

[23] *Ibid.*

[24] See Fernández-Aráoz et al. (2015).

[25] Asia Competitiveness Institute interviews of senior management staff of OUE Limited (2015).

plagued by debtors. He received the opportunity to apply the financial concepts he had been taught in school and at the same time received important lessons about banking from his father. Subsequently, he was assigned to another position, where he had to collect debts from those who owed money to the bank:

> *"So, I did all this, and after two years my father told me that since I had experience with being on the borrower's side, he wanted to switch me to the lender side. So, I started working in the bank side after working on the company side and knowing how the borrower thinks. It was not an easy job, as all the bad loans would go to me, and I would write a two-page report for all the bad loans, asking why the executive committee signed their approval four or five years ago, but then it turned into a bad loan. So I would ask about the things they didn't see, and question them on why they ended up approving these loans. I learned a lot from that experience."*[26]

Accordingly, the on-the-job training provided by Mochtar Riady exposed Dr Riady to the different environments and challenges of leading a business. Although Dr Riady was born in Indonesia, he received most of his early education in Singapore and completed his higher education in the United States, graduating from the University of Southern California. He also obtained a Master of Business Administration degree from the Golden Gate University and was awarded an honorary Degree of Doctor of Business Administration from Napier University in the United Kingdom. His education and experience in finance provided him with command of a language that was useful in the investment and business world, which in turn enabled him to take on a more hands-on approach in key business decisions.

In the 1990s, Dr Riady entered the Hong Kong business environment and in 2003, he decided to base himself in Singapore. In 2006, Dr Riady purchased a stake in OUE Limited and became the Executive Director of the company. Besides assuming the position of OUE Limited's Executive Chairman, Dr Riady is also the Executive Director of Lippo Limited and has been its chairman since 1991.[27] Dr Riady also holds executive positions at Lippo's overseas offices in China and Hong Kong. Both Dr Riady and his brother James Riady have been entrusted with overseeing the business, with the former being in charge of Singapore and overseas while the latter runs the Indonesian operations.

3.3.1 GROOMING A NEW "FIRST GENERATION"

The importance of educating and training the next generation to sustain the family business is clear from the grooming which even the next generation of Riadys has received.

For the Riadys, the "internal curriculum" for grooming the next generation involves not just equipping them with a good education but also helping them grasp the technicalities of running a business, since "a university education can prepare the next generation for business roles, but not for ownership roles in family businesses".[28] The emphasis on education also relates to Dr Riady's belief

---

[26] *Ibid.*

[27] See Lippo Limited (2008).

[28] See Schwass (2013, p. 6).

that rationality, and not emotion, should guide business decisions. Brian Riady, Dr Riady's son, was also educated overseas and returned to Asia to prepare for his role as the Chief Executive Officer of a cinema company called "Cinemaxx".[29]

Dr Riady has applied some important lessons learned from his own experiences with his father in grooming the next generation, including the importance of receiving training akin to the experiences of the first generation, so that the second generation "effectively becomes the first generation again".[30] This "first generation training" means that rather than being given an already optimised and efficient business to manage, the next generation is assigned to be in charge of an entirely new project in an area that they have expressed an interest in. Dr Riady explains that this kind of first-hand experience will enable the next generation to understand the challenges and struggles of starting a new business from scratch:

> *"If Brian runs an operation that is already running smoothly, he will not learn. But now, he's facing all kinds of things, like people giving him pressure on why his payment is late — this is real. So that is what we want him to experience, rather than treating him as a second or third generation."*[31]

Similar to Mochtar Riady's on-the-job exposure for Dr Riady, Brian Riady also accompanies his father to attend important board meetings and key events so he can be exposed to the company. This parallel learning is useful for the next generation as the early exposure to the business, and the stories that are shared and passed down by the older generation will enable the next generation to internalise and uphold the company values that sustain the family business. This practice is advocated by studies which stress that each generation in a family owned business should understand its history or story. Since "personal values and visions leave an indelible imprint on the businesses", an understanding of what has come before empowers subsequent generations to assert themselves while firmly situating them in a multi-generational continuity.[32]

In the case of the Riady family, the goal has been, as much as has been possible, to enable the next generation to carve a niche and pursue an area that interests them. Successful multi-generational family-owned businesses understand the "natural diversity of interests and needs of family members, based on their respective positions".[33] For example, Brian Riady shared during ACI's interviews that the younger generation is encouraged to pursue areas where they demonstrate potential,[34] and that there are frequent discussions with the older generation about their interests and goals. Therefore, the company finds ways to accommodate and integrate the interests and talents of the next generation into the business to expand into new areas. Dr Riady did however acknowledge that as the family grows in size and more branches are added to the family tree, succession planning could become more complicated, and conflicts between family members could arise, which could in turn necessitate changes to existing approaches.[35]

---

[29] Asia Competitiveness Institute interviews of senior management staff of OUE Limited (2015).

[30] *Ibid.*

[31] *Ibid.*

[32] See Schwass (2013, p. 3).

[33] *Ibid* (p. 5).

[34] Asia Competitiveness Institute interviews of senior management staff of OUE Limited (2015).

[35] *Ibid.*

CHAPTER 4

COMPETITIVE BUSINESS POLICIES FOR ASSET ENHANCEMENT: STRATEGIC POLICIES INTRODUCED FOR THE TURNAROUND OF MANDARIN ORCHARD SINGAPORE AND MANDARIN GALLERY

Chapter 3 discussed the ways in which a strong management ethos has moulded a company culture that emphasises quality, empowerment and compassion. It also outlined how this focus on quality is also tangible in the branding strategy of OUE Limited, which is predicated on the securing of iconic assets, and their transformation into exponentially more valuable, high-quality assets. The following chapter will correspondingly explore the specific strategic business policies that were designed and implemented in order to transform the MOS and MG.

4.1 PRODUCTIVITY, COST AND PRICE COMPETITIVENESS: DELIVERING VALUE

Most of the restructuring that took place following the acquisition of MOS was aimed at expanding the retail space of MG. Yet, it must be noted that MOS itself also rose significantly in terms of valuation and profitability after its acquisition. This rise in profitability was driven largely by the company's efforts to keep costs under control while raising revenue — a challenging task for an organisation operating within a labour-intensive industry, located in labour-scarce Singapore.

This section discusses the measures taken to increase productivity and price competitiveness, and their resultant effects on the financial performance of the hotel and gallery.

4.1.1 PRODUCTIVITY DRIVE

In the asset enhancement of both MG and MOS, Dr Riady consistently prioritised the drive for productivity in the use of both capital and labour inputs by streamlining and optimising both the investment and operational aspects of business policy in order to allow MOS and MG to mount a turnaround.

With specific reference to Dr Riady's investments into MG and MOS in particular, a significant factor that influenced him was his belief in adding value via driving capital productivity. This can be examined in two stages. Firstly, he observed that due to the building standards which were the norm when MOS and MG were constructed, their initial configurations were not spatially efficient. They had a relatively low ratio of net floor area to gross floor area.[1] In this, he perceived an opportunity to add value. As such, with the enhancement of both MOS and MG,

[1] See Asia Competitiveness Institute conference conversation with industry captains with Dr Stephen Riady (2014).

the initial priority was to increase the productivity of the buildings, ensuring that a larger proportion of square footage could be used, given the building area available.

Secondly, Dr Riady showed his commitment to driving productivity through his choice of building utilisation. While MOS was originally a property almost wholly focused on hospitality, Dr Riady introduced an integrated retail concept for MG due to his observation of market trends. He believed that branching into retail could prove lucrative as the sector was experiencing an upswing and could potentially be more productive than hospitality in generating returns for OUE Limited.[2] The results of this decision speak for themselves — annual revenue at the MGs increased from S$8 million to S$30 million, and a favourable valuation of the MG places its worth at S$500 million, despite the S$190 million investment outlay.[3]

Operationally, Dr Riady also introduced various policies to drive average labour productivity (ALP), and therefore increase MG's competitiveness. In 2010, two factors made it vital that ALP growth was driven. The first factor was internal and had to do with the company's mandate becoming more focused on improving operational efficiency. The second, external factor consisted of the government's tightening of foreign labour policies, which made it substantially more difficult for MOS to attract and retain talent through the avenues which it had previously used. As such, we can accordingly dissect the drive for ALP into two constituents, namely, increasing the operational revenue per worker — "working hard" or increasing value-added (VA) per unit of operational revenue (OR) — "working smart".[4] Evidently, Dr Riady approached his productivity drive by maximising smart work:

> *"We are here because, for everything we do, we expect a certain value to be created. This is because OUE Limited as a group is ultimately about value creation. I think the culture is different."*[5]

Consequently, investments in capital goods such as machinery and robots such as self-guided vacuum robots or motorised devices used to lift beds were made in the interest of maximising productivity.[6] These goods either aided the staff in their duties, increasing their output/time spent, or replaced them, allowing remaining staff to concentrate on more value-added activities, increasing the ratio of VA to OR, and hence ALP. Furthermore, staff were also provided with training to improve efficiency and work faster and smarter. As such, this allowed MOS's manpower requirements to be streamlined from 800 to 700.[7]

The effectiveness of Dr Riady's productivity-driven strategic policies enabled MOS to not only increase its net operating profits by 80 percent over two and a half years but also maintain

[2] Asia Competitiveness Institute interviews of senior management staff of OUE Limited (2015).

[3] *Ibid.*

[4] See Tan and Tan (2014).

[5] Asia Competitiveness Institute interviews of senior management staff of OUE Limited (2015).

[6] *Ibid.*

[7] *Ibid.*

a profit margin of 55 percent at the high end of the spectrum, relative to comparable hospitality properties.[8]

4.1.2 COST EFFICIENCY

The aforementioned productivity drive and associated initiatives were implemented to allow MOS to avoid the need for further downsizing, after it was rocked by initial waves of redundancies. As a senior executive reveals:

> *"I think we started really cutting costs in 2009. A lot of staff were trimmed down because when we looked at it, a lot of fat had accumulated over the years."*

A direct result of this was said to be a fall in the general morale of the hotel's staff, along with growing concerns regarding the potential loss of the experience and expertise which had made Mandarin such a venerable institution to begin with. As such, prioritising cost efficiency became a priority for MOS's management, and numerous additional initiatives were put into place to facilitate it. As can be seen from Figure 4.1, the hotel's expenses plateaued between 2000 and 2014, despite revenues growing at a significantly higher rate. Specifically, operating revenues for the hotel grew at a compound annual growth rate (CAGR) of 4.7 percent between 2000 and 2014, while operating expenses grew at 1.7 percent. This illustrates how MOS's

Figure 4.1 MOS Revenues and Expenses

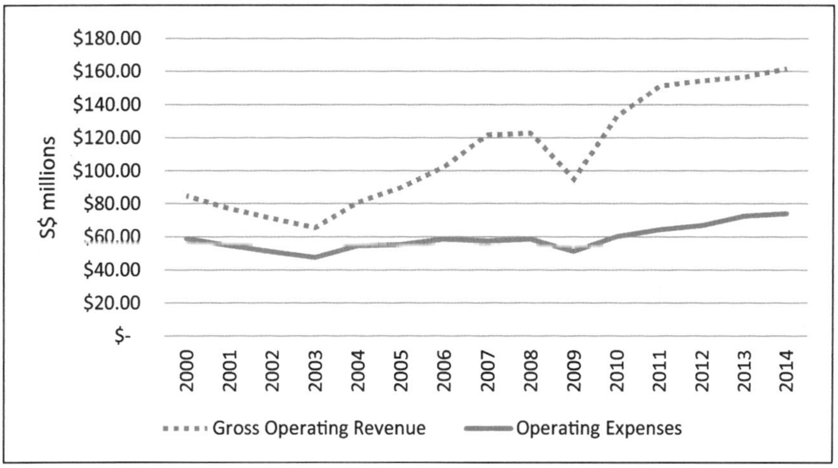

Source: Asia Competitiveness Institute; OUE Limited

[8] *Ibid.*

Figure 4.2 Value-Added per Employee of MOS

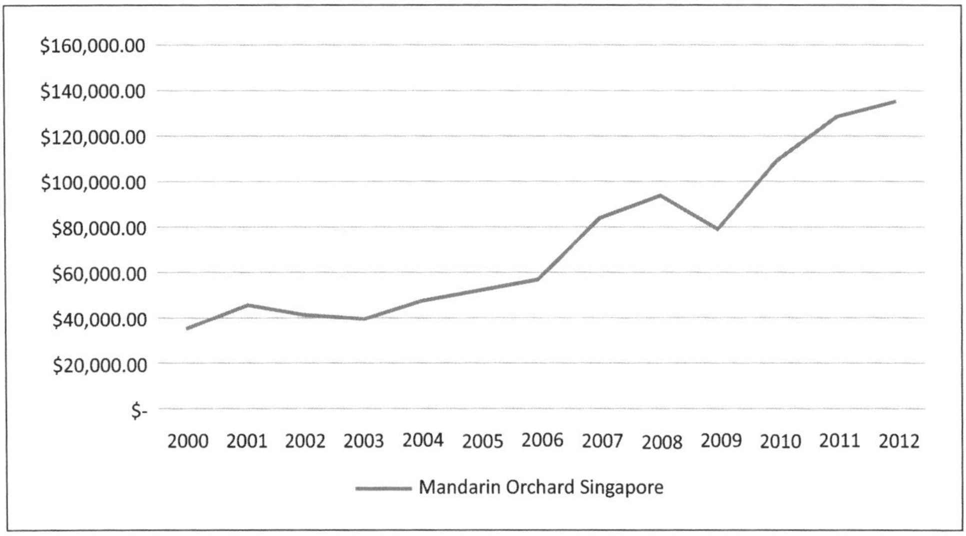

Source: Asia Competitiveness Institute; OUE Limited

productivity-driven policies allowed it to streamline its operations, hence increasing cost efficiency.

Furthermore, with respect to labour cost efficiency, we see vast improvements with regard to value-added per employee. With reference to Figure 4.2, overall value-added per employee of MOS increased from approximately S$35,000 in the year 2000 to S$135,000 in the year 2012. Most significant, however, was its increase upon the OUE Limited takeover in 2006 from approximately S$60,000 to just over S$80,000. Resultantly, we can conclude that OUE Limited's management of MOS allowed for significant improvements in both operating ratio and labour cost efficiency.

4.1.3 PRICE COMPETITIVENESS

A competitive pricing strategy is central to improving the profitability and valuation of MOS and MG. However, the differing competition dynamics inherent to the retail and hospitality markets dictated that OUE had to adopt two different competition strategies for MOS and MG, each with its own implications on pricing and marketing policies.

As for the competitive pricing policies, for a hotel like MOS with more than 1,000 rooms (Figure 4.3), the primary focus is to achieve a high room occupancy rate while maintaining an average room price comparable to other hotels in the same market segment. The performance of MOS can be evaluated based on three critical dimensions: average occupancy rate (AOR), average room rate (ARR) and revenues per available room (RevPAR) (Figure 4.4). As a general guideline, AOR examines the hotel's ability to fill up its available guest rooms while ARR examines how much a room in the hotel would cost on average. Together, these constitute RevPAR,

Figure 4.3 Total Number of Hotel Rooms in MOS

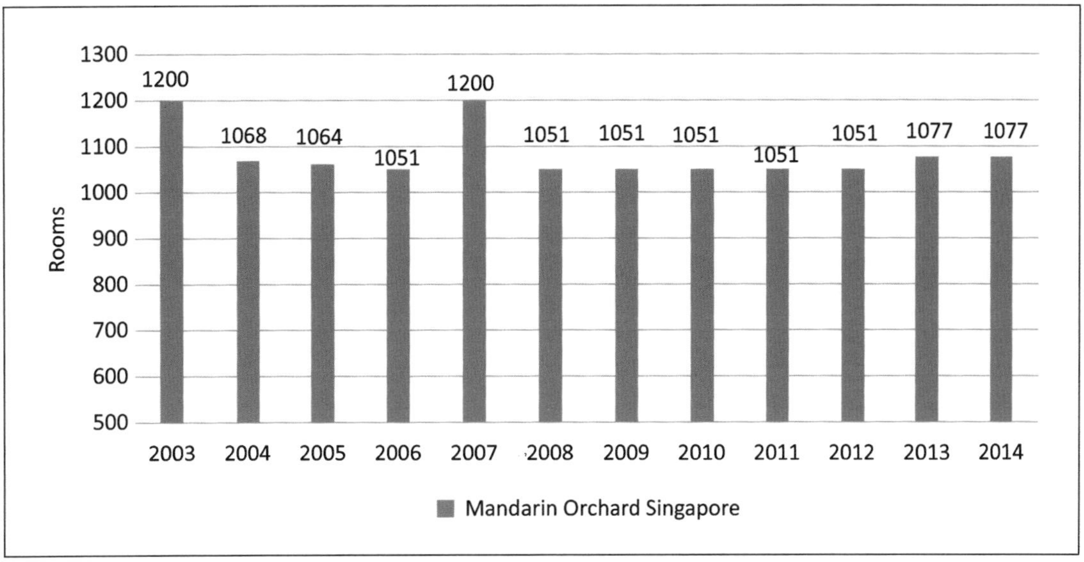

Source: Asia Competitiveness Institute; OUE Limited

Figure 4.4 Indicators for Hotel Performance[9]

Name of Indicator	Definition
Average Occupancy Rate (AOR)	= [Gross lettings (Room Nights)/Available room nights] × 100
Average Room Rate (ARR)	= Total room revenues/Gross lettings
Revenues per Available Room (RevPAR)	= Average occupancy rate × Average room rate

Source: Adapted from Singapore Tourism Board (2015)[10]

which captures the revenue performance that is attributable to each guest room over the course of a year.

ARRs for hotels in Singapore are impacted by several factors, such as location, quality, branding, target customer market and seasonality. Based on Figure 4.5, it is apparent that, relative to its own historical performance, the ARR for MOS had been on an upward trend between 2003 and 2008. This suggests that at the time of its acquisition in 2006, there was already an upward trend for room rates which was not necessarily due to a shift in business direction by the new owners. In fact, since 2008, the ARR has essentially remained stable in nominal terms, implying that it has declined in real terms.

[9]The Singapore Tourism Board defines gross lettings and available room nights using the following formulas: "Available room nights = Maximum rooms – Rooms under renovation, for staff use, others" and "Gross lettings (Room Nights) = Adjusted Paid lettings + Complimentary lettings", see Singapore Tourism Board (2015).

[10]See Singapore Tourism Board (2015).

Figure 4.5 Average Room Rate of MOS

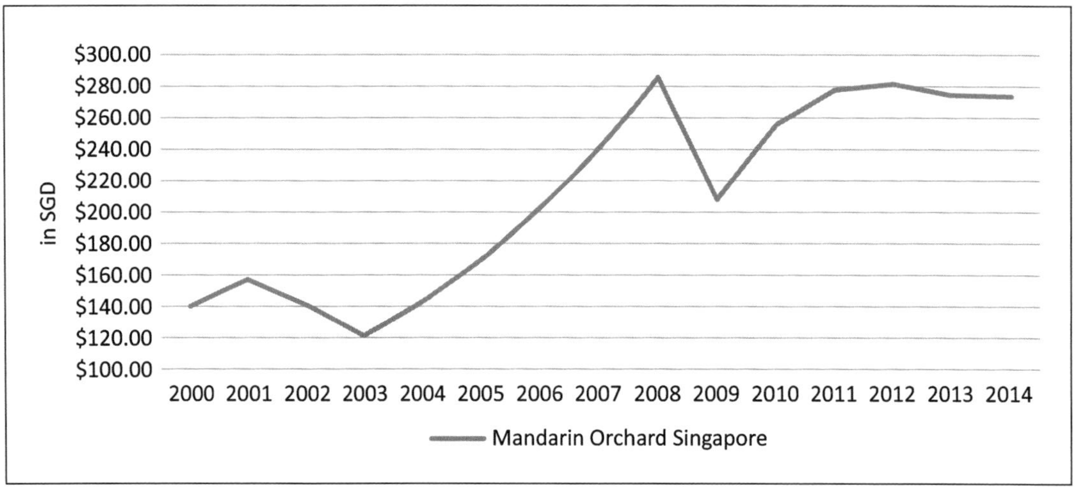

Source: Asia Competitiveness Institute; OUE Limited

Figure 4.6 Average Room Rate Comparison for MOS and Industry

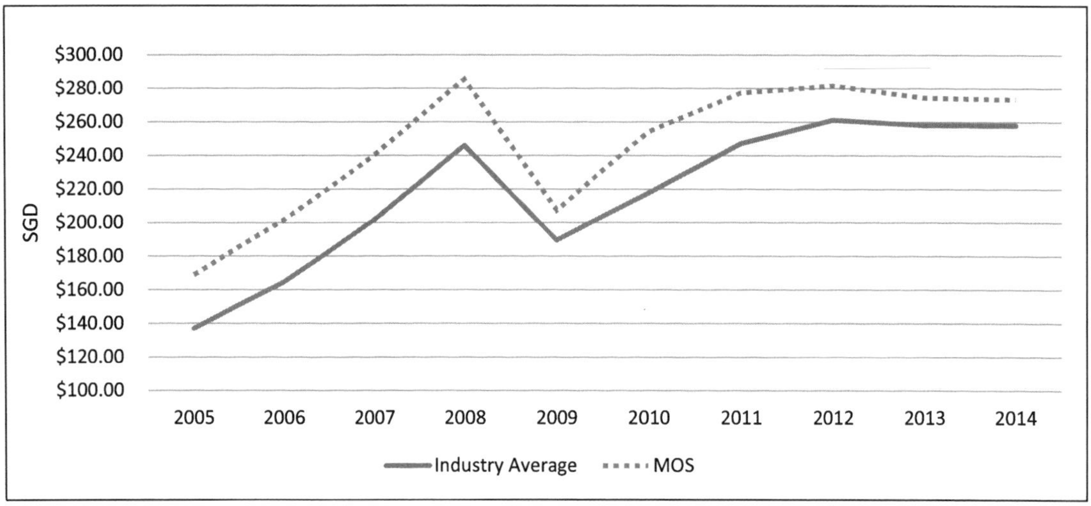

Source: Asia Competitiveness Institute; OUE Limited

Based on Figures 4.5 and 4.6, it is clear that MOS has continued to charge a higher ARR relative to the industry's ARR between 2005 and 2014. This is not surprising as MOS is positioned as a five-star hotel. However, of greater relevance is the fact that between 2011 and 2014, the gap has narrowed between the industry's performance and MOS, particularly when visualised as

Figure 4.7 Ratio of Average Room Rates for MOS to Industry

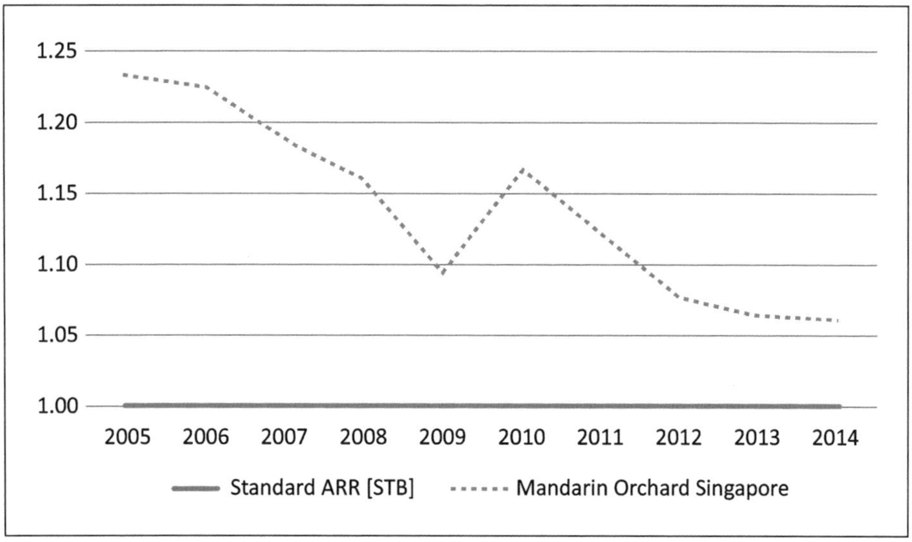

Source: Asia Competitiveness Institute; OUE Limited

a ratio with industry average values brought to unity for comparison (Figure 4.7). Based upon anecdotal accounts, this could be in part due to market pressures:

> "*Occupancy is not that bad now, it is just that the competitor hotels are lowering their rates. So if we increase our rates, our occupancy falls.*"[11]

Consistent with the above, we see that the CAGR of the ARR for MOS for the decade from 2005 to 2014 was 5.5 percent, below the industry average of 7.3 percent for the same period.

In considering whether the pricing strategy pursued by MOS is comparable to competing hotels of similar standing, it would be more illustrative to compare the performance of MOS relative to the hotel tier it is situated within.[12] The Singapore Tourism Board (STB) introduced a tiered system for hotels, classifying them as luxury, upscale, mid-tier or economy (Figure 4.8). In a market report prepared by CB Richard Ellis in 2013 for the OUE Hospitality Trust prospectus, MOS was classified within the upscale hotel tier.[13]

Comparing the ARR of MOS to other hotels in the upscale tier to which it belongs, it is apparent that the pricing closely follows the average price for hotels of that tier (Figure 4.9). This would appear to be in response to the highly price-elastic demand for hotel rooms in

[11] Asia Competitiveness Institute interviews of senior management staff of OUE Limited (2016).

[12] Since data for hotel tier performance were only made publicly available from 2011 onwards by STB, consistent hotel tier data from STB over a longer time period are not available.

[13] See CB Richard Ellis (2013).

Figure 4.8 Hotel Tiers and Definitions

Hotel Tier	Defining Features
Luxury	Includes hotels in the luxury segment which are predominantly in prime locations and/or in historical buildings.
Upscale	A degree of luxury as well as quality in the furnishings, decor and equipment in every area of the hotel. Bedrooms will offer more space and are usually well designed. It provides services, such as concierge and porter services, 24-hour room service, laundry and dry cleaning. Restaurants will provide high-quality cuisine.
Mid-Tier	Significantly greater quality and range of facilities, such as bars, restaurants, meeting rooms and in-room dining. All bedrooms will be spacious with fully en-suite bathrooms and offer a good standard of comfort and amenities.
Economy	Comfortable, no-frills and well-equipped accommodation with standard facilities, internet connection and an en-suite bath/shower room. Rooms are simple, with basic furnishings and sizes ranging from 12 to 18 square metres. It offers restaurants serving breakfast, lunch and dinner.

Source: Adapted from CB Richard Ellis (2013)[14]

Figure 4.9 Average Room Rates for MOS and Respective Hotel Tiers

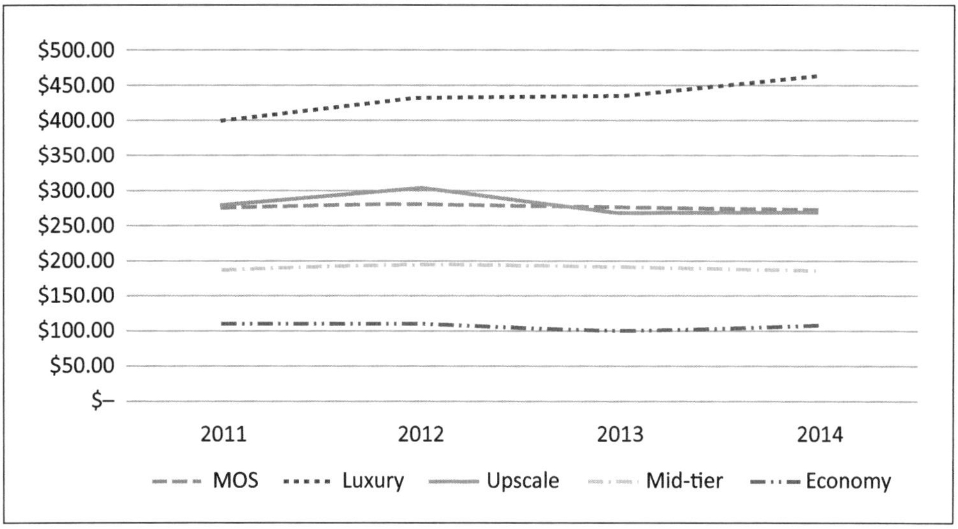

Source: Asia Competitiveness Institute; OUE Limited; Singapore Tourism Board

Singapore, given the high degree of competition in the industry. Based on the disaggregated data for ARR by hotel tiers, it appears that the increase of industry average ARR levels was driven largely by increases within the luxury hotel tier, while MOS has closely tracked the upscale hotel tier in terms of room pricing. It can be seen that the ARR for MOS has been slightly higher than its corresponding hotel tier up until 2012, but since then, its ARR is almost completely aligned with its tier. The slower growth of ARR for MOS compared to the industry

[14] See CB Richard Ellis (2013).

Figure 4.10 Average Room Rates for MOS and Competitive Set

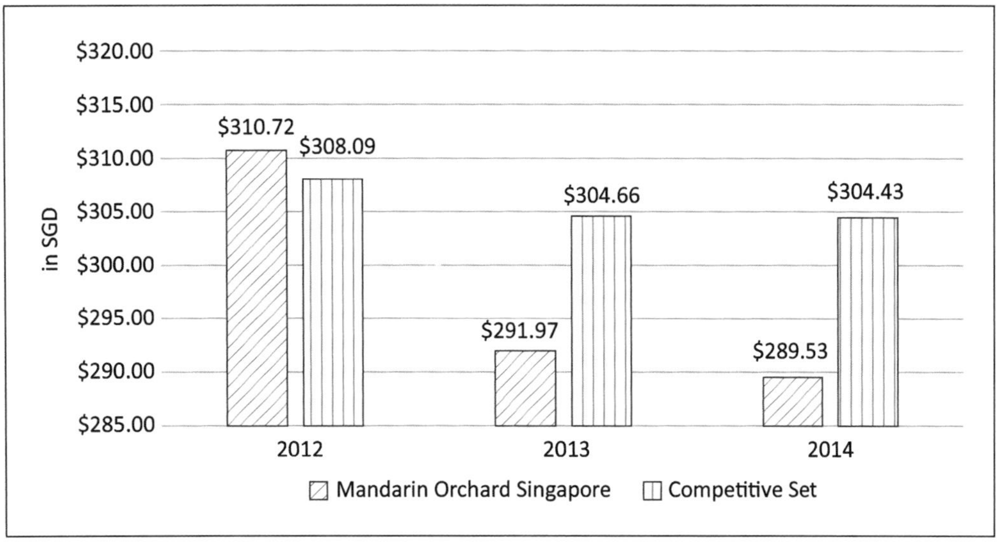

Source: Asia Competitiveness Institute; OUE Limited; STR Global (2015)

at large would appear to be a common feature for hotels within the upscale tier, at least in the years between 2011 and 2014.

To ensure appropriate comparisons, the scope of comparison was further narrowed to a set of six hotels within the same area as MOS, chosen on the basis of key factors, such as size, quality of service, facilities and branding. Six hotels were selected: Hotel Royal Plaza on Scotts, Grand Park Orchard, Sheraton Towers Singapore, Hilton Singapore Hotel, Shangri-La Singapore Tower & Garden Wing and Swissotel The Stamford, based upon a report by STR Global comparing the performance of MOS to this competitive set for the years 2012–2014.[15]

Relative to this set, using year to date values, MOS has experienced a sharper ARR decrease, with a CAGR of –3.5 percent, compared to the competitive set's CAGR of –0.6 percent (Figure 4.10). This is consistent with the findings of our study that an elastic demand for hotel rooms in the Singapore hospitality industry would make price differentiation difficult to achieve.

Next, we examine the component for hotel room revenues performance, viz. occupancy rates (Figure 4.11). Prior to the acquisition, the AOR increased slightly between 2000 and 2005, with a trough of 61.6 percent in 2001 and a peak of 76.9 percent in 2005. However, after the acquisition, following an initial dip, the AOR for MOS has rose noticeably, experiencing a more marked increase between 2006 and 2014 — with the actual AOR value surpassing 90 percent in 2013 and 2014.

Comparing the AOR trends for MOS and the industry, it can be seen that AORs for MOS have tracked industry trends closely and that, while they were in fact performing below industry levels

[15] See STR Global (2015).

Figure 4.11 Average Occupancy Rate of MOS

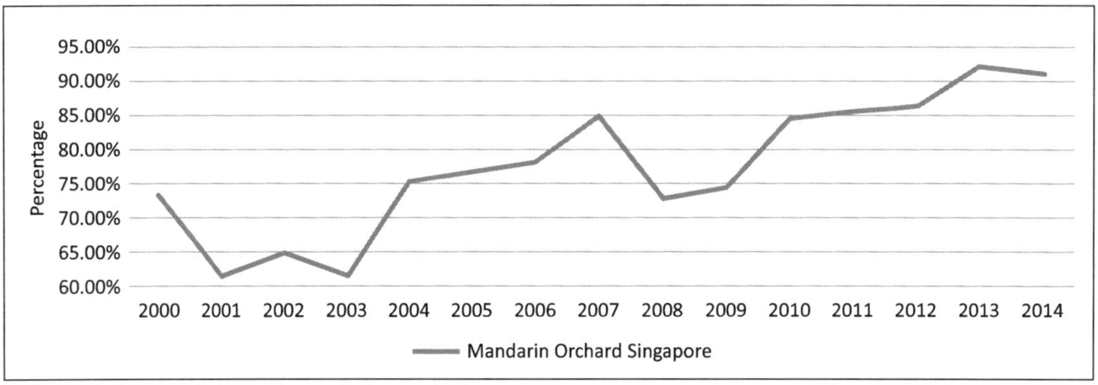

Source: Asia Competitiveness Institute; OUE Limited

Figure 4.12 Average Occupancy Rate Comparison for MOS and Industry

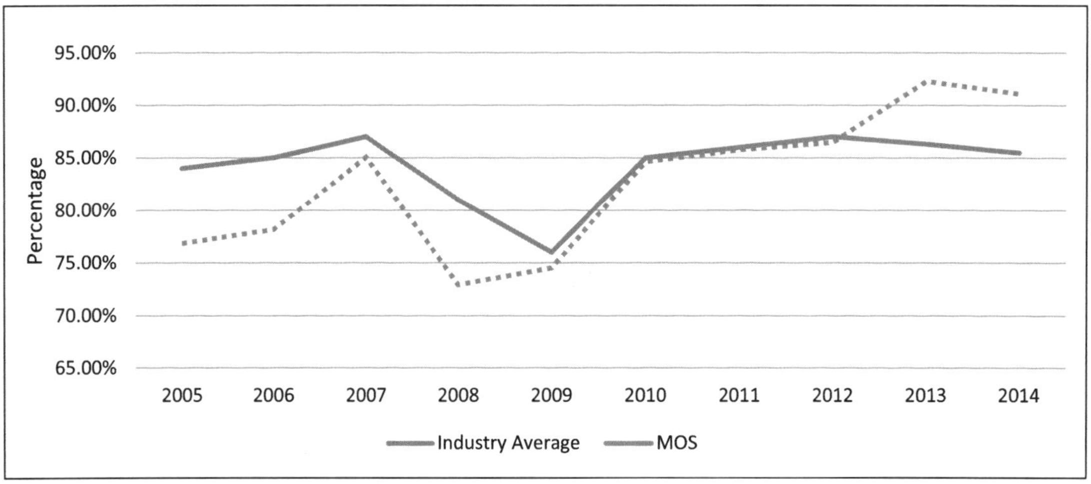

Source: Asia Competitiveness Institute; OUE Limited; Singapore Tourism Board

from 2005 to 2009, they closed the gap from 2010 to 2012 and indeed outperformed the industry by a clear margin in 2013 and 2014 (Figure 4.12). Industry-level AORs have remained largely around the 85 percent mark, except in 2008 and 2009, which coincides with the global downturn causing downward pressures on business performance across the board.

In terms of performance by hotel tiers, a comparison of MOS to its counterparts in the upscale hotel tier reveals that there could be different average AORs across the various categories.[16] In

[16]As previously mentioned, consistent STB public data disaggregated into respective hotel tiers were only available beginning from 2011, limiting the observable time period for AORs.

Figure 4.13 Average Occupancy Rates for MOS and Respective Hotel Tiers

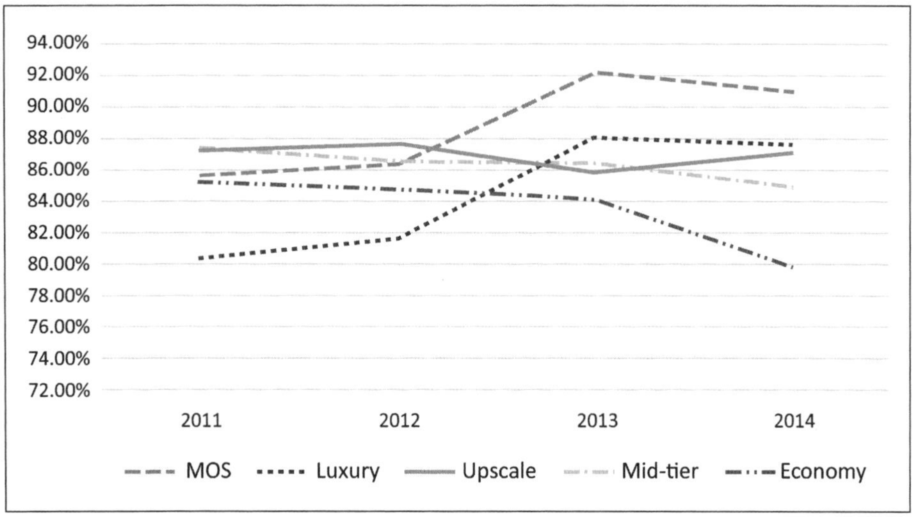

Source: Asia Competitiveness Institute; OUE Limited; Singapore Tourism Board

terms of AOR, for the years 2013 and 2014, it is apparent that MOS has not only outperformed its own tier of upscale hotels, but in fact fares better than the average for all other hotel tier categories, which do not exceed the 90 percent AOR mark at any point in the four observed years (Figure 4.13). While the timeframe for this performance comparison is relatively short and it is consequently difficult to draw comprehensive conclusions from this information, we can gather that for this period, MOS performed above average in terms of AOR compared both to the industry at large, as well as in relation to its own specific hotel tier.

Based on the year to date values for the performance of MOS relative to the aforementioned competitive set of six comparable hotels, it is apparent that MOS was able to maintain an exceptional AOR, which consistently remained above 90 percent (Figure 4.14). Achieving a high occupancy rate allowed MOS to outperform even established international brand name hotels in terms of this indicator.

Combining the findings that have been gathered from analysing ARR and AOR together leads in turn to RevPAR, which is defined as the revenue performance attributable to each available guest room on a per-night basis. RevPAR, derived by multiplying AOR with ARR, indicates how well a hotel has managed to generate revenues based upon a pricing strategy applied per room, while factoring in how effectively the hotel is able to ensure that as many of its available hotel rooms are occupied at a given time.

RevPAR is arguably a more effective indicator of the performance of a hotel than ARR, as a higher RevPAR demonstrates the ability of a hotel to maximise revenues with its available inventory of rooms in mind. Although a hotel such as MOS would ideally want to command a high ARR, a high ARR without a correspondingly high AOR would ultimately mean a missed

Figure 4.14 Average Occupancy Rates for MOS and Competitive Set

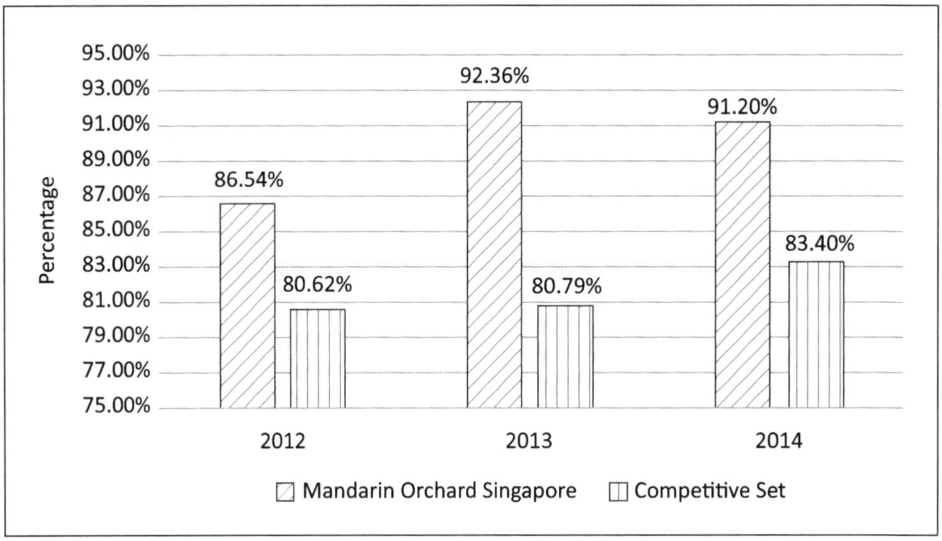

Source: Asia Competitiveness Institute; OUE Limited; STR Global (2015)

Figure 4.15 Revenues per Available Room of MOS

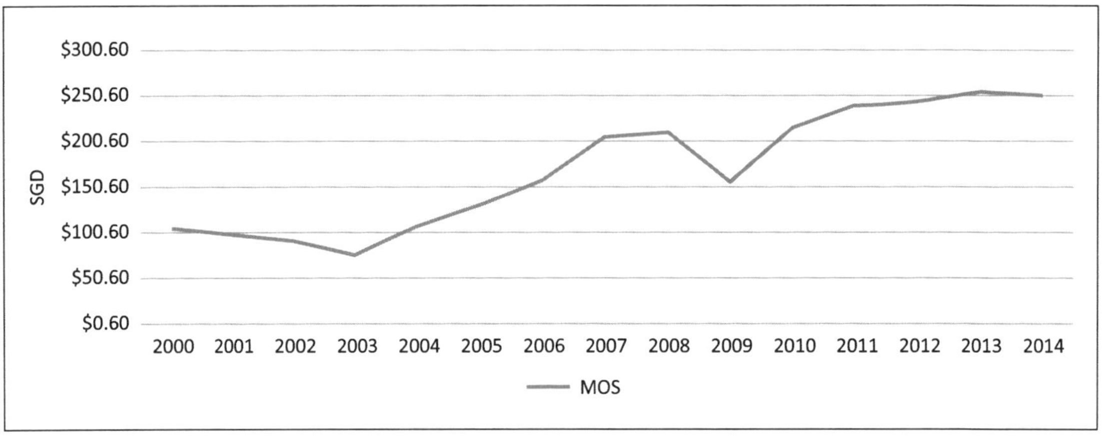

Source: Asia Competitiveness Institute; OUE Limited

opportunity to generate higher revenues, as available rooms are left idle. Quoting a senior executive at MOS:

> *"Price has a correlation with occupancy. One goes up and the other goes down. You must try and find the right balance."*[17]

As shown in Figure 4.15, the RevPAR of MOS has been improving markedly over time, with a CAGR of 6.5 percent between 2000 and 2014. In comparison to the industry average,

[17] Asia Competitiveness Institute interviews of senior management staff of OUE Limited (2016).

Figure 4.16 Revenues per Available Room Comparison for MOS and Industry

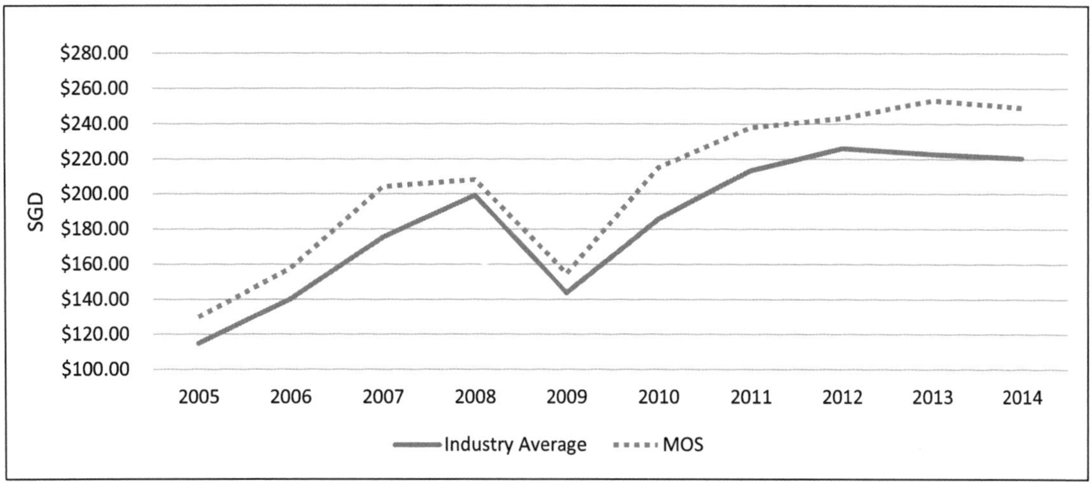

Source: Asia Competitiveness Institute; OUE Limited; Singapore Tourism Board

Figure 4.17 Ratio of Revenues per Available Room for MOS to Industry

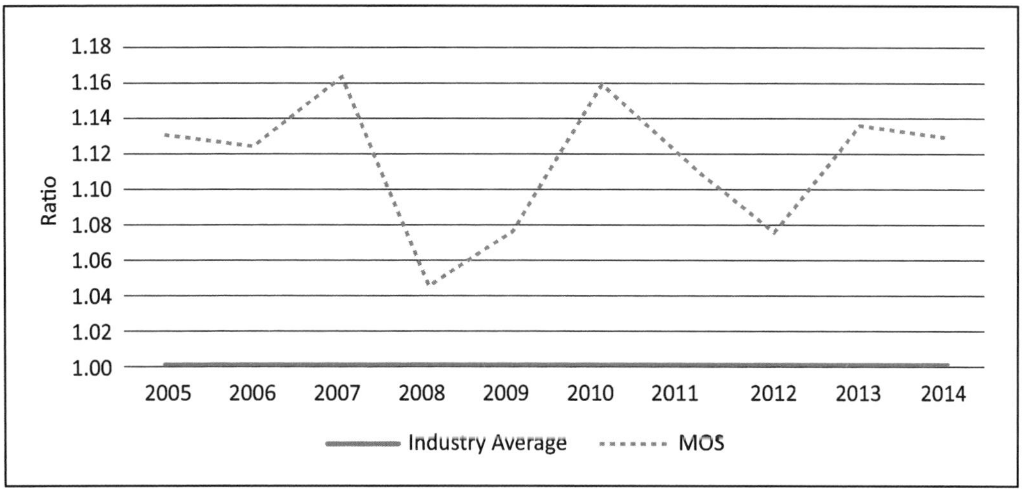

Source: Asia Competitiveness Institute; OUE Limited; Singapore Tourism Board

MOS has an improving RevPAR that continues to remain above industry-level performance (Figure 4.16).

Taken as a ratio to visualise how the RevPAR for MOS compares to the industry, with industry RevPAR values taken as unity so as to form a baseline, the challenge to maximise RevPAR as discussed by the managers of MOS and OUE Limited becomes readily apparent. MOS's performance with regard to RevPAR fluctuates considerably without a clear upward trend to indicate a consistently improving RevPAR when compared to the industry (Figure 4.17). This suggests that MOS has not been able to implement a strategy for RevPAR that can consistently outperform the industry average by an improving margin annually.

Figure 4.18 Revenues per Available Room for MOS and Respective Hotel Tiers

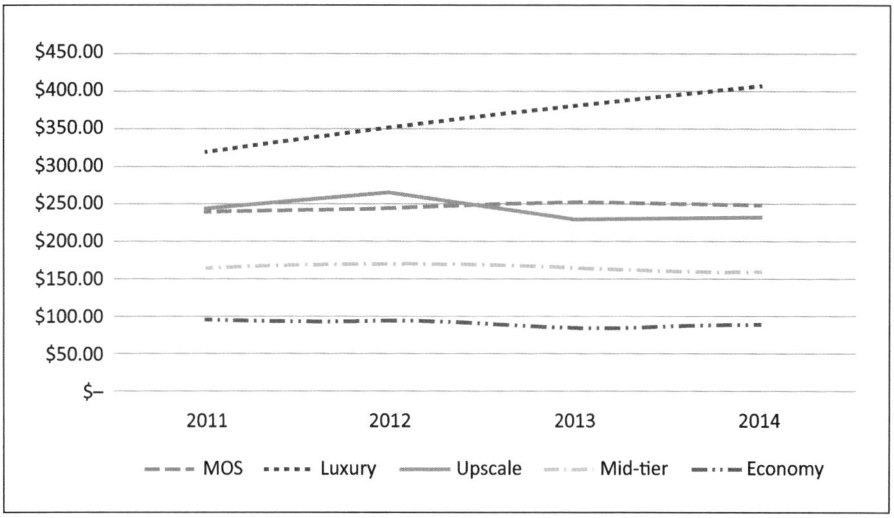

Source: Asia Competitiveness Institute; OUE Limited; Singapore Tourism Board

In considering the performance of MOS relative to the hotel tiers, the RevPAR for MOS, although coming in slightly higher than its own tier of upscale hotels in 2013 and 2014, does not vary much from average values for the upscale tier (Figure 4.18). However, when considered in relation to the aforementioned competitive set,[18] based upon year to date values from the STR Global report, MOS commands a higher RevPAR in comparison to the set of mostly international brand name hotels, though this lead is beginning to shrink (Figure 4.19).[19]

This suggests that, after acquisition, the hotel revenue performance of MOS has been driven primarily by maximising occupancy rates of the hotel, while pricing its hotel rooms at a suitably high price point. Considering that MOS is the largest hotel by room count along Orchard Road with over a 1,000 rooms (Figure 4.20), the fact that its AOR has outpaced most of its competitors and the industry as a whole is a notable achievement.

The high RevPAR is achieved through a systematic approach to hotel pricing and marketing. For MOS, pricing has been an important (but not the only) element of what has clearly been a successful strategy to raise and maintain AORs at a high level. The key difference underpinning the profitability of MOS is the systematic approach it takes towards maximising its RevPAR by striking a careful balance between its ARR and AOR. Following the acquisition, OUE Limited took a number of concrete steps to raise the performance of MOS's RevPAR.

[18]The six hotels in this competitive set were listed in the earlier discussion on average room rates.

[19]An additional noteworthy point is that, with the exception of "Swissotel The Stamford", the other hotels in the competitive set have fewer than 620 rooms each. Whether the lower combined RevPAR for the competitive set is due to a drag on the values from an outlying underperforming hotel is not immediately clear from the data, but *ceteris paribus*, MOS having a higher RevPAR despite having more rooms to fill relative to its competitive set is a commendable feat in itself.

Figure 4.19 Revenues per Available Room for MOS and Competitive Set

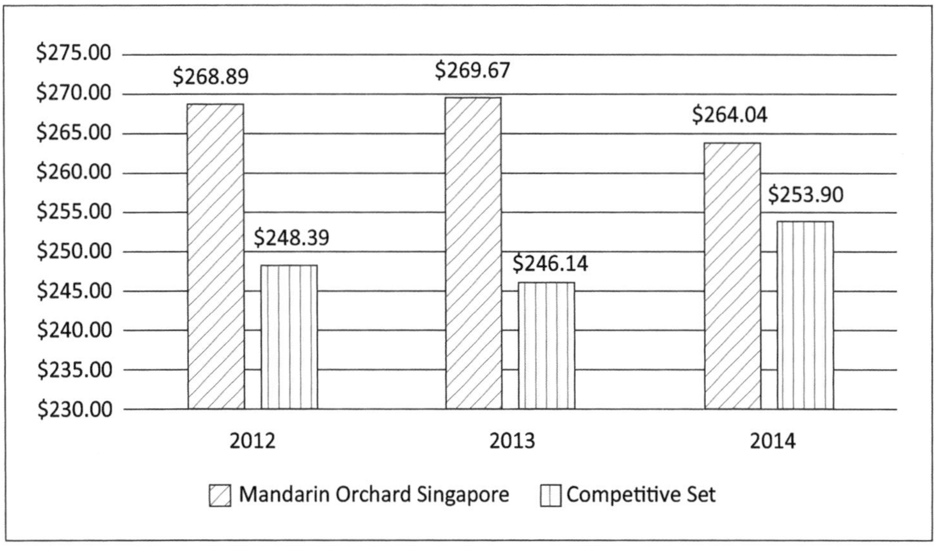

Source: Asia Competitiveness Institute; OUE Limited; STR Global (2015)

Figure 4.20 Hotels by Room Count in Orchard Area

Hotel Name	Number of Rooms
Mandarin Orchard Singapore	1,051
Grand Hyatt Singapore	662
Orchard Hotel Singapore	656
Traders Hotel Singapore (now Hotel Jen)	546
Royal Plaza	511
Regent Singapore	440
Hilton Singapore Hotel	422
York Hotel Singapore	407
Concorde Hotel Singapore	407
Singapore Marriott Hotel	393

Source: Adapted from CB Richard Ellis (2013)[20]

Firstly, Meritus Hotels and Resorts, as overall manager of the OUE Limited hotels, embarked upon marketing and online distribution initiatives such as the upgrading of their Global Distribution Systems to allow for the availability of supply to be managed in real time.[21] MOS also participated in special rate programmes on reservation systems such as

[20] See CB Richard Ellis (2013).

[21] See Overseas Union Enterprise Limited (2008, p. 36).

Galileo, Abacus and Amadeus to ensure higher occupancies of its hotel rooms, as well as partnered with "global third-party e-intermediaries" to increase bookings within their respective regional markets.[22] MOS has demonstrated its ability to keep pace with and even outperform the industry in terms of filling up its available rooms — no small challenge given the large number of rooms MOS has and the highly competitive nature of the hospitality environment in Singapore.

Secondly, the hotel is also gradually shifting its identity from being a leisure to a business-oriented hotel by expanding into other markets to diversify the guest profile. The guest profile for MOS has historically been visitors from Indonesia, some of whom travel from Indonesia to seek medical treatment in Singapore. The proximity of MOS to the Mount Elizabeth hospital attracts many such guests, with a good number of them being return customers. Presently, the bulk of the customers to MOS consists mainly of Indonesians and travellers from the People's Republic of China (PRC):

> *"Indonesians and PRC travellers are our best customers. Mandarin is near Mount Elizabeth hospital and it is in the middle of all the shopping centres, so they love it. They love our chicken rice and our lobster laksa, too!"*[23]

Steps have been taken to change the composition of the customer profile towards a more corporate clientele for MOS, with a noticeable improvement of 5.0 percent in 2014 from 23.0 percent in 2013, for the customer profile based on the revenue of MOS.[24] These initiatives have been taken as part of the strategy to pursue a higher ARR, as this group is able to afford higher room rates:

> *"Corporate customers are the ones who will pay you the high room rates, so the room rate has been improving because there has been a lot of work done to target the corporate customer."*[25]

Thirdly, strict revenue management was put in place as revenue managers were hired by the company with the goal of maximising RevPAR. These managers had to calibrate average room rates, as well as average occupancy rates, to ensure revenues were maximised on a daily basis.

Thus, the new management moved away from relying on bookings by airline companies offering lower rates to proactively focusing on identifying groups that could potentially pay higher room rates, such as corporate guests and individual travellers. The hotel also reviews the occupancy profile and examines the breakdown of customers from the various categories,

---

[22] *Ibid.*

[23] Asia Competitiveness Institute interviews of senior management staff of OUE Limited (2016).

[24] See OUE Hospitality Trust (2014a, p. 46, 2015, p. 57), respectively.

[25] Asia Competitiveness Institute interviews of senior management staff of OUE Limited (2016).

namely, wholesale, travel, online bookings, corporate, individuals and free individual travellers. To quote a member of senior management:

> *"Even now, we're looking at some of the travel agents. They give us a lot of business, but they charge really high commissions. However, if it is my Internet business or my corporate business, I do not have such big discounts. So in terms of money to the company, I would get more."*[26]

Maintaining a high RevPAR requires constant vigilance, and a keen eye for hospitality trends, evident from the hotel's AOR, which averaged 89.9 percent between 2012 and 2014 (see Table A4 in Appendix 5). Moving forward, the company hopes to increase its weekend occupancy rates by introducing promotions based on the concept of "staycations" to local guests:

> *"If you take the corporate business, they're always working late but on weekends they go home. So to generate weekend business, we try and encourage what they call 'staycations'. Singaporeans, come in and have a weekend in our hotel. They do not have to cook, wash, or anything. And some of these locals do take it up."*[27]

As for competitive pricing policies for the Mandarin Gallery or MG, compared with the highly homogenised competitive landscape of the hospitality sector, retail space provides more niches for differentiation. However, the contractual nature of rental retail space implies high switching costs, resulting in relatively high and stable occupancy rate (Figure 4.21). To maximise profit, the effective rental price becomes the main focus. As a new entrant in the prime retail space scene, functioning on the perennially crowded Orchard Road, MG strived

Figure 4.21 Occupancy Rate (Committed) of MG

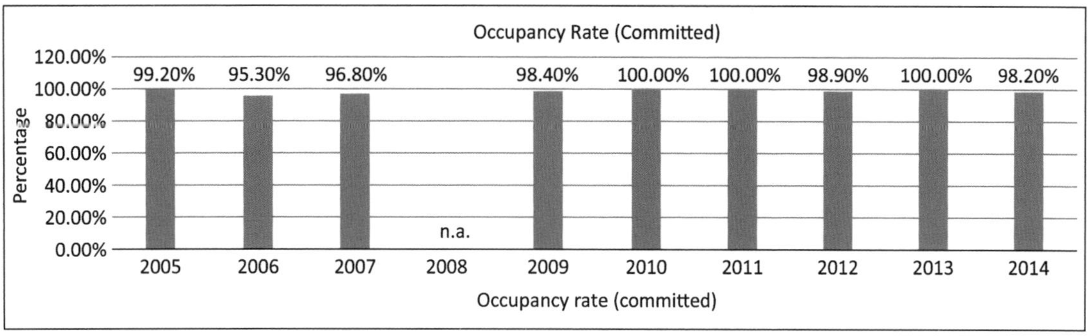

Source: Asia Competitiveness Institute; OUE Limited

[26] *Ibid.*

[27] *Ibid.*

Figure 4.22 Effective Monthly Gross Retail Rent per Square Feet of MG

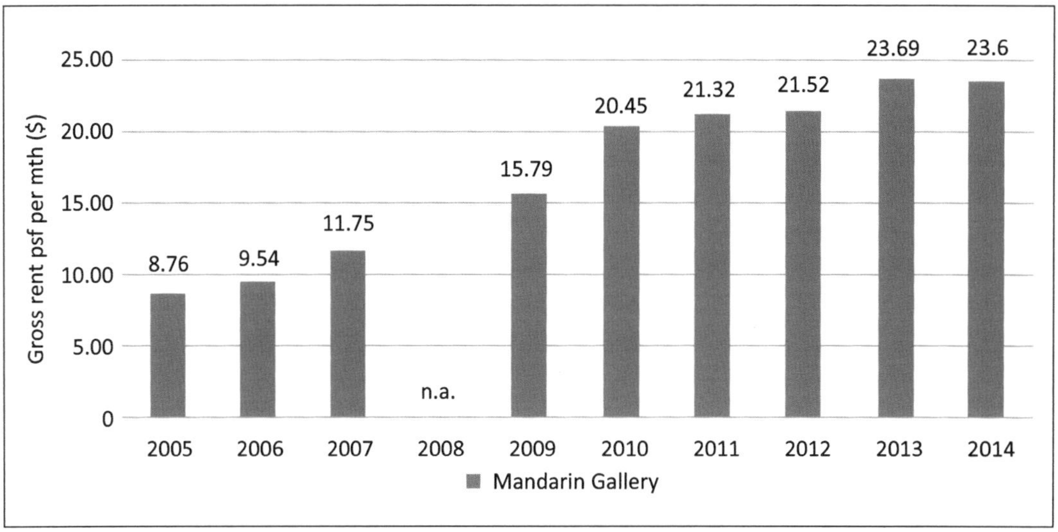

Source: Asia Competitiveness Institute; OUE Limited

to increase its profitability and valuation through differentiation in order to command a higher rental price.

Following the physical renovation and transformation into an upscale retail space, the effective monthly gross retail rent per square foot for MG almost tripled from S$8.76 in 2005 to S$23.60 in 2014 (Figure 4.22). Overall effective retail rent for the property includes prime retail space rentals and rentals for other units spread across other parts of the mall. 98 percent of MG's rental income comprises of fixed rent,[28] while retailers for the first and second floors "form more than 50 percent of the rental for the mall".[29] Significantly, it was estimated that with the refurbishments, the expected ground floor prime rent of S$50 to S$60 per square foot per month for MG would produce "about four times what OUE would earn from renting out the function rooms".[30] When taken in conjunction with the high levels of committed occupancy for the gallery, the reasons underlying the increase in revenues generated by MG become more readily apparent.

[28] Fixed rents comprise lease agreements between the landlord and lessee, fixing the price of rentals for a pre-discussed term, decreasing the uncertainty surrounding the future inflow of rental income. For the official statement declaring the source of this proportion of MG's rental income, see OUE Hospitality Trust (2014b, p. 2).

[29] See Warden (2015).

[30] The space absorbed by MG from what was the fourth floor of the hotel had comprised mostly event spaces such as a banquet hall and large function rooms, and it has been observed that despite losing these rooms to MG, MOS hotel still has a considerable amount of function space, providing a sense of the sheer scale of the building. For the article discussing the potential gains to be made from the MG refurbishments, see Tay (2008).

Figure 4.23 Approximate Singapore Prime Retail Rents by Submarket Type

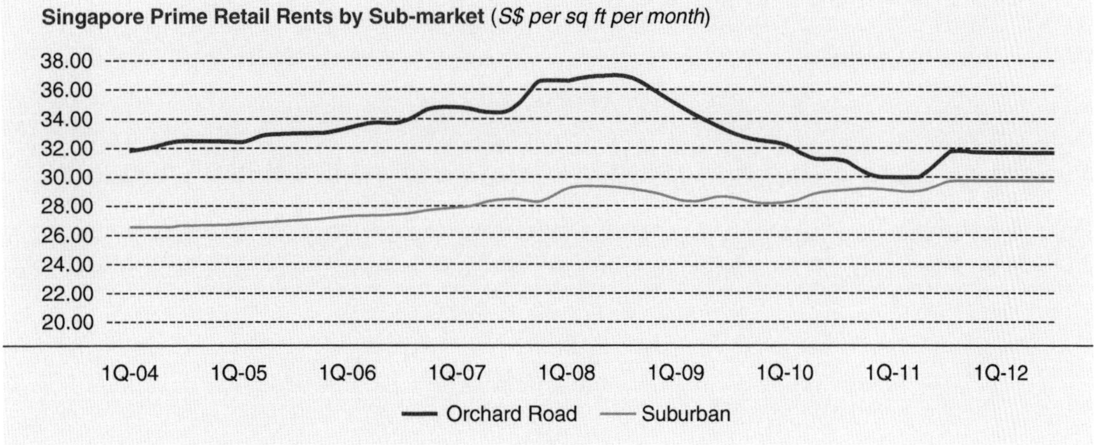

Source: Asia Competitiveness Institute; CapitaMall (2012); CB Richard Ellis

Redeveloping the gallery to take aim at the prime retail rental market was a deliberate strategy adopted by OUE Limited's management. The decision to redevelop the gallery to have a wide frontage of 152 metres is correspondingly an example of this conscious effort to cater to the needs of such retailers. The advantage of catering to prime retailers is clear, as the estimated range of S$50 to S$60 per square foot per month for MG in 2008 was above the aggregated prime retail rental rate prevailing on Orchard Road in the first quarter of 2008 — which was closer to the S$38 per square foot per month mark (Figure 4.23). The prime retail rent rates for the Orchard area have continued on within the S$30 to S$40 per square foot per month range between 2012 and 2014.[31]

4.2 HUMAN RESOURCE POLICIES: REVAMPING AND REJUVENATION

The policies initiated to improve productivity and pricing also had impact on human resources. When the Lippo Group acquired OUE Limited in 2006, MOS had already experienced a series of leadership changes, since it had previously undergone two rounds of acquisitions. Hence, the group had to ensure that due diligence for human resource integration was executed properly, as employee morale was low after the acquisition. This was further exacerbated by the lack of clear human resource processes related to career planning, performance appraisal, compensation and benefits, and employee record keeping at MOS. The new management had a clear plan for turning around the hotel, and one key challenge included streamlining existing human resource processes and work procedures, which had become inefficient due to numerous changes in management.

[31] See Colliers International (2014).

The resultant human resource strategy focused on weeding out underperformers and recruiting new front-line hotel employees, improving hotel operations and processes to enhance productivity, and retraining workers to upgrade their competencies while introducing automation.

4.2.1 CHANGE OF CULTURE: SPEED, NIMBLENESS AND ADDING VALUE

Following the change of management, OUE Limited and the staff working in MOS had to adjust to a new management philosophy and company culture — one that was very bottom-line conscious and focused on the notion of adding value. To quote a senior member of staff:

> *"We are here because we expect a certain value to be created in everything we do, because ultimately OUE Limited as a group is about value creation. I think the culture is different."*[32]

One of the first few measures taken by the new management when they came on board in 2006 was replacing staff in various departments and functions, who were not performing to expectation. These included functions such as housekeeping, marketing and security. For example, younger bellboys were hired for their speed, with their uniforms redesigned without pockets in order to discourage the soliciting of extra tips which had affected levels of service.

> *"In the past you had older people there, but that just would not do with our smaller hotel driveway. You need speed — get the luggage and go. When designing the clothes, do not design them with pockets, because if you want to work fast you should not put pockets in, where they can put keys and so on, because it is bulky."*[33]

In 2010, the company focused on improving operational efficiency and undertook cost-cutting measures such as reducing food wastage and saving electricity, as the hotel manager was given a mandate to reduce operational costs and streamline internal processes. Hotel employees were also provided with training to improve efficiency by working faster and smarter.[34]

The number of rooms at the hotel also posed certain problems which affected service standards and delivery. On days where hotel occupancy rates were high, for example, the hotel's restaurant would struggle to cope with the number of guests, resulting in long lines at the breakfast buffet. In order to improve service standards, the buffet choices were redesigned and food options were streamlined so that diners could finish their meals promptly and vacate the restaurant. Again, the focus of the new management was to enhance speed and efficiency to improve lagging service standards.

---

[32] Asia Competitiveness Institute interviews of senior management staff of OUE Limited (2015).

[33] *Ibid.*

[34] The hotel management consciously invested in the training and development of staff, with a range of workforce skills qualification (WSQ) courses offered to staff to improve the quality of responsiveness, leadership, work safety, service culture, language and even F&B module, to name a few examples. See Meritus Hotels and Resorts (2015).

4.2.2 AUTOMATION OF PROCESSES AND INVESTING IN EMPLOYEES

Aligned with the move to improve productivity was the human resource initiative undertaken by the hotel to invest in process automation and the upgrading of equipment. These measures were implemented to accommodate older employees who worked in housekeeping operations, and support and improve the overall capabilities of hotel staff.[35] The automation of processes was necessary, as Singapore's ageing population and new restrictions on hiring foreign labour had exacerbated MOS's ability to attract and retain talent. Some initiatives included the use of self-guided vacuum robots to clean long walkways in the hotel so that staff could be allocated for more complex tasks.

The hotel thus embraced automation to address the lack of manpower and encourage older workers to be more efficient and productive. This particular initiative entailed investments in installing motorised devices for use by the housekeeping staff, so that they would no longer need to physically lift beds to change bedsheets. Accordingly, repetitive or especially arduous housekeeping activities such as the changing of sheets, the cleaning of long corridors and garbage disposal could now be executed using mechanised equipment. Such job redesign initiatives enabled work to be completed with greater ease and efficiency, thus enabling management to offset the constraints in hiring housekeeping staff:

> "*You have to clear rubbish and things like that, but old people cannot push the carts or carry things that are heavy, so we have robots or engines attached to these trays, so that they are easier to push. Even an old man can push a hundred kilograms of weight*!"[36]

Apart from procuring labour-saving equipment, the company also examined ways to improve the efficiency of processes by adopting motion studies, workflow analysis and other such measures. Additional initiatives included offering management trainee programs and internships to new recruits and rotating interns across different functions to expose them to various hotel operations. This ensured that there was a ready pool of talent to be allocated to different departments based on the organisation's needs. These measures enabled MOS to not only raise average productivity levels of staff, but led to it achieving the position of overall champion of the Productivity Story 2011 competition, organised by local agencies to encourage the adoption of innovative and effective productivity initiatives.[37]

4.2.3 INTRODUCTION OF THE "WE CARE" PROGRAM

As a result of these aforementioned business policies to increase value through productivity and efficiency, the hotel's gross operating profit jumped from approximately S$60 million in 2008

---

[35] See Meritus Hotels and Resorts (2015).

[36] Asia Competitiveness Institute interviews of senior management staff of OUE Limited (2015).

[37] The competition was organised by the Pacific Asia Travel Association (PATA) and Singapore's Workforce Development Agency (WDA) to recognise the efforts in promoting the adoption of productivity measures among companies in Singapore, and MOS was chosen from a shortlist which included five other illustrious and innovative finalists as the winner of the hotel category (Workforce Development Agency, 2012).

to S$90 million in two and a half years.[38] However, adapting to the new OUE Limited company culture, with its focus on efficiency, speed and nimbleness through streamlining and corporate governance measures came at a price.

Since employees had already experienced two previous mergers and acquisitions, the new corporate culture of speed inadvertently led to employee burnout and fatigue as some employees could not adjust to the new performance-based environment. This was exacerbated by a booming hospitality industry which provided opportunities for those who were seeking to leave, leading to an unusually high attrition rate perhaps best exemplified by the loss of 200 employees in 2010. This led to the realisation that the company had to consider more sustainable people management strategies. To quote a senior manager who recalled the situation:

> "*That's when we at the corporate office got some signals that something was wrong. The engine got overheated. You can push profit, but at the end of the day brand equity is affected because people can only work so much.*"[39]

The management realised that it was critical to look at the low morale and fatigue issues of its employees, as employee dissatisfaction could potentially affect service levels at MOS. This spurred the creation of the "We Care" program, a series of initiatives to look after the needs of its employees. Since 2012, initiatives such as restoring policies on compensation, the reemployment of retirees, staff engagement programs and flexible benefits schemes have been implemented to engage and retain employees.[40] The management also revamped human resource processes and compensation policies pertaining to overtime pay, annual wage supplements, job roles and responsibilities, and proper maintenance of employee records. The clarity of processes brought about by these wide-ranging initiatives was successful in improving management–industrial relations.

Given the fairly flat organisation structure and the executive chairman's leadership style of practicing management by walking the hotel, open communication between employees and management was encouraged. Even rank-and-file employees were empowered to provide feedback to upper management. This sent a strong signal to the organisation that employee welfare and care is fundamental, especially in a service-driven industry where the effects of low employee morale can be particularly damaging.

During interviews with employees of MOS, it was additionally discovered that many staff have been employed by the hotel since it was first built in the 1970s, with several staff even having received their 40-year long service awards. Furthermore, the current management values employees who have been with the organisation for long periods of time and encourages them to continue their services through job redesign and the reorganisation of roles:

> "*Notwithstanding any problems, the executive chairman always says that these are our staff, so we cannot fire them, because where do they go, and what do you want them to do? We should find ways to help them and reorganise them.*"[41]

---

[38] See Appendix 5.

[39] Asia Competitiveness Institute interviews of senior management staff of OUE Limited (2015).

[40] See Meritus Hotels and Resorts (2015).

[41] See Asia Competitiveness Institute interviews of senior management staff of OUE Limited (2015).

4.2.4 OUTCOME OF HUMAN RESOURCE MEASURES AND INITIATIVES

The human resource measures that were implemented to improve morale and performance proved to be successful. These successes came about despite ongoing expansion efforts, which resulted in an increase in the number of hotel rooms from 1,051 in 2006 to 1,077 in 2014.[42]

The culture of MOS has also evolved into one that is not only results-oriented but also familial in character. Most of the senior management described the corporate culture of the firm as being open, informal and team-oriented, where everyone is "like a member of the family".[43] Even rank-and-file employees such as the hotel doorman are able to approach and channel feedback to senior management.

The management recognises that cultural transformation requires both timely and regular communication, prompting them to initiate a monthly tea session for staff, giving them an opportunity and platform to channel feedback on how to improve processes and performance:

> *"Our purpose is to find out how we help them in terms of their performance — give them the tools that they need to do well in their job. Then we get closer, and build this bond. If there are any working issues, they can always approach us, instead of complaining or making grievances."*[44]

Apart from building staff morale and improving productivity, MOS has also focused on building a service culture to sustain its competitive advantage, specifically since the property has received a new lease of life, with its transformation. The management hopes that the "caring" approach championed through human resource practices will instil a service culture that is aligned to an organisational culture of "caring". The hotel's management are particularly determined to see MOS live up to the reputation it had cultivated in the earlier years of its operation as a provider of uniquely excellent service:

> *"If we can do well with service, I think our guests will appreciate (us) more. And then, I think we want to just focus on building up this great service culture of caring."*[45]

4.3 TRANSFORMATION WITH REPOSITIONING AND DIFFERENTIATION: A DYNAMIC METAMORPHOSIS

Prior to its acquisition by the Lippo Group, MOS had undergone several rounds of refurbishment. For instance, in the late 1990s, traditional food and beverage (F&B) business operators faced competition from the new generation of food courts and restaurants that had sprung up along Orchard Road. This led to the hotel embarking on a refurbishment exercise, relaunching "Mandarin Singapore" with upgraded guest rooms, lobby, F&B outlets and conference facilities.[46]

---

[42] Indicated by the consistency of improvements in the ratio of occupied rooms per employed full-time equivalent. See Appendix 5.

[43] See Asia Competitiveness Institute interviews of senior management staff of OUE Limited (2015).

[44] *Ibid.*

[45] *Ibid.*

[46] See Overseas Union Enterprise Limited (1992) and (1993).

In 2000, extensive renovations were carried out on the main hotel building. After UOB acquired the hotel in 2001, renovations costing S$52 million to revamp guest rooms in the main tower were completed,[47] while in 2004, it was announced that four floors of the South Towers were to be converted into 47 executive rooms, an executive club lounge and two executive suites, all of which cost S$6 million in total.[48] In late 2005, restaurants such as Chatterbox,[49] home of the famous Mandarin Chicken Rice, along with other F&B outlets, were also refurbished.[50] As part of ongoing refurbishments, upgrading works were carried out in the hotel in 2006, where the Deluxe, Premier and Club Rooms located on floors 29 to 32 at the Grand Tower of the hotel were refurbished. Other areas such as the guests' lifts, hotel driveway, Mandarin Ballroom, and The Club Lounge at the Grand Tower were also renovated.[51]

4.3.1 REPOSITIONING AND PLANNING THE PHYSICAL TRANSFORMATION

In 2006, asset enhancement plans for MG were announced under the new management.[52] The key goal of the transformation was to maximise the potential rental income of the property due to its strategic location and was driven by Dr Riady's vision to transform and reposition MG as a high-end luxury shopping mall.

The timing of the refurbishment was favourable and coincided with numerous initiatives by the Singapore government in support of tourism and retail activities. In January 2005, then Minister for Trade and Industry Lim Hng Kiang announced that a S$2 billion Tourism Development Fund would be set up to support tourism-related infrastructure, initiatives and activities.[53] Following that, in March 2005, the Urban Redevelopment Authority (URA) launched incentives to encourage the development and rejuvenation of Orchard Road, such as gross floor area (GFA) incentives and the "relaxation of guidelines to allow buildings to expand their shopping podium up to their boundaries".[54] In addition, the STB announced in 2007 that it was embarking on a S$40 million plan to support events and undertake infrastructural enhancements of Orchard Road, slated for completion in April 2009, which coincided with the opening of Singapore's Integrated Resorts in 2009 and 2010.[55] Retailers along Orchard Road were encouraged to create attractive and high-quality designs to capitalise on the expected increase in visitor arrivals, an opportunity that OUE Limited seized upon:

> *"At that time URA had already started encouraging the owners along Orchard Road to create high quality designs — vibrant streetscapes and stuff like that along that. I think the opportunities were*

---

[47] See *Business Times* (2002).

[48] See Overseas Union Enterprise Limited (2005, p. 5).

[49] The Mandarin chicken rice in Chatterbox has won numerous awards for its signature Chicken rice dish. The secret recipe was put together by the restaurant's German Executive Chef Peter Gehrmann, who decided to put the hawker dish on the menu of Chatterbox when it first opened at Mandarin Orchard Singapore in August 1971.

[50] See Overseas Union Enterprise Limited (2006).

[51] See Overseas Union Enterprise Limited (2007).

[52] *Ibid* (pp. 8–9).

[53] See Singapore Tourism Board (2005, p. 12).

[54] These development incentives were announced by then Minister for National Development, Mr Mah Bow Tan, in Parliament on 7 March 2005. See Urban Redevelopment Authority (2005).

[55] See Channel NewsAsia (2007).

there to do something about it because of the valuable frontage that we have, which at that time was a driveway — a driveway and a drop off for the hotel."[56]

Prior to the transformation of MOS, a large portion of the hotel's frontage consisted of a driveway with a drop off and the main entrance. The original building also featured an ageing shopping arcade with small shops at ground level and a second and third storey populated by stores selling mainly touristy souvenirs:

"*The configuration of the shops was very old-fashioned and out-dated, and it was not very attractive to shoppers. It was bit dingy, with lots of dead end corner. So, it was not a very attractive mall and it was not a very attractive shopping centre. It was called Mandarin Gallery at that time. So, I think there was already potential to enhance the value of that particular space, especially the podium.*"[57]

The refurbishment plans included revamping the hotel's façade by maximising the property's 152-metre-long frontage, which ran along a prime stretch of Orchard Road. Much of this area was to be absorbed into space for the new and improved MG. With plans drawn up to reallocate space from the hotel to the gallery, GFA from the hotel could be absorbed and built into the retail podium, presenting considerable potential for the development of a bigger and much improved retail space.[58] With regard to the gallery, the design concept for prime retail shops included a double-volume shopfront to maximise the Orchard Road frontage:

"*Because if you just do a ground level frontage then you only have one floor, but if you go with duplex or a double volume format then your exposure doubles with two floors. That was one of the things we did to maximise and take advantage of the Orchard Road frontage. That also added value to the shops.*"[59]

The major change made for the refurbishment was relocating the hotel's reception from the first to the fifth floor to maximise the amount of space available for the gallery. In planning the physical transformation of MOS, it was held to be imperative that any transfer of space from the hotel to the gallery did not compromise the hotel's room count. Hence, the additional space was reallocated by reducing the number of function rooms and banquet halls instead. Even more space for the new hotel lobby on the fifth floor was created by repurposing space from the swimming pool and the attached pool deck. Additional GFA was also obtained from basement one of the hotel, which contained designated areas for engineering, maintenance and storage operations. Several of these operations were accordingly relocated to other parts of the hotel, with the basement being converted into carpark space instead.[60]

[56] Asia Competitiveness Institute interviews of senior management staff of OUE Limited (2015).

[57] *Ibid.*

[58] See Appendies 5 and 6.

[59] Asia Competitiveness Institute interviews of senior management staff of OUE Limited (2015).

[60] See Appendix 6.

To enhance the guest experience,[61] four F&B outlets were added to the new fifth floor hotel lobby. A dedicated lift was also constructed to take guests to the fifth floor, but since there were two wings, two sets of lifts were required. By centralising all the F&B outlets on the same floor, the property was able to operate with just one central kitchen, rather than having separate kitchens for each F&B establishment spread across the hotel's floors.

4.3.2 PHYSICAL RESTRUCTURING OF MANDARIN ORCHARD SINGAPORE AND MANDARIN GALLERY

In pursuing the physical transformation of MOS, Dr Riady and his team faced a number of challenges. The first was seeking approval from the government for the proposed changes. This was ultimately obtained fairly quickly, as URA was "pleased that we were converting (the hotel frontage) into a pedestrian walkway, and that the space was an open space".[62]

Next came convincing the old tenants of Mandarin Gallery to cooperate with the refurbishment plans. This proved to be challenging, as tenants felt that they had not been given sufficient notice of the impending redevelopment.[63]

Being an additions and alterations (A&A) project, the third major challenge during the refurbishment was working within the constraints of existing infrastructure. Because the building was constructed in 1970, the existing plans or "as-built-drawings" had some inherent deficiencies as they did not reveal certain structural details, which proved to be particularly significant during the refurbishment.[64]

> *"The architects and the engineers had designed everything in accordance to what they felt was the actual on-site situation, as based on the 'as-built-drawings'. But when we actually began construction we found that, for example, what we thought were just brick walls were actually structural walls."*[65]

In addition to issues with having to work around structural walls, the team was also constrained by the low head room on the higher floors, which posed a problem for the design of the new ceilings.

The fourth challenge was that during the refurbishment, it was determined that the hotel would still operate normally, so managing the flow of traffic within a large hotel with over 1,000 rooms, which was also undergoing significant renovations, became something the management team had to overcome. The architect, together with the hotel operations team, had to anticipate

[61] The iconic Chatterbox restaurant was relocated from floor 39 to the fifth floor, and the other F&B outlets adjacent to the new lobby were an international buffet restaurant called Triple Three, a café called Coffee & Crust and a hotel bar, Bar on 5. See Overseas Union Enterprise Limited (2010).

[62] Asia Competitiveness Institute interviews of senior management staff of OUE Limited (2015).

[63] An article presenting the views of tenants of MG affected by the redevelopment appeared in the *Straits Times* on 26 May 2007, see Yip (2007).

[64] See Appendix 6.

[65] Asia Competitiveness Institute interviews of senior management staff of OUE Limited (2015).

possible disruptions and assess how best to reorganise core hotel functions to keep MOS operational during the refurbishment phase. Since the old spacious lobby had been relocated to the fifth floor to facilitate the redevelopment of MG, a temporary lobby had to be built with check-in equipment. Additionally, while the construction work was ongoing, the team had to create safe passages and divert existing walkways so that guests could still access the lobby. Temporary passages were erected and decorated to camouflage the construction and minimise complaints from guests:

> "*Whenever we created temporary passage ways for guests which went through construction sites, we tried to make them as pleasant as possible. We dressed them up so that they did not look like construction sites. You would walk through a passage way and not realise that the areas just outside the passages above you were under construction.*"[66]

The exercise inevitably had a major impact on the hotel operations unit, as it required a large amount of shifting the "back of house" and "front of house" components so that the hotel could continue to be operational,[67] while the fifth-floor new reception area was completed. This led to numerous complaints from hotel guests during the refurbishment phase, particularly when hacking and demolition work was being carried out. Although the work was limited to a specific number of hours a day, it still resulted in some loss of business due to dissatisfaction on the part of some guests. Nevertheless, these measures were deployed until the completion of redevelopment work in November 2009.[68]

4.3.3 DIFFERENTIATING FOR UNIQUENESS AND CHARACTER

Costing a total of S$200 million to refurbish, the upgrading work for MOS and MG was completed towards the end of 2009.[69] With the gallery refurbishments, the revamped hotel featured a prominent 152 metre glass frontage running along Orchard Road, while the new fifth-floor hotel reception area featured a striking multi-coloured crystal-pixel artwork suspended from the ceiling, which was designed entirely by a Singaporean artist.[70]

The structure of the new MG did not replicate the typical layout for a mall, since it had been repurposed from space originally designated for MOS. The first two levels of the gallery showcased high-end international labels while the third level reflected casual sports labels. The fourth level provided a variety of dining experiences as well as essentials to complete the retail shopper's lifestyle needs. The mall was also more easily accessible, as pedestrians and customers could enter along Orchard Road through an escalator located near the front of the mall's entrance and be connected directly to the mall's second floor.

---

[66] *Ibid.*

[67] "Back of house" refers to hospitality operations and processes that typically take place outside of the view of hotel guests, while "front of house" are the client-facing staff and services.

[68] See Overseas Union Enterprise Limited (2010, p. 11).

[69] MG had a soft launch at the end of 2009 and was fully open and operational by early 2010. See Ramchandani (2009).

[70] See Overseas Union Enterprise Limited (2010).

The refurbishment of MOS and MG was driven by the company's differentiation strategy of creating a quality "Class A" asset, with the recurring theme being that the property should cater to the niche, rather than just the mass market. Additionally, due to the smaller, less traditional layout of the mall, one of the strategies adopted by the team was to offer a complementary, rather than competing, shopping experience in relation to the other malls in the vicinity:

> "*What our competitors could offer would be ten times more than what we could. How do we then fit into this puzzle? That is to take the route of being an intimate-sized mall and to complement. The whole idea is that after they shop at our competitors, they will walk here and they will not be seeing the same things, so it is about ensuring that what we offer completes their whole shopping experience.*"[71]

The mall was thus positioned to offer shoppers a more holistic retail experience and provide other complementary retail categories, such as "Living & Lifestyle", "Food & Beverage", and "Hair & Beauty". The team carefully selected tenants to align with the company's motto of striving for differentiated quality. Potential tenants were selected based on their ability to offer the high-end retail experience that MG envisaged, which motivated the leasing team to source for new entrants who could provide novel and sophisticated products and services. Following a careful selection process, the gallery was successful in securing many first-time entrants to Singapore. The tenants included a mix of 103 high-end fashion, lifestyle and F&B tenants, encompassing both international and local brands:

> "*These were brands that I call brands with attitude. They were a little bit different, not run of the mill, mainstream luxury. They were always brands that had a designer behind them that had a bit of attitude in terms of how they viewed their designs and how they put it forward.*"[72]

Given that the mall's core focus is fashion apparel, it accounted for 45.7 percent of the tenant mix of MG based on retail rental income in the first quarter of 2013. Accessories formed 14 percent, and watches and jewellery made up 13 percent, collectively comprising the top 3 categories by rental income for the tenant mix of the gallery.[73]

---

[71] Asia Competitiveness Institute interviews of senior management staff of OUE Limited (2015).

[72] *Ibid.*

[73] See OUE Hospitality Trust (2013, pp. 5–6).

CHAPTER 5

CORPORATE FINANCE STRATEGY: STRATEGIES FOR ADDING VALUE

This chapter will explore the evolution of the corporate finance strategy towards MOS and MG, which shifted from a dominant focus on the hotel business to a focus on asset transformation after the acquisition of OUE Limited. This strategy is one that aims to be sustainable over the long term by utilising OUE Limited as a vehicle to both pursue growth opportunities and purchase underperforming assets ripe for redevelopment. The instruments used for this purpose were publicly listed Real Estate Investment Trusts (REITs), such as the OUE Hospitality Trust. The trusts control stabilised assets such as MOS and MG while unlocking created value and recycling capital.

5.1 THE OUE HOSPITALITY TRUST (OUE H-TRUST)

The OUE H-Trust is a Singapore listed REIT. The corporate strategies initiated by the REIT Manager (see Figure 5.1 for the REIT Manager profiles) adopt a broad and aggressive investment strategy that includes, but is not limited to, investing capital in a "portfolio of income-producing real estate which is used primarily for hospitality and/or hospitality-related purposes, whether wholly or partially, as well as real estate-related assets."[1]

Such a strategy has translated into the strategic transformation — both physical and operational — of OUE's real estate assets to diversify its footprint in retail and hospitality that caters to different groups of customers, as well as commercial and entertainment sectors. This in

Figure 5.1 OUE REIT Manager Profiles

Board of Directors of the REIT Manager			
Mr Christopher James Williams Chairman and Non-Executive Director	**Mr Lee Yi Shyan** Deputy Chairman and Non-Independent Non-Executive Director	**Mr Chong Kee Hiong** Chief Executive Officer and Executive Director	**Mr Sanjiv Misra** Independent Director
Mr Liu Chee Ming Independent Director	**Professor Neo Boon Siong** Independent Director	**Mr Ong Kian Min** Independent Director	
Executive Team of the REIT Manager			
Mr Chong Kee Hiong Chief Executive Officer	**Mr Eric Gan Chee Tei** Chief Financial Officer	**Ms Goh Lillian** Senior Vice President, Investor Relations	**Mr Chen Yi Chung** Vice President, Investments

[1] See OUE Hospitality REIT Management.

Figure 5.2 Valuation Graph of MOS and MG

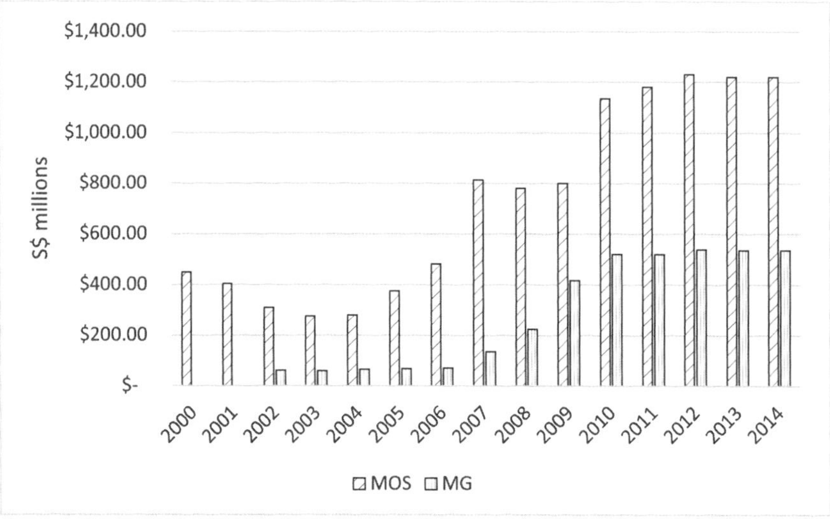

Source: Asia Competitiveness Institute; OUE Limited

turn ensures that sustainable sources of income are cultivated across industry sectors. Such a diversified portfolio allows the REIT managers to maintain a healthy balance sheet, thereby avoiding the need for secondary offerings and the reissuing of bonds to raise capital.

The strength of this strategy has helped OUE Limited achieve a CAGR of 19.5 percent for the total value of assets owned between 2006 and 2014, which was all notably executed without requiring a secondary offering to raise additional shareholder equity.[2]

In 2014, both the hotel and gallery were collectively valued at S$1.7 billion, with the hotel being valued at S$1.2 billion and the mall at S$536 million (see Appendix 5).[3] Valuations of MOS went from a low of S$276.0 million in 2003 to a staggering S$1,220.0 million in 2014, with the largest increase in value taking place from 2006 to 2007, when the property's valuation grew by 68.7 percent (Figure 5.2). MG went from S$61.5 million in 2002 to S$536.0 million in 2014, with highest annual growth occurring between 2006 and 2010, which coincided with the period of the redevelopment and reopening of the gallery.

5.1.1 ADOPTING A GOVERNMENT-ALIGNED CORPORATE STRATEGY

Differences in valuation methodologies aside, the considerable increase in market value of MOS and MG suggests that an effective business model underpins these results, with higher valuations representing significant capital gains. Part of the backdrop for the implementation of a successful corporate finance strategy is a favourable policy environment, as established by the local government. The company believes that the business and investment strategy must be aligned with and

[2] See Overseas Union Enterprise Limited (2007, p. 33, 2015a, p. 30).

[3] See OUE Hospitality Trust (2015, pp. 36–38).

support the local government's policies and initiatives, as articulated in Dr Riady's business philosophy:

> "*You must pay attention to where the government is moving, and where they are going — especially if the leader or central banker is a determined person. Then you have to follow — do not fight against it! And my investments, generally, are doing okay.*"[4]

Alignment with the Singapore government's initiatives is also evident in the Lippo Group's initial decision to purchase OUE Limited in 2006, when the government introduced regulations requiring local banks to divest from their non-core assets. Furthermore, in 2005, due to the declining market share of tourists in Asia Pacific, the Ministry of Trade and Industry (MTI) put forward a case for developing Integrated Resorts (IR) in Singapore to reinvent Singapore as a global cosmopolitan city.[5] The management believed that the government's push for developing the tourism sector was a positive cue for the company to further invest in the hospitality and retail business, as the increased focus on tourism would have positive spillover effects on these industries:

> "*So, the Singapore government start debating whether Singapore should have Integrated Resorts, should have gaming. And here you go, I think you see a lot of plans have been implemented by the government today that we can see, like Formula One, of course Integrated Resorts, Universal Studios, River Safari, Gardens by the Bay, the new Kallang stadium (the Sports Hub) and so on. So, I think what we do is very simple; I see the government's vision, and I try to follow, and fit into the government's vision.*"[6]

Thus, the company embarked on a strategy to diversify its portfolio to include a mix of hospitality, retail, residential and commercial properties aimed at sustaining a steady revenue stream, together with "value-enhancing development projects".[7] These were some of the considerations behind the purchase of OUE Limited, as well as the impetus for the transformation of MOS and MG — the full realisation of which necessitated an effective corporate finance strategy.

5.1.2 CAPITAL AND RISK MANAGEMENT

A core feature of sustainable growth models favoured by OUE required it to maintain a strong balance sheet while securing a diverse source of capital inflow — both from financial and institutional investors as well as through open capital markets (see Appendix 5 for a snapshot of selected financial statements). Active management and the (re)structuring of corporate debt was also another strategy adopted by OUE and took into account credit and repayment risks.

[4] Asia Competitiveness Institute interviews of senior management staff of OUE Limited (2015).

[5] See Ministry of Trade and Industry (2006).

[6] Excerpt from Dr Riady's speech at the 2014 Asia Competitiveness Institute Annual Conference, on 26 November 2014.

[7] See Overseas Union Enterprise Limited (2008, p. 2).

Exposure to market turbulence and fluctuations in interest rates, as well as foreign exchange volatility, serve as yet further sources of financial uncertainty. These uncertainties have been addressed in part through an active diversification and hedging strategy, which has included the acquisition of new assets (see Appendix 3) and branching out to integrate the hospitality, commercial and entertainment sectors into the umbrella of its MG premises.

5.2 RISK AND RETURN ANALYSIS

The strategic decision to undertake the transformation of MOS and MG had several underlying motivations. When OUE Limited acquired the property, it was a relatively old building that had been around for more than 30 years and was configured to focus predominantly on the hotel aspect of the business. OUE Limited's management team assessed the property and quickly picked up on the fact that it was being underutilised, given its prime location on Orchard Road:

> *"30 years later, 40 years later, retail is more valuable than the hotel, because the rent can go higher than fifty dollars per square feet. For the parent, the bank owner, (it was) 30 years ago when they built it, and this probably was not their main line of business, so they did not look at it, but the utilisation has changed."*[8]

5.2.1 OPTIMISING TRANSFORMATION

With an understanding of how OUE's asset base was being underutilised, the immediate priority for the company became the maximisation of the property's value, given the higher rental yields that neighbouring retail assets were earning compared to MG before the refurbishment. Based on the team's evaluation, the ground floor, which consisted of a large lobby, carpark, coffeehouse, bank and some shops, was underutilised, and the ground floor space could generate more yield if it was converted to retail:

> *"We said, listen — in Orchard Road, for ground floor spaces, the best and most optimised use is retail. But we have got a hotel lobby now, right? So, we looked at the hotel with consultants, and we found that the hotel podium was zoned for commercial (use). That meant we could convert it to shops. I don't have any additional plot ratio, but I can convert (existing space) to shops."*[9]

The team was additionally willing to adopt a radically new design by relocating the lobby to the fifth floor, as they had come across designs in luxury hotels overseas, such as the Ritz Carlton and the Four Seasons in Chicago, which have their lobbies located on the 12th and seventh floors, respectively. For MOS, the fifth floor was chosen as the new space for the lobby due to the availability of open areas, as well as space that could be taken from the swimming pool. This arrangement thus allowed the ground floor of the hotel to be freed up. The combined effect of all these

---

[8] Asia Competitiveness Institute interviews of senior management staff of OUE Limited (2015).

[9] Asia Competitiveness Institute interviews of senior management staff of OUE Limited (2016).

measures released approximately 180,000 square feet of GFA from the hotel, which could be used for the redevelopment of the refurbished MG (see Appendix 6).

The initial numbers confirmed that the asset could potentially provide far higher yield, especially since the option of converting it to commercial space was possible. This likely factored in to an assessment of higher terminal values for the property, as discussed earlier in Chapter 2.

With regard to the expansion of retail space and the restructuring of the hotel, the strategy of adding value through asset enhancements was driven by the company's vision of creating mixed-use developments.[10] The asset enhancement resulted in the conversion of hotel space into retail space for an upscale mall, complemented by an adjoining hotel to collectively provide an integrated hospitality and retail experience for shoppers and hotel guests. The proposed facelift of the asset by increasing retail net lettable area (NLA) space proved to be a viable strategy to maximise rental yield,[11] as both the internal and external façades of the hotel were enhanced to attract shoppers and guests. This was especially critical given the aforementioned strong push from government statutory boards and agencies such as STB and URA to revive the Orchard Road district, along with all attendant initiatives. Furthermore, since the hotel is a sizeable establishment with more than 1,000 rooms, it provides a potential "captive customer base" of shoppers that would patronise the mall.[12]

These were encouraging signs that lowered the possible development risks around the project, as discussed earlier in Chapter 2. Furthermore, as one of the first significant and high-profile transformation projects undertaken by the new OUE Limited management team under the Lippo Group, the asset refurbishment took on additional significance as a way to shape the expectations of the market for the business and the new owners and to communicate the quality and value that could be expected of the OUE brand.

5.2.2 MAXIMISING EFFICIENCY AND DELIVERING OPERATIONAL EXCELLENCE

A critical component of OUE's risk and return strategy remains its need to preserve a high standard of operational excellence, along with ensuring that assets yield the highest possible returns. Operating under a REIT model and a corporate trust allows OUE to leverage on the various stakeholders within the trust structure to achieve the optimal utilisation of available talent, resources and growth opportunities. As illustrated in Figure 5.3, a key strategy for OUE would be to rely on the strategic expertise of its main sponsor (OUE Limited) to deliver top-notch hospitality services. As the largest hotel along Orchard Road, maintaining a customer-focused commitment to service excellence would naturally translate to customer loyalty and positive brand

[10] A mixed-use development essentially provides an optimal mix of property utilisation, as chosen among the commercial, residential, hospitality and retail segments.

[11] See Appendix 5 for the historical values detailing the distribution of space between MOS and MG within the property.

[12] See Warden (2010).

Figure 5.3 OUE Hospitality Trust Structure

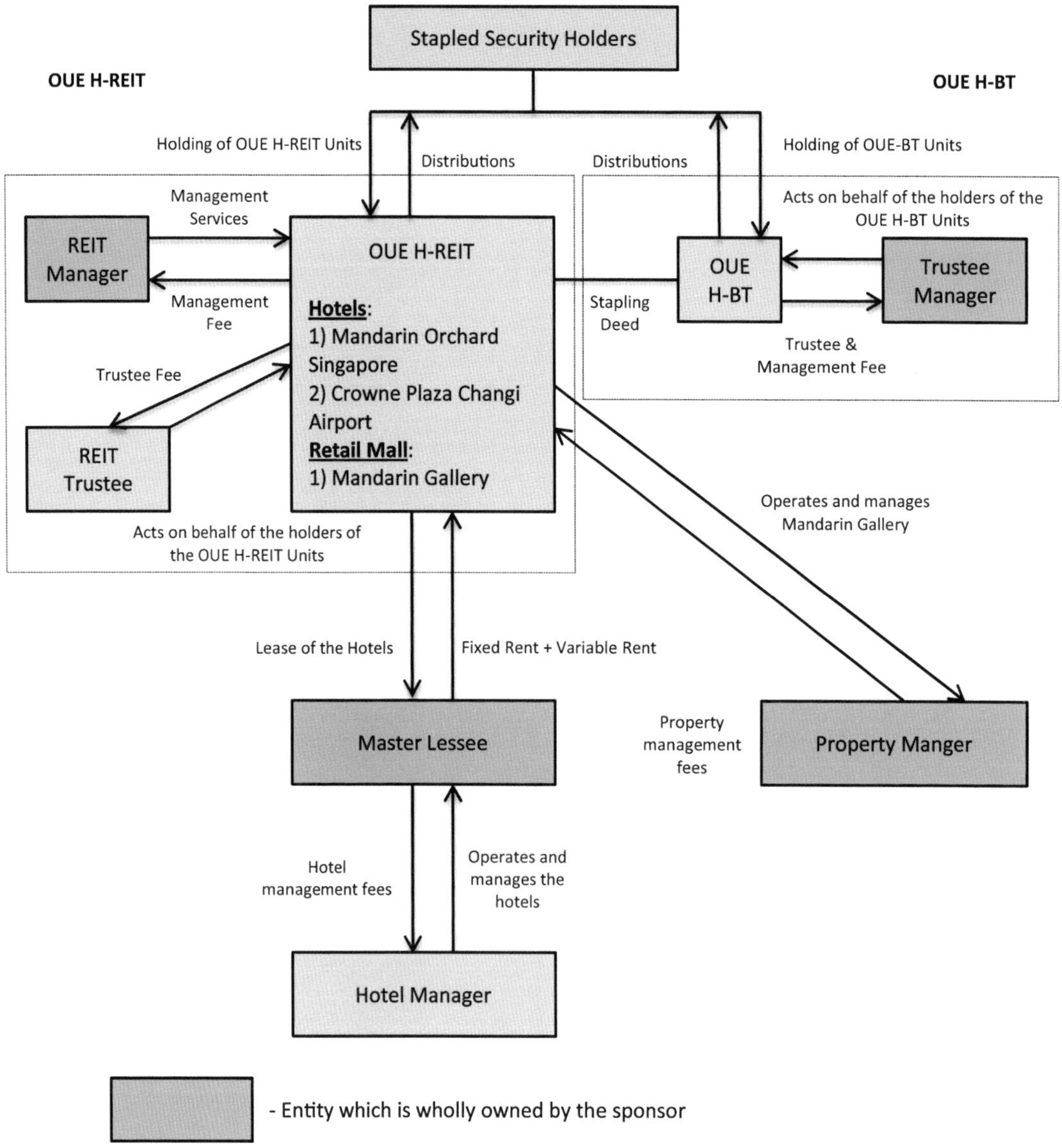

Source: Adapted from OUE Hospitality REIT Management organisational chart

development, which would in turn create a self-sustaining revenue cycle and a growing customer base.

Additionally, operational optimisation and strategic growth and development must be maintained through forging close working relationships with Master Lessees. A strong working relationship with the Master Lessees and other trustees within the trust structure would ensure that growth opportunities continue to develop, while preserving an overall commitment to operational excellence for staff and customers alike.

5.3 FINANCING OPTIONS

Having identified MG as one of the suitable assets for transformation, the financing that was allocated for the redevelopment would come from internal resources within OUE Limited as part of the purchase of the company:

> "*For the Mandarin Gallery, the large part of it was funded through internal resources, because ... at the point when we bought over the group, there was a fair bit of cash resources still sitting within the group. And for the whole redevelopment for Mandarin Gallery, the budget was about $190 million.*"[13]

It was important that this decision was made with the joint venture partner, which was agreeable to the arrangement for the use of the acquired company's resources:

> "*At that point of time the joint venture partner had already agreed with the redevelopment of Mandarin Orchard Singapore and Mandarin Gallery, so it was an on-going project through 2009.*"[14]

As discussed in Chapter 2, decisions for how to finance a given undertaking depend largely upon available resources and the structure of the company. In this case, it was decided that the internal resources within OUE Limited which were purchased during the acquisition were sufficient to fund the initial transformation of MG. Thereafter, the financing approach for subsequent projects would have to be evaluated, as taking on external borrowings could prove to be far more cost effective as an efficient use of available capital:

> "*I think the rationale for the original capital expenditure for Mandarin Gallery was that the plan was made based on the assumption that it'll be funded through internal resources. At that point in time, there were sufficient internal resources to fund the work. Whereas for this project, when we were evaluating the redevelopment of this building, the assumption was that there would be project financing taken up.*"[15]

5.3.1 BUILDING CORPORATE AND INSTITUTIONAL MOMENTUM

As suggested in Chapter 2, the ownership and capital structure of a company has bearings upon the financing options available to a company. In considering the ownership structure of the joint venture company Lippo Property Investment Private Limited when OUE Limited was first acquired,[16] we are able to note that the company was 60 percent owned by the Lippo Group and 40 percent owned by Malaysian businessman Ananda Krishnan.[17] Just over 55 percent of

[13] Asia Competitiveness Institute interviews of senior management staff of OUE Limited (2015).

[14] *Ibid.*

[15] *Ibid.*

[16] See United Overseas Bank (2006).

[17] See AFX Asia (2006).

Figure 5.4 Breakdown of "Overseas Union Enterprise Limited" Shares Sold in the Divestment

Company Name	Number of "Overseas Union Enterprise Limited" Shares	Percentage of "Overseas Union Enterprise Limited" Shares	Purchase Consideration (S$)
United Overseas Bank Limited	57,436,565	32.58%	$585,852,963.00
Overseas Union Holdings Private Limited	21,324,219	12.09%	$217,507,033.80
Overseas Union Facilities (Private) Limited	8,207,899	4.66%	$83,720,569.80
Overseas Union Insurance Limited	10,076,250	5.71%	$102,777,750.00
Total	**97,044,933**	**55.04%**	**$989,858,316.60**

Source: Asia Competitiveness Institute; United Overseas Bank (2006)

"Overseas Union Enterprise Limited" shares were owned by the joint venture company at the time of sale (see Figure 5.4).[18]

Having crossed the 33 percent ownership threshold, the new owners of "Overseas Union Enterprise Limited" had to then launch a mandatory unconditional cash offer for the remaining shares at the acquisition price of S$10.20 per share, which fuelled talk in the market at the time of the possibility that the company was being taken private.[19] On 12 July 2006, the shares in the capital of "Overseas Union Enterprise Limited" were suspended from trading when the public float fell below 10 percent with acceptance of the aforementioned cash offer. However, in December 2006, "Overseas Union Enterprise Limited" conducted a private placement of 20 million new ordinary shares of the company at S$10.50 per share, raising the public float to more than 10 percent and allowing trading of "Overseas Union Enterprise Limited" shares to resume on 3 January 2007, thereby ensuring that the company remained public.[20]

Under the new ownership, the shareholding structure became considerably more intricate (Figure 5.5). The division of ownership between affiliates of the Lippo Group and Ananda Krishnan was evident based upon the structure of substantial shareholders. This, coupled with the financial crisis of 2008, may have led to difficulties in determining the financing options available for potential projects, which may be a factor for the lack of investment activity from OUE Limited between 2006 and 2010.

This situation subsequently changed in 2010, when the Lippo Group's direct and indirect interests in OUE Limited rose from 64.67 percent to 88.52 percent. The group paid S$957 million to acquire Ananda Krishnan's share of OUE Limited, and ownership of OUE Limited was finally consolidated.[21] Yet again, speculation was rife that OUE Limited might be required to de-list should the public float of OUE Limited shares fall below 10 percent.[22] However,

[18] For the joint acquisition of "Overseas Union Enterprise Limited", OUE Realty Private Limited was the immediate holding corporation, while the ultimate holding corporation was Lippo ASM Asia Property LP, a limited partnership established in the Cayman Islands. See Overseas Union Enterprise Limited (2007, pp. 8 and 86).

[19] See Jayasankaran (2006).

[20] See Overseas Union Enterprise Limited (2007, p. 8).

[21] See *Business Times* (2010). The remainder of the company was held by retail and institutional investors.

[22] See Goh (2010).

Figure 5.5 Substantial Shareholders of OUE Limited After Acquisition in 2006

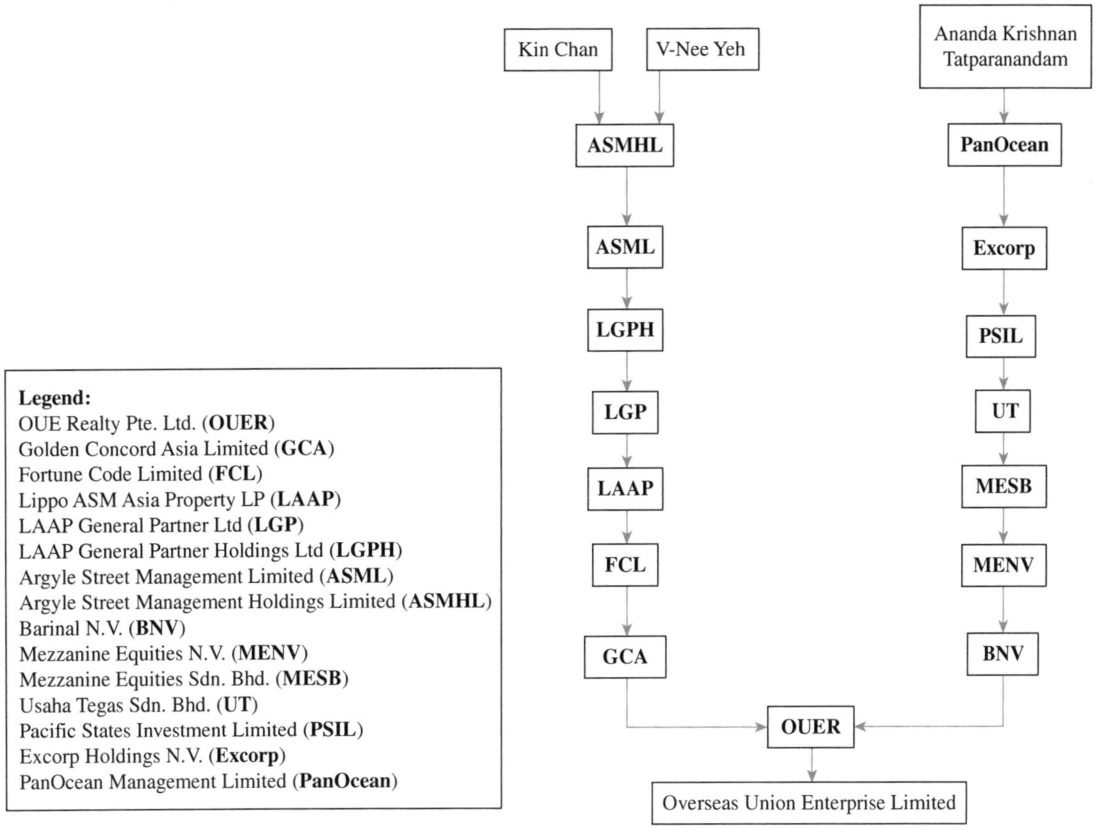

Source: Asia Competitiveness Institute; Overseas Union Enterprise Limited (2007)

under the consolidated management of OUE Limited by the Lippo Group, the company remained committed to staying a publicly traded firm, and this was made apparent when OUE Limited increased its public float substantially after the consolidation from 11.44 percent in 2010 to 31.43 percent in 2011.[23] This was another key decision for the company, as was described here:

> *"The other thing that was defining for us is that at one time, OUE Limited, (when) we took over it was not very well-known. There was not a single analyst that wrote anything about OUE Limited. And for one and a half years, we went on a road trip… Because, you see when we took over from the Malaysians, Dr Riady ended up owning nearly 90 percent of the company. So, we went on a road show to place shares. Went to see a lot of people, fund managers, we went to see a lot of analysts, from all over Singapore, to Hong Kong, to London, to Zurich, to Holland, the United States. And we talked and talked and talked our heads off. Now I think there are 15 analysts writing about OUE Limited. Before, not a single one. So, it is quite a well-known company now, and of course they managed to place the shares out."*[24]

---

[23] See Overseas Union Enterprise Limited (2010, p. 149, 2011, p. 163).

[24] Asia Competitiveness Institute interviews of senior management staff of OUE Limited (2016).

This strategy has helped OUE Limited to remain within the public eye, leading to wide analyst coverage of the company's stock, with some 15 analysts researching the performance of the company and forming their recommendations, allowing OUE Limited to more easily access additional financing in the market from institutional investors.[25] Part of the benefit of OUE Limited remaining public is also the ability for their stock to trade in the secondary market, making the stock more liquid and providing another financing option for the company.

5.3.2 INVESTMENT PLANNING: UNLOCKING VALUE WITH REAL ESTATE INVESTMENT TRUSTS

For OUE Limited, the main investment thesis appears to be to find prime or undervalued assets ripe for transformation while maintaining "active lease management and ongoing asset enhancement activities to increase the recurring income base", so as to strike a balance between improving recurring income while pursuing strategic investment opportunities.[26] An important part of the challenge is a matter of timing the investments:

> *"I mean if you look at the transactions that we've done after he (Dr Riady) has control, I think he has very good timing, and I think that when it comes to property, you know, timing is very critical."*[27]

While OUE Limited's approach to investment has been a concerted and focused strategy, another important part of the challenge to executing this strategy was to lay out a plan for securing the financial resources to fund future projects to ensure continued growth of the OUE Limited business. The determination of the sources of funding is an important decision which affects the cost of capital of a company, as explained in Chapter 2. Planning for transformation can furthermore be a very costly exercise and requires careful financial management:

> *"And a lot of this was done basically through revitalising and doing asset enhancement to the property portfolio that OUE Limited has at the point when we got the company in 2006. And the best thing about this whole transformation, it was done without any further fund raising from the shareholders, it was all done by internal resources, recycling and external borrowing."*[28]

This was one of the important factors behind the deliberate choice for OUE Limited to remain as a publicly traded company, as discussed earlier in this chapter. OUE Limited acknowledged that a company's capital investment policies "considerably affect firm value and market reactions of stock prices", and the performance of the investment policy makes "the value of the firm and the price of the equity vary".[29] Hence, the company declared that the company will "remain

---

[25] See OUE Limited (2015b).

[26] See *Singapore Business Review* (2017).

[27] Asia Competitiveness Institute interviews of senior management staff of OUE Limited (2015).

[28] *Ibid*.

[29] See Lu, Hwang and Lin (2016, p. 344).

committed to enhancing shareholder value",[30] an indication of the influence of investors and their continued confidence on a company's corporate finance strategy.

An innovative part of the OUE Limited plan to finance investments into future projects was the use of REITs as a vehicle to unlock the capital value of the assets, providing liquidity for new undertakings.

OUE Limited has achieved its current standing by employing an adroit business model for seizing opportunities and fuelling future growth. The use of REITs was also a key tool for growing the business. From as early as 2008, the team at OUE Limited had already been considering the possibility of having REIT components in the group, the obstacles being timing, as well as the high requirements from the Monetary Authority of Singapore (MAS) which had to be met in order to launch an REIT:

> "*In 2008, when we first came in two years younger… we have always been toying with the idea of having a hospitality REIT, an asset light strategy. In other words, all the assets on my balance sheet can be sold into the REIT, goes into them, but we control the management company. So, it is taken off from the balance sheet, we collect the money, then we control the manager, and we have got 30 percent of significant interest that then becomes our recurring income. That is the model.*"[31]

Since its acquisition, OUE Limited has been able to grow without needing to raise additional capital from shareholders. Coupled with astute business timing and acumen, as well as a focus upon quality and adding value, the speedy growth of the market valuation of the assets meant that as of 31 December 2013, MOS alone had an open market fair value of S$1.22 billion, with a carrying amount, or book value, of S$115.4 million, creating a valuation surplus of approximately S$1.1 billion.[32] However, this surplus was an unrealised gain, which could either be unlocked by selling the asset or by transferring it to an REIT. With the capital gains made on the two redeveloped assets of MOS and MG, the next innovative step taken was the use of REITs to capture the value that was created and to redeploy the capital into the business projects under OUE Limited. The goal was to realise some of this surplus, as well as to purse an asset light balance sheet strategy to deleverage and free additional resources to pursue growth opportunities. Hence, the company moved MOS and MG off its balance sheet to an affiliated REIT in order to monetise the fair market value of the building, derive interest as recurring income while maintaining an element of control over the management company of the REIT. The challenge in realising this model, unsurprisingly, was in the details.

OUE Limited launched two REITs in quick succession within a span of 12 months: OUE Hospitality REIT, which had its initial public offering (IPO) in July 2013, and OUE Commercial REIT, listed January 2014. REITs provide a form of indirect exposure to the property market for investors and generate investment returns in two ways: through yield via rental income from the properties held and capital growth via increases in the property value.[33] A significant challenge

[30] See *Singapore Business Review* (2017).

[31] Asia Competitiveness Institute interviews of senior management staff of OUE Limited (2015).

[32] See OUE Limited (2015a, p. 139).

[33] See Fitzpatrick (2013).

OUE Limited faced in setting up its REITs was timing the hiring of the management team to promote the REIT with the remaining window of opportunity to launch the REIT, as it had to enter the market at the right moment to be viable. Hiring a strong team of people to run a REIT is essential, and even though OUE Limited had already been hiring people with REIT expertise as early as 2009 in a move of considerable foresight, a challenge for REITs listed in Singapore is the hiring of suitably experienced personnel from the industry for key positions in the REITs, as per the requirements of the regulatory authority.[34]

MOS and MG formed the initial asset base of OUE Hospitality REIT, which comes under OUE Hospitality Trust. OUE Hospitality Trust is a stapled entity that consists of both OUE Hospitality REIT as well as OUE Hospitality Business Trust, with the business trust component intended to remain dormant.[35] Through its Singapore IPO, OUE Hospitality Trust managed to raise S$600 million.[36]

The use of REITs by OUE Limited was a considered financial strategy that has allowed the company to further improve its standing among investors as well as the financing capacity of the group. In particular, the REITs have allowed OUE Limited to deploy a sophisticated use of corporate financial structures to preserve control while developing deeper capabilities for business expansion. Furthermore, with the right of first refusal agreement between OUE Hospitality Trust and OUE Limited as sponsor, OUE Hospitality Trust is given the first opportunity to grow its portfolio of high-quality properties by acquiring suitable properties from OUE Limited, enhancing returns for REIT unit holders and allowing capital to be unlocked for OUE Limited.[37] With this arrangement, OUE Limited is well positioned to continue pursuing larger business opportunities with more capital at its disposal without having to give up prime assets.

[34] For example, in order to fulfil the conditions to obtain the necessary Capital Market Services Licence (CMSL) to manage a REIT from the MAS, applicants had to have managers with at least five years of relevant experience in the property industry, see Monetary Authority of Singapore (2014, p. 8). In 2013, Mr Chong Kee Hiong, who had previously been the CEO of CapitaLand's serviced residence segment The Ascott Ltd, was appointed as CEO of OUE Hospitality Trust; see *Business Times* (2013).

[35] Within the OUE Hospitality Trust IPO prospectus, it was stated that OUE Hospitality Business Trust would be dormant as its primary purpose was to be a master lessee of last resort, meaning if OUE Hospitality REIT is unable to appoint a mater lessee for MOS or a newly acquired hospitality asset, OUE Hospitality Business Trust would then become active and be appointed as the master lessee for such a property. It was also stipulated that OUE Hospitality Business Trust may become active if there are certain projects that may not be suitable for OUE Hospitality REIT. For more, see OUE Hospitality Trust (2013, pp. 80–81).

[36] See Hammond (2014). In terms of investors, S$346 million of OUE Hospitality REIT was to be allocated to institutional investors and S$46 million to retail accounts, with a free float of 52.1 percent; see *EuroWeek* (2013).

[37] The ability for the REIT to draw upon the resources of OUE Limited was further strengthened through a right of first refusal agreement, which gives OUE Hospitality Trust privileged access to asset acquisition opportunities from OUE Limited; see OUE Hospitality Trust (2013, pp. 267–268).

CHAPTER 6
LEADERSHIP LESSONS FOR TRANSFORMATION: A MAN WITH A DISTINCT LEADERSHIP STYLE

Having discussed the various competitive business policies that were designed and implemented to assist in the turnaround of MOS and MG, the final section of the report will feature key leadership lessons learned from Dr Riady, whose role was instrumental in the transformational change process.

Under the leadership of Dr Riady, MOS improved considerably in terms of profitability, while MG was transformed into an upscale niche mall comprising four levels of high-end boutiques, shops and restaurants. The success of the transformation can be attributed to Dr Riady's leadership and foresight in being able to capitalise on the retail potential of the property during the growth of the tourism industry, as well as being able to assemble a competent team to steer the organisation to achieve the project goals.

This chapter will discuss some of the leadership lessons that can be drawn from the transformation of MOS and MG, evaluated in the context of existing literature on leadership and family-owned businesses.

6.1 THE THINKING CHAIRMAN: VISION AND FOCUS

A notable aspect of Dr Riady's leadership is his ability to strategise and effectively articulate his vision to his employees. With the redevelopment of MOS and MG, Dr Riady was clear from the onset that re-allocating space from the hotel to the gallery would maximise profits, given the property's unique location. He was also able to clearly translate his vision of value enhancement by describing what the finished product should look like, both structurally as well as from a branding perspective:

> "*So, for example, he (Dr Riady) was the one who was very much for relocating the lobby to the fifth floor to free up prime area... He did the same thing with our OUE Downtown... He is very good in the sense that he comes from an angle, a very much commercial angle, but then he determines the way we design.*"[1]

Hence, Dr Riady was able to balance the commercial goals of a project while challenging the boundaries of transformation to deliver a quality product. In the case of MOS, Dr Riady convinced his employees that moving the hotel lobby from the ground floor to the fifth floor was not unusual, as during his travels he had encountered many top hotels that had adopted this strategy. He constantly reminded the project management team that the refurbished mall should

[1] Asia Competitiveness Institute interviews of senior management staff of OUE Limited (2015).

be high-end, focusing on targeting a niche client base by featuring new brands or entrants into the market which could draw crowds as a destination shopping mall.

The ability to visualise or present the "big picture" is also complemented by Dr Riady's strength of being an "out-of-the-box" thinker with many ideas. He is unafraid of thinking or dreaming big, and part of the reason for this appears to be the fact that he is not solely driven by commercial or monetary considerations. Instead, his focus is on creating a "wow" or quality product that excites the consumer. During the interviews, many employees shared that Dr Riady encourages innovative ideas rather than ideas that are easily executed. The combination of creativity and practicality is a quality that was often discussed by his employees:

> "*...It is an option that nobody really considered (asset enhancement). It is a lot of work and it is much more straightforward to pull it (the hotel) down and redo it... People just never looked at it as a viable option until we did... for Mandarin Gallery, okay maybe (they might say) that is one off, but then we did it again for our OUE Downtown. So people now open their eyes, and it is from things like this that they start to recognise what OUE Limited is, the value and the ideas that they never thought about.*"[2]

The leadership trait of envisioning is exemplified by Dr Riady, who describes himself as a "thinker" who "dreams a lot" and believes in having "an international perspective and vision".[3] This quality personifies the notion of transformational thinking, where he is constantly reviewing potential investments such as MOS and MG, which can be revitalised. During his interview, he shared his personal goal of envisioning one project every year:

> "*That's important, that way you're thinking about those things every week, you have a list, what are you really excited about this year, what do you look forward to, then you dream: "Oh this year US Bank Towers are opening, it will look like this", you dream about it... Yes, visioning. Or when that opens, what would it look like. So you're already there, you think and think, and the design is one thing, the tenant mix is another thing.*"[4]

His reflective disposition is also common knowledge amongst his employees, who presented him with a hand-drawn caricature for his birthday, with the words "The Thinking Chairman".

6.2 A BLEND OF EAST AND WEST: HANDS-ON AND RESULTS-DRIVEN LEADERSHIP

Based on the interviews and analysis, it appears that Dr Riady encompasses a blend of modern and traditional approaches to leading his organisation. During the interviews, Dr Riady was constantly described as a hands-on or participative leader, defined as one who "consults with subordinates, obtains their ideas and opinions, and integrates their suggestions into the

---

[2] *Ibid.*

[3] *Ibid.*

[4] *Ibid.*

decisions".[5] His leadership embodies a mix of both Eastern and Western leadership styles as he is hands-on and involved in the company, firm but not autocratic. This balance is significant as in family-owned businesses, decision making should not be limited to a few family members as this practice can "breed an overly introspective culture that impedes the reinvention and adaptability necessary to respond to new market dynamics and to stay ahead of competitors."[6]

Unlike laissez-faire leadership or a more hands-off style where a leader provides limited feedback and direction, a collaborative or participative leadership style is particularly important in transformational change, as it enables the leaders to share the new vision and encourage organisational buy-in. Employees in the company are also given the freedom or autonomy to execute their roles which motivates them to take ownership and deliver results:

> *"I think he gives all his heads a lot of autonomy... gives us a lot of opportunity ... you in turn actually feel a lot more responsible. And you feel like you really want to run the division very well. And I think that is how it is, because he doesn't clip you and then you find that you cannot do this or you cannot do that. That is when you lose your whole enthusiasm and steam for what you do. Whereas he gives you the autonomy. You explore and you explain to him. He supports you. That is where you dare to try."*[7]

This aspect of his leadership was more visible following the end of the joint venture partnership in 2010 as the spilt from Ananda Krishnan gave Dr Riady free rein in moving the company closer to his strategic vision and assuming a more hands-on approach.

> *"I think that in the last few years he is a bit more hands on, a lot more intimately involved. I think at that time he was fairly new to Singapore so he was probably still finding his way around, and I think I can see that he is a lot more confident in the sense of what he wants and in his direction to us. Especially in the last few years."*[8]

Known for having a keen eye for detail, Dr Riady constantly provides feedback to his team and closely monitors all his developments. In the case of MOS, he recommended process improvements upon the reopening of the hotel to improve service, productivity and traffic flow at the property. During the room renovations, Dr Riady was personally involved in reviewing the designs and provided suggestions before the renovations began. He was also closely involved in the decisions relating to the positioning of the mall and ensured that the tenant list included only high-end retailers and outlets.

Dr Riady's hands-on leadership style has also ensured that quality standards are maintained. He has a reputation of being reluctant to cut corners and delivers a good quality product through his close involvement and attention to detail. Being personally involved in the projects also means that he is not afraid to make changes to a project which may prove costly or inconvenient.

---

[5] See Northouse (2010, p. 128).

[6] See Koh, Tong and Waltermann (2012, p. 15).

[7] Asia Competitiveness Institute interviews of senior management staff of OUE Limited (2015).

[8] *Ibid.*

This trait is evident in the other OUE Limited projects such as the conversion of the old DBS towers to OUE Downtown, where he requested a change in the façade of the property to increase visibility and quality, amounting to several additional million dollars of costs:

> *"So he drives down the highway and sees the OUE Limited sign and he said, "The first thing, when you go down the highway, is you are going to see this building (OUE Downtown). And he wanted it to look good because that OUE Limited name is there at the top... So he asked for quite a well-known architect to come and propose how to revamp the façade. And of course for me it is a dream because my boss is willing to spend this money."*[9]

Dr Riady also obtained first-hand knowledge of potential issues and challenges present in the hotel and gallery by practicing Management By Walking About (MBWA). Popularised by management guru Tom Peters, this practice advocates that managers who walk the floors have a better grasp on the pulse of the organisation as they are able to comprehend challenges, connect with employees, and provide feedback on issues in an organisation.[10] In fact, MBWA was particularly beneficial during the initial years when MOS was first purchased by OUE Limited, as it enabled Dr Riady to confront the process and people issues facing the organisation. By being involved, he has been able to ensure that the company goals, specifically those related to value enhancement, can be met smoothly. The dedication and drive to correct errors was also a sign to customers and investors that the company was serious about delivering quality.

[9] *Ibid.*

[10] See *The Economist* (2008).

CHAPTER 7
CONCLUSION

The objective of this report is to present the factors that contributed to the turnaround of Mandarin Orchard Singapore and Mandarin Gallery, focusing specifically on the business practices and decisions involved in transforming both assets from underutilised investments into profitable and contemporary developments.

The property, developed in 1971 underwent a series of ownership transfers before finally being purchased by the Lippo Group in 2006 via a joint venture. Dr Stephen Riady assumed the position of Executive Director of OUE Limited in 2006 and in the same year, the property underwent a significant refurbishment exercise which was completed in 2010.

The methodology used for data collection in the report included conducting structured interviews and correspondences with key office holders at OUE Limited and MOS, reviewing documents such as archival data and current reports, and conducting a tour of the hotel and gallery. Secondary information from annual reports, financial reports, media releases and restructuring plans were also used in the preparation of this report.

The report is divided into eight key chapters: (i) the history of the asset; (ii) a literature review of the transformational change model developed for the study; (iii) the role of corporate culture in transformational change; (iv) competitive business policies and (v) financial strategy implemented as part of the transformation of the entity. The last two chapters (vi and vii) focused on the role of leadership in managing change.

The findings of the report support the transformational change model developed as part of the case study to explain the various factors that can impact change management efforts. The transformational journey of MOS began with the change of ownership to OUE Limited in 2006. The vision and foresight of its leader, Dr Riady, provided the impetus to execute OUE Limited's business strategy of asset enhancement and value creation for the property, culminating in both the tangible and intangible transformation of MOS and MG. The decision to allocate greater gross floor area from the hotel and build a bigger retail gallery to maximise value was a crucial strategic decision in enhancing the value of the iconic asset.

> "*Driven by transformation, we are focused on executing our strategy to transform the function, perception and value of our developments through innovative asset repositioning and enhancement initiatives.*"

Executive Chairman, OUE Limited
March 2016

Based on the transformational change model, we find that three key drivers must be aligned for change to be successful. These include the following:

(a) Inculcating an organisation culture that promotes and champions change, driven by a leader's vision. In the case of MOS and MG, the participative leadership style and support of management enabled the company to eradicate the old culture of complacency and replace it with one that valued efficiency and results.
(b) Devising sound business policies that emphasised productivity through streamlining costs and automation enabled MOS to achieve operational efficiency and increase its net profits. In addition, MOS's strategy of offering competitive pricing and maximising occupancy rates enabled the hotel to outperform its competitors. Human resource policies were also revamped to further promote staff training and workplace programs, to boost retention and morale.
(c) Adopting a corporate finance strategy that focused on using instruments such as REITs to stabilise assets and recycle capital, while aligning efforts with government initiatives and policies in the industry environment.

These three drivers facilitated the repositioning and rebranding of MOS to a business-oriented hotel and transforming MG into a four-storey retail asset offering a holistic and unique shopping experience to capture a niche market.

Finally, the report also identified key leadership traits of Dr Riady, such as having a clear vision, commitment to the business strategy, and adopting a hands-on approach, to spearhead change management efforts. By adopting a leadership style that promotes empowerment, open communication and innovation, MOS was able to push its boundaries and achieve its goal of unlocking the hidden value of one of the oldest hotels in Singapore.

The report should benefit entrepreneurs, government officials, small and medium enterprises (SMEs), family-owned businesses and researchers keen on understanding the challenges faced in managing assets in the hospitality and retail sector. The report will also be useful for family-owned businesses as it discusses some best practices adopted by the Riady family to sustain the family business into the next generation.

BIBLIOGRAPHY

"New name for Meritus Mandarin Singapore." ETurboNews (eTN). January 29, 2010. Accessed August 08, 2017. https://eturbonews.com/14100/new-name-meritus-mandarin-singapore.

"Orchard Road to undergo S$40m rejuvenation: STB." Channel NewsAsia. October 29, 2007. Accessed August 01, 2017. http://www.wildsingapore.com/news/20070910/071030-1.htm.

Achua, Christopher F., and Robert N. Lussier. Leadership: Theory, Application & Skill Development. Mason: South-Western Cengage Learning. 2013.

Adenike, Adeniji, Osibanjo Omotayo, and Abiodun Abolaji. "Organizational change and human resource management interventions: An investigation of the Nigerian banking industry." *Serbian Journal of Management* 8, no. 2 (2013): 139–154.

AFX Asia. "Singapore's UOB sells 55 pct stake in OUE to Indonesia's Lippo Group." *AFX Asia.* May 28, 2006.

Al-Haddad, Serina, and Timothy Kotnour. "Integrating the organizational change literature: a model for successful change." *Journal of Organizational Change Management* 28, no. 2 (2015): 234–262.

Albert, Stuart, and David A. Whetten. "Organizational Identity." *Research in Organizational Behavior* 7, (1985): 263–293.

Amit, Raphael. "Cost leadership strategy and experience curves." *Strategic Management Journal* 7, no. 3 (1986): 281–192.

Bae, Johngseok, Shyh-Jer Chen, Tai Wai David Wan, John J. Lawler, and Fred Ochieng Walumbwa. "Human resource strategy and firm performance in Pacific Rim countries." *The International Journal of Human Resource Management* 14, no. 8 (2003): 1308–1332.

Barney, Jay B., and Delwyn N. Clark. *Resource-based Theory: Creating and Sustaining Competitive Advantage*. Oxford: Oxford University Press, 2007.

Barney, Jay. "Firm resources and sustained competitive advantage." *Journal of Management* 17, no. 1 (1991): 99–120.

Beer, Michael, and Nitin Nohria. "Cracking the code of change." *Harvard Business Review* 78, no. 3 (2000): 133–139.

Berrone, Pascual, Jordi Surroca, and Josep A. Tribó. "Corporate ethical identity as a determinant of firm performance: A test of the mediating role of stakeholder satisfaction." *Journal of Business Ethics* 76, no. 1 (2007): 35–53. doi:10.1007/s10551-006-9276-1.

Boehe, Dirk Michael, and Luciano Barin Cruz. "Corporate social responsibility, product differentiation strategy and export performance." *Journal of Business Ethics* 91, no. 2 (2010): 325–346.

Boyne, George A., and Kenneth J. Meier. "Environmental change, human resources and organizational turnaround." *Journal of Management Studies* 46, no. 5 (2009): 835–863.

Business Times. "OUE sheds more light on JV with UOL." *Business Times*. May 3, 2006.

Business Times. "Three-Minute Digest." *Business Times*. June 5, 2013.

Caza, Arran, Brianna A. Barker, and Kim S. Cameron. "Ethics and ethos: The buffering and amplifying effects of ethical behavior and virtuousness." *Journal of Business Ethics* 52, no. 2 (2004): 169–178.

Chang, Aihwa, Hsu Hsin Chiang., and Tzu Shian Han. "A multilevel investigation of relationships among brand-centered HRM, brand psychological ownership, brand citizenship behaviors, and customer satisfaction", *European Journal of Marketing* 46, no.5 (2012): 626–662 (accessed 26 September 2017).

Chatterjee, Sayan. "Types of synergy and economic value: The impact of acquisitions on merging and rival firms." *Strategic Management Journal* 7, no. 2 (1986): 119–139.

Cheng, Bor-Shiuan, Li-Fang Chou, Tsung-Yu Wu, Min-Ping Huang, and Jiing-Lih Farh. "Paternalistic leadership and subordinate responses: Establishing a leadership model in Chinese organizations." *Asian Journal of Social Psychology* 7, no. 1 (2004): 89–117.

Chilkoti, Avantika. "Mochtar Riady, chairman, Lippo Group." Financial Times. February 29, 2016. Accessed August 08, 2017. https://www.ft.com/content/2e63aaca-ca6a-11e5-be0b-b7ece4e953a0.

Chua, Alvin. "Overseas Union Bank (OUB)." Infopedia. February 24, 2011. Accessed August 08, 2017. http://eresources.nlb.gov.sg/infopedia/articles/SIP_1787_2011-02-24.html.

Collins, Jim. "Level 5 leadership: The triumph of humility and fierce resolve." *Harvard Business Review* 79, no. 1 (2001): 66–79.

Conner, Kathleen R. "A historical comparison of resource-based theory and five schools of thought within industrial organization economics: do we have a new theory of the firm?" *Journal of Management* 17, no. 1 (1991): 121–154.

Conroy, Stephen J., and Tisha LN Emerson. "Business ethics and religion: Religiosity as a predictor of ethical awareness among students." *Journal of Business Ethics* 50, no. 4 (2004): 383–396.

Corley, Kevin G. "Defined by our strategy or our culture? Hierarchical differences in perceptions of organizational identity and change." *Human Relations* 57, no. 9 (2004): 1145–1177.

Corley, Kevin G., and Dennis A. Gioia. "Identity ambiguity and change in the wake of a corporate spin-off." *Administrative Science Quarterly* 49, no. 2 (2004): 173–208.

Cornelissen, Joep P., S. Alexander Haslam, and John MT Balmer. "Social identity, organizational identity and corporate identity: Towards an integrated understanding of processes, patternings and products." *British journal of management* 18, no. s1 (2007).

Cornelius, Nelarine, James Wallace, and Rana Tassabehji. "An analysis of corporate social responsibility, corporate identity and ethics teaching in business schools." *Journal of Business Ethics* 76, no. 1 (2007): 117–135.

Crook, T. Russell, David J. Ketchen, James G. Combs, and Samuel Y. Todd. "Strategic resources and performance: a meta analysis." *Strategic Management Journal* 29, no. 11 (2008): 1141–1154.

Cunningham, J. Barton, and Philip Gerrard. "Characteristics of well-performing organisations in Singapore." *Singapore Management Review* 22, no. 1 (2000): 35.

Covey, Stephen R. "Sense of Stewardship." *Executive Excellence* 17, no. 7 (1997): 3.

Damodaran, Aswath. *Investment Valuation: Tools and Techniques for Determining the Value of Any Asset.* Hoboken, NJ: Wiley, 2002.

Denison, Daniel, Colleen Lief, and John L. Ward. "Culture in family owned enterprises: recognizing and leveraging unique strengths." *Family Business Review* 17, no. 1 (2004): 61–70.

Denning, Stephen. "Transformational innovation: A journey by narrative." *Strategy & Leadership* 33, no. 3 (2005): 11–16.

Dent, Eric B., and Susan Galloway Goldberg. "Challenging 'Resistance to Change'." *Journal of Applied Behavioural Science* 35, no. 25 (1999): 25–41.

Dickson, Peter R., and James L. Ginter. "Market segmentation, product differentiation, and marketing strategy." *The Journal of Marketing* (1987): 1–10.

Dierickx, Ingemar, and Karel Cool. "Asset stock accumulation and sustainability of competitive advantage." *Management Science* 35, no. 12 (1989): 1504–1511.

Directorate, OECD Statistics. "The OECD Glossary of Statistical Terms." The OECD Glossary of Statistical Terms. Accessed August 08, 2017. https://stats.oecd.org/glossary/.

Dollinger, Marc J. "Confucian ethics and Japanese management practices." *Journal of Business Ethics* 7, no. 8 (1988): 575–584.

Dorfman, Peter W., Jon P. Howell, Shozo Hibino, Jin K. Lee, Uday Tate, and Arnoldo Bautista. "Leadership in Western and Asian countries: Commonalities and differences in effective leadership processes across cultures." *The Leadership Quarterly* 8, no. 3 (1997): 233–274.

Dowling, Grahame R. "Developing your company image into a corporate asset." *Long Range Planning* 26, no. 2 (1993): 101–109.

Dreyer, Brent J., and Kieran Mathieson. "Ensuring consistency in the estimation of vacancy rates." *Appraisal Journal* 63, (1995): 209–209.

Eisenstat, Russell, Bert Spector, and Michael Beer. "Why Change Programs Don't Produce Change." *Harvard Business Review* 68, no. 6 (1990): 158–166.

Euroweek. "Cornerstone support helps Reit return after sell-off." *Euroweek*. July 12, 2013.

Fama, Eugene F.. "The effects of a firm's investment and financing decisions on the welfare of its security holders." *The American Economic Review* 68, no. 3 (1978): 272–284.

Fama, Eugene F, and Merton H. Miller. *The Theory of Finance*. Holt Rinehart & Winston, 1972.

Fernandez-Araoz, Claudio, Sonny Iqbal, and Jorg Ritter. "Leadership lessons from great family businesses." *Harvard Business Review* 93, no. 4 (2015): 82–88.

Finnerty, John D. "Financial engineering in corporate finance: An overview." *Financial Management* (1988): 14–33.

Fitzpatrick, Damian. "Warming to hot property." *Money Management* 27, no. 14 (2013): 20.

Fort, Timothy L. "Religion and business ethics: the lessons from political morality." *Journal of Business Ethics* 16, no. 3 (1997): 263–273.

Gerstner, Eitan, James Hess, and Wujin Chu. "Demarketing as a differentiation strategy." *Marketing Letters* 4, no. 1 (1993). 49–57.

Gilley, Ann, Jerry W. Gilley, and Heather S. McMillan. "Organizational change: Motivation, communication, and leadership effectiveness." *Performance Improvement Quarterly* 21, no. 4 (2009): 75–94.

Glew, David J., Anne M. O'Leary-Kelly, Ricky W. Griffin, and David D. Van Fleet. "Participation in organizations: A preview of the issues and proposed framework for future analysis." *Journal of Management* 21, no. 7 (1995): 395–421. Accessed 26 September 2017. https://doi.org/10.1016/0149-2063(95)90014-4.

Goh, Shannon. "Lippo buys Krishnan's OUE stake for $957m." *The Business Times*. March 10, 2010.

Goss, Tracy, and Richard Pascale. "The reinvention roller coaster: Risking the present for a powerful future." *Harvard Business Review* 71, no. 6 (1993): 97–106.

Gotsi, Manto, and Alan Wilson. "Corporate reputation management:"living the brand"." *Management Decision* 39, no. 2 (2001): 99–104.

Hammond, Clare. "Institutional demand muted for 'undervalued' OUE Reit." *Euroweek*. January 20, 2014.

Hatch, Mary Jo, and Majken Schultz. "The dynamics of organizational identity." *Human Relations* 55, no. 8 (2002): 989–1018.

Heng, Janice. "Prefab saves time for Changi hotel." AsiaOne. February 12, 2016. Accessed August 08, 2017. http://www.asiaone.com/singapore/prefab-saves-time-changi-hotel.

Hill, Charles WL. "Differentiation versus low cost or differentiation and low cost: a contingency framework." *Academy of Management Review* 13, no. 3 (1988): 401–412.

Ho, Stephanie. "Singapore Tourism Board." Infopedia. February 05, 2015. Accessed August 08, 2017. http://eresources.nlb.gov.sg/infopedia/articles/SIP_31_2005-01-31.html.

Hofstede, Geert. *Culture's Consequences: Comparing Values, Behaviors, Institutions and Organizations Across Nations.* Vol. 2nd ed. California: Sage Publications, 2001.

Holland, Daniel, and Chad Albrecht. "The worldwide academic field of business ethics: Scholars' perceptions of the most important issues." *Journal of Business Ethics* 117, no. 4 (2013): 777–788.

House, Robert, Mansour Javidan, Paul Hanges, and Peter Dorfman. "Understanding cultures and implicit leadership theories across the globe: an introduction to project GLOBE." *Journal of World Business* 37, no. 1 (2002): 3–10.

House, Robert J, Paul Hanges, Mansour Javidan, Peter W Dorfman, and Vipin Gupta. Culture, Leadership, and Organizations: The GLOBE Study of 62 Societies. Thousand Oaks: Sage Publications Inc. 2004.

Huselid, Mark A. "The impact of human resource management practices on turnover, productivity, and corporate financial performance." *Academy of Management Journal* 38, no. 3 (1995): 635–672.

Ionescu, Vladimir-Codrin. "Leadership, culture and organizational change." *Manager* 20, (2014): 65.

Jayasankaran, S. "OUE may be taken private, says M'sian businessmen". The Business Times, June 19, 2006, 2.

Jensen, Michael C., and William H. Meckling. "Theory of the firm: Managerial behavior, agency costs and ownership structure." *Journal of Financial Economics* 3, no. 4 (1976): 305–360.

Kaiser, Kevin., and S. David Young. *Blue Line Management: What Value Creation Really Means* (Fontainebleau: INSEAD 2009).

Kanter, Rosabeth M. "Leaders with passion, conviction and confidence can use several techniques to take charge of change rather than react to it." *Ivey Business Journal* 64, no. 5 (2000): 32–36.

Kanter, Rosabeth Moss., Barry A. Stein, and Todd D. Jick. *The Challenge of Organizational Change: How Companies Experience it and Leaders Guide it.* New York: Free Press, 1992.

Kapferer, Jean-Noel. *The New Strategic Brand Management: Advanced Insights and Strategic Thinking.* Kogan page publishers, 2012.

Kaufmann, Hans R., Demetris Vrontis, Michael Czinkota and Alvin Hadiono. "Corporate branding and transformational leadership in turbulent times." *Journal of Product & Brand Management* 21, no. 3 (2012): 192–204.

King, Peter, and Wei Zhang. "Chinese and western leadership models: A literature review." *Journal of Management Research* 6, no. 2 (2014): 1.

Koh, D., Dean Tong., and Bernd Waltermann. *Defying the Odds: Building Family Businesses that Last* (Singapore: Boston Consulting Group 2012).

Koller, Timoty. "What is value-based management?" *McKinsey Quarterly*, no. 3 (1994): 87–101.

Kotter, John P. "Accelerate." *Harvard Business Review* 90, no. 11 (2012): 45–58.

Kotter, John P. "Leading change: why transformation efforts fail." *Harvard Business Review* 73, no. 2 (2009).

Kraaijenbrink, Jeroen. "A Value-Oriented View of Strategy." Working Paper. University of Twente. 2011.

Kuhn, Thomas S. *The Structure of Scientific Revolutions*. Chicago, IL: The University of Chicago Press, 1970.

Lam, Patrick TI, Yat Hung Chiang, and Stephen H. Chan. "Financing real estate development using bonds in Asia." *International Journal of Strategic Property Management* 15, no. 4 (2011): 340–355.

Lien, Ying Chow., and Louis Kraar. *From Chinese Villager to Singapore Tycoon: My Life Story*. Singapore: Times Books International, 1992.

Littler, D. 1999. "Cost-leadership strategy", *Wiley Encyclopedia of Management* (Wiley Online Library), 9:1.

Liu, P., and Quan D. (2011). *Measuring hotel risk and financing* [Electronic version]. Retrieved [1 August 2017], from Cornell University, School of Hospitality Administration site: http://scholarship.sha.cornell.edu/articles/285.

Lu, Jin-Ray, Chih-Chiang Hwang, and Chien-Yi Lin. "Do shareholders appreciate capital investment policies of corporations?." *International Review of Economics & Finance* 43, (2016): 344–353.

Lussier, Robert N., and Christopher F. Achua. *Leadership: Theory, Application, Skill Development*. Mason, OH: South-Western, 2013.

Mahoney, Joseph T., and J. Rajendran Pandian. "The resource based view within the conversation of strategic management." *Strategic Management Journal* 13, no. 5 (1992): 363–380.

Mayhew, Brian W., and Michael S. Wilkins. "Audit firm industry specialization as a differentiation strategy: Evidence from fees charged to firms going public." *Auditing: A Journal of Practice & Theory* 22, no. 2 (2003): 33–52.

Singapore Ministry of Trade and Industry. *Ministerial Speeches and Comments for Integrated Resorts* (Singapore: Ministry of Trade and Industry 2006) Accessed March 22, 2016. https://www.mti.gov.sg/MTIInsights/Pages/Ministerial-Speeches-and-Comments-for-Integrated-Resorts.aspx.

Modigliani, Franco, and Merton H. Miller. "Corporate income taxes and the cost of capital: a correction." *The American Economic Review,* (1963): 433–443.

Moingeon, Bertrand. "From corporate culture to corporate identity." *Corporate Reputation Review* 2, no. 4 (1999): 352–360.

Monetary Authority of Singapore. *Banking (Amendment) Bill — 2nd reading speech — By Mr Lee Hsien Loong, DPM, Singapore and Chairman, MAS* (Singapore: Monetary Authority of Singapore 2001) Accessed March 10, 2015. http://www.mas.gov.sg/news-and-publications/speeches-and-monetary-policy-statements/speeches/2001/banking-amendment-bill-2nd-reading-speech-by-dpm-lee-16-may-2001.aspx.

Monetary Authority of Singapore. *Extension of Grace Period for Banks Divestment of Non-Financial Businesses* (Singapore: Monetary Authority of Singapore 2003) Accessed March 10, 2015. http"//www.mas.gov.sg/news-and-publications/media-releases/2003/extension-of-grace-period-for-banks.aspx.

Monetary Authority of Singapore. *MAS Issues Banking (Amendment) Regulations 2004* (Singapore: Monetary Authority of Singapore) Accessed March 10, 2015. http://www.mas.gov.sg/news-and-publications/media-releases/2004/mas-issues-banking-amendment-regulations-2004.aspx.

Monetary Authority of Singapore. *Guidelines on Criteria for the Grant of a Capital Markets Service Licence Other Than for Fund Management [Guideline No SFA04-G01]* (Singapore: Monetary

Authority of Singapore) Accessed November 12, 2015. http://www.mas.gov.sg/regulations-and-financial-stability/regulations-guidance-and-licensing/securities-futures-and-funds-management/guidelines/2014/guidelines-on-critera-for-the-grant-of-a-capital-markets-services-licence-guideline-no-sfa04_g01.aspx.

Muzellec, Laurent, and Mary Lambkin. "Corporate rebranding: destroying, transferring or creating brand equity?." *European Journal of Marketing* 40, no. 7/8 (2006): 803–824.

Muzellec, Laurent, Manus Doogan, and Mary Lambkin. "Corporate rebranding-an exploratory review." *Irish Marketing Review* 16, no. 2 (2003): 31.

Myers, Stewart C. "Determinants of corporate borrowing." *Journal of Financial Economics* 5, no. 2 (1977): 147–175.

Northouse, Peter G. *Leadership: Theory and practice*. 7th ed. California. Sage publications, 2010.

O'Toole, James. "Connecting the dots between leadership, ethics and corporate culture." *Ivey Business Journal Online* 73, no. 5 (2009): 3.

One Raffles Place. "Tower 2." Onerafflesplace.com.sg 2014. http://www.onerafflesplace.com.sg/tower2-about.shtml (Accessed April 20, 2016).

OUE Hospitality REIT Management. "OUE Hospitality Trust Profile". Accessed 8 October 2017. https://oueht.com/index.php?/trust-profile.

OUE Hospitality Trust. *OUE H-Trust IPO Prospectus* (Singapore: OUE Hospitality Trust 2013) Accessed March 5, 2015. http://oueht.com/publications.

OUE Hospitality Trust. *Annual Report 2013: Making Our Mark* (Singapore: OUE Hospitality Trust 2014) Accessed May 7, 2015. http://oueht.com/publications.

OUE Hospitality Trust. *Annual Report 2014: Setting the Future in Motion* (Singapore: OUE Hospitality Trust 2015) Accessed May 7, 2015. http://oueht.com/publications.

OUE Hospitality Trust. 2016. "Mandarin Orchard Singapore." OUEHT.com. http://oueht.com/properties/mandarin-orchard-singapore (accessed March 31, 2016).

OUE Limited. "OUE unveils new corporate identity". OUE.com.sg June 19 2013. http://www.oue.com.sg/doc/Press%20Release_OUE%20Unveils%20New%20Corporate%20Identity.pdf (accessed April 1, 2016).

OUE Limited. *Annual Report 2013: Transformational Future* (Singapore: OUE Limited 2014). Accessed April 27, 2015. http://www.oue.com.sg/investor-relations/financial-report.

OUE Limited. *Annual Report 2014: Transforming Potential* (Singapore: OUE Limited 2015) Accessed April 27, 2015. http://www.oue.com.sg/investor-relations/financial-report.

OUE Limited. *OUE Limited — Analyst Coverage* (Singapore: OUE Limited 2015) Accessed October 29, 2015. http://www.oue.com.sg/investor-relations/analyst-coverage.

Overseas Union Enterprise Limited. *Annual Report 1969* (Singapore: Overseas Union Enterprise Limited 1970).

Overseas Union Enterprise Limited. *Annual Report 1970* (Singapore: Overseas Union Enterprise Limited 1971).

Overseas Union Enterprise Limited. *Annual Report 1971* (Singapore: Overseas Union Enterprise Limited 1972).

Overseas Union Enterprise Limited. *Annual Report 1972* (Singapore: Overseas Union Enterprise Limited 1973).

Overseas Union Enterprise Limited. *Annual Report 1973* (Singapore: Overseas Union Enterprise Limited 1974).

Overseas Union Enterprise Limited. *Annual Report 1978* (Singapore: Overseas Union Enterprise Limited 1979).

Overseas Union Enterprise Limited. *Annual Report 1980* (Singapore: Overseas Union Enterprise Limited 1981).

Overseas Union Enterprise Limited. *Annual Report 1981* (Singapore: Overseas Union Enterprise Limited 1982).

Overseas Union Enterprise Limited. *Annual Report 1985* (Singapore: Overseas Union Enterprise Limited 1986).

Overseas Union Enterprise Limited. *Annual Report 1990* (Singapore: Overseas Union Enterprise Limited 1991).

Overseas Union Enterprise Limited. *Annual Report 1994* (Singapore: Overseas Union Enterprise Limited 1995).

Overseas Union Enterprise Limited. *Annual Report 1997* (Singapore: Overseas Union Enterprise Limited 1998).

Overseas Union Enterprise Limited. *Annual Report 2002* (Singapore: Overseas Union Enterprise Limited 2003).

Overseas Union Enterprise Limited. *Annual Report 2003* (Singapore: Overseas Union Enterprise Limited 2004).

Overseas Union Enterprise Limited. *Annual Report 2004* (Singapore: Overseas Union Enterprise Limited 2005).

Overseas Union Enterprise Limited. *Annual Report 2006: Diversifying with the Changing Face of Asia.* (Singapore: Overseas Union Enterprise Limited 2007) Accessed December 16, 2014. http://www.oue.com.sg/investor-relations/financial-report.

Overseas Union Enterprise Limited. *Annual Report 2007: We go Beyond* (Singapore: Overseas Union Enterprise Limited 2008) Accessed December 16, 2014. http://www.oue.com.sg/investor-relations/financial-report.

Overseas Union Enterprise Limited. *Annual Report 2008: Building value, Shaping our future* (Singapore: Overseas Union Enterprise Limited 2009) Accessed December 16, 2014. http://www.oue.com.sg/investor-relations/financial-report.

Overseas Union Enterprise Limited. 'OUE Acquires Iconic DBS Towers for S$870.5M'. OUE.com.sg August 11, 2010. http://www.oue.com.sg/doc/OUE_Press_release_DBS_Towers_Acquisition.pdf (accessed April 20, 2016).

Overseas Union Enterprise Limited. *Annual Report 2009: Unveiling A New Phase of Growth* (Singapore: Overseas Union Enterprise Limited 2010) Accessed December 16, 2014. http://www.oue.com.sg/investor-relations/financial-report.

Overseas Union Enterprise Limited. 'OUE acquires the iconic Crowne Plaza Changi Airport Hotel'. OUE Limited: Announcements, April 15, 2011. http://www.oue.com.sg/investor-relations/announcements (accessed April 20, 2016).

Overseas Union Enterprise Limited. *Annual Report 2010: Enhancing Assets, Driving Growth* (Singapore: Overseas Union Enterprise Limited 2011) Accessed December 16, 2014. http://www.oue.com.sg/investor-relations/financial-report.

Overseas Union Enterprise Limited. 2012. *Annual Report 2011: Enduring Values* (Singapore: Overseas Union Enterprise Limited 2012) Accessed Decemeber 16, 2014. http://www.oue.com.sg/investor-relations/financial-report.

Pérez, Andrea, and Ignacio Rodríguez Del Bosque. "Organizational and corporate identity revisited: Toward a comprehensive understanding of identity in business." *Corporate Reputation Review* 17, no. 1 (2014): 3–27.

Peteraf, Margaret A. "The cornerstones of competitive advantage: A resource based view." *Strategic Management Journal* 14, no. 3 (1993): 179–191.

Porter, Michael E. *Competitive Advantage Creating and Sustaining Superior Performance: With a New Introduction*. New York: Free Press, 1985.

Porter, Michael E. *Competitive Strategy: Techniques for Analysing Industries and Competitors*. New York: The Free Press. 1980.

Reid, Gavin. *Small Business Enterprise: An Economic Analysis.* New York, NY: Routledge 1993.

Reitsperger, Wolf D, Shirley J. Daniel, Stephen B. Tallman, and William G. Chismar. "Product quality and cost leadership: compatible strategies?." *MIR: Management International Review*, (1993): 7–21.

Rooke, David, and William R. Torbert. "Seven transformations of leadership." *Harvard Business Review* 83, no. 4 (2005): 66–76.

Ruediger Kaufmann, Hans, Demetris Vrontis, Michael Czinkota, and Alvin Hadiono. "Corporate branding and transformational leadership in turbulent times." *Journal of Product & Brand Management* 21, no. 3 (2012): 192–204.

Schein, Edgar H. "Coming to a new awareness of organizational culture." *Sloan Management Review* 25, no. 2 (1984): 3–16.

Schwass, J. *Family Businesses: Successes and Failures* (Lausanne: International Institute for Management Development 2013).

Sims, Ronald R. *Changing the Way We Manage Change.* London: Quorum Books, 2002.

Singapore Business Review. "OUE's full-year profit down 7.7% to $144.4m." SBR.com.sg February 21 2017. http://sbr.com.sg/commercial-property/news/oues-full-year-profit-down-77-1444m (accessed February 26, 2017).

Singapore Tourism Board. *Singapore Tourism Board Annual Report 2004/2005: Unique Moments in a Unique Year* (Singapore: Singapore Tourism Board 2005) Accessed March 22 2016. https://www.stb.gov.sg/news-and-publications/publications/Pages/Annual-Reports.aspx.

Singapore Visitor. "A New Palace for Modern Mandarins in Singapore… The Mighty Mandarin Hotel is Open!" *Singapore Visitor*. December 1971.

Spencer, X. Sarah Yang, Therese A. Joiner, and Suzanne Salmon. "Differentiation strategy, performance measurement systems and organizational performance: Evidence from Australia." *International Journal of Business* 14, no. 1 (2009): 83.

Stahl, Michael J., and David W. Grigsby. *Strategic Management: Total Quality and Global Competition.* Hoboken, NJ: Wiley 1997.

Stalk, George, and Henry Foley. "Avoiding Traps That Can Destroy Family Businesses." *Harvard Business Review* 90, (2012): 25–27.

Stansbury, Jason. "Reasoned moral agreement: Applying discourse ethics within organizations." *Business Ethics Quarterly* 19, no. 1 (2009): 33–56.

Steingard, David S. "Spiritually-informed management theory: Toward profound possibilities for inquiry and transformation." *Journal of Management Inquiry* 14, no. 3 (2005): 227–241.

Stuart, Albert, and David A. Whetten. "Organizational Identity." *Research in Organizational Behavior* 7, (1985): 263–295.

Sunder, Shyam. "Management control, expectations, common knowledge, and culture." *Journal of Management Accounting Research* 14, no. 1 (2002): 173–187.

Tan, Angela. "UOL and OUE to swap assets worth \$73m." *The Business Times*. March 13, 2006.

Tan, Khee Giap, and Yan Yi Tan. "Promoting SMEs and enhancing labor productivity in Singapore: A policy analysis." *Journal of International Commerce, Economics and Policy* 5, no. 03 (2014): 1440012 (12 pages).

Teo, Joyce. "DBS Towers sold to OUE for \$871m." *The Straits Times*. August 12, 2010.

Termeer, Catrien JAM, Art Dewulf, and G. Robbert Biesbroek. "Transformational change: governance interventions for climate change adaptation from a continuous change perspective." *Journal of Environmental Planning and Management* 60, no. 4 (2017): 558–576.

United Overseas Bank. *Annual Report 2001: United for Growth* (Singapore: United Overseas Bank 2002) Accessed March 31, 2016. http://www.uob.com.sg/assets/pdfs/reports2001.pdf.

United Overseas Bank. "OUE Divestment Notice." UOBgroup.com May 26 2006. http://www.uobgroup.com/assets/pdfs/about/news/2006/news_27may_01.pdf (Accessed March 5, 2015).

Urban Redevelopment Authority. "URA Launches Development Incentives to Enhance and Rejuvenate Orchard Road." URA.gov.sg March 7 2005. http://www.ura.gov.sg/uol/media-room/news/2005/mar/pr05–10.aspx (accessed March 22, 2016).

Utterback, James M., and William J. Abernathy. "A dynamic model of process and product innovation." *Omega* 3, no. 6 (1975): 639–656.

Vasko, Lydia. "Crowne Plaza Changi Airport is crowned world's best airport hotel by Skytrax." *The Straits Times*. March 18, 2015.

Verbos, Amy Klemm, Joseph A. Gerard, Paul R. Forshey, Charles S. Harding, and Janice S. Miller. "The positive ethical organization: Enacting a living code of ethics and ethical organizational identity." *Journal of Business Ethics* 76, no. 1 (2007): 17–33.

Vincent, Roger. "Singapore firm buys U.S. Bank Tower in downtown LA." *Los Angeles Times*. June 19, 2013.

Vincent, Roger. "U.S. Bank Tower owner plans to build a rooftop observatory for tourists." *Los Angeles Times*. July 14, 2015.

Warden, Goola. "Remaking OUE in Lippo's mould." *The Edge Singapore*. 24 May 2010.

Wheelen, Thomas L., and J. David. Hunger. *Strategic Management and Business Policy: Achieving Sustainability*. 14th ed. Essex: Pearson Education Limited, 2010.

Wheelen, Thomas L, J. David Hunger, Alan N. Hoffman and Charles E Bamford. Concepts in Strategic Management and Business Policy: Globalization, Innovation, and Sustainability. Harlow: Pearson Education Limited, 2015.

Whetten, David A. "Albert and Whetten revisited: Strengthening the concept of organizational identity." *Journal of Management Inquiry* 15, no. 3 (2006): 219–234.

Whetten, David A., and Stuart Albert. "Organizational Identity." *Research in Organizational Behaviour* 7, (1985): 263–295.

Wiegelmann, Thomas Wolfgang. "Risk Management in the Real Estate Development Industry." *Robina: Institute of Sustainable Development & Architecture* (2012).

Worden, Skip. "Religion in strategic leadership: A positivistic, normative/theological, and strategic analysis." *Journal of Business Ethics* 57, no. 3 (2005): 221–239.

Yang, Liu-Qin, Russell E. Johnson, Xichao Zhang, Paul E. Spector, and Shiyong Xu. "Relations of interpersonal unfairness with counterproductive work behavior: the moderating role of employee self-identity." *Journal of Business and Psychology* 28, no. 2 (2013): 189–202.

Younes, Elie, and Russell Kett. "Hotel investment risk: what are the chances?." *Journal of Retail & Leisure Property* 6, no. 1 (2007): 69–78.

Yukl, Gary. *Leadership in Organizations*. 15th ed. Boston: Pearson Education, 2013.

Zenger, Todd. "What is the theory of your firm?." *Harvard Business Review* 91, no. 6 (2013): 72.

APPENDIX 1
METHODOLOGY FOR DATA COLLECTION

STRUCTURED INTERVIEWS

Interviews were conducted between 9 February 2015 and 31 July 2016:

1. Executive Chairman of OUE Limited
2. Chief Executive Officer/Group Managing Director of OUE Limited
3. Chief Corporate Officer of OUE Limited
4. Hotel Manager of Mandarin Orchard Singapore
5. Head of Investor Relations of OUE Limited
6. Senior Vice President (Development & Projects) of OUE Limited
7. Senior Vice President (Finance) of OUE Limited
8. Senior Vice President (Retail, Marketing & Leasing) of OUE Limited
9. Senior Vice President (Property Management & Technical Support) of OUE Limited
10. Assistant Vice President (Investor Relations) of OUE Limited

DOCUMENT REVIEW

1. Annual reports (1969–2014)
2. Media releases/reports
3. OUE Limited website
4. Organisational chart of OUE Limited, Mandarin Orchard Singapore and Meritus Hotels and Resorts
5. Restructuring plans/drawings for refurbishment of Mandarin Orchard Singapore and Mandarin Gallery
6. Business and financial data of Mandarin Orchard Singapore and Mandarin Gallery
7. Pictures of old Mandarin Orchard Singapore and Mandarin Gallery property and the refurbished property

DATA ANALYSIS

1. Collection of available quantitative data from public and private sources, and verification of the integrity of data
2. Application of necessary calculations to the data and examination of the trends, and evaluation of further data analysis and collection requirements

OBSERVATION

1. Tour of the hotel and gallery on 18 September 2015
2. Speech by Dr Stephen Riady at a leadership forum on family businesses on 24 July 2015

APPENDIX 2

SUPPLEMENTARY INFORMATION ON MANDARIN ORCHARD SINGAPORE, MANDARIN GALLERY AND MERITUS HOTELS AND RESORTS

Table A1 Facilities Available at Mandarin Orchard Singapore in the 1970s

Facility name			
Act One	Chatterbox	Clipper Bar	Kasbah
Mezzanine	Pine Court	Sandbar & Pool	Mandarin Shopping Arcade
The Belvedere	The Library	The Stables	Top of the M

Source: Adapted from OUE Limited

BACKGROUND INFORMATION ON MERITUS HOTELS AND RESORTS

When it opened its doors in the 1970s, the "Mandarin Singapore" hotel gained a reputation in the industry of providing service synonymous with authentic Asian hospitality. Representing this hospitality was the Meritus Ambassador, a beautifully dressed Asian girl in cheongsam or silk sarong, captured by the trademark golden ribbon, symbolising silk, the highly sought-after item that first linked the East with the West.

The Mandarin brand became a successful formula in the hotel industry, providing patrons from the likes of presidents, kings and queens, to sojourners from both near and far, a distinguished venue to meet, dine and stay. Its mission was to offer excellence of service no matter who you were or where you were from. Everyone on a journey merited Mandarin's enchantment.

The company kept the image of the Seal of Quality to signify its commitment to consistently deliver its Asian hospitality to their guests. Subsequently, the group also introduced the new name "Meritus" signifying excellence and worth to highlight its ambition to offer this blend of service culture comprising "Asian grace, warmth, and care" to the rest of the world. This prompted the group to establish Meritus Hotels and Resorts, under the Hospitality Division of OUE Limited to manage and operate its hotels and resorts based in Singapore, Malaysia and China.

The Meritus Hotels and Resorts group has won numerous awards which reflect the strong recognition of its home-grown name and reputation. Meritus is a three-time winner of the most popular heritage brand at the Singapore Prestige Brand Award and was also conferred the accolade of global winner for a luxury hotel chain at the prestigious world luxury hotel awards in 2013.

Timeline for the incorporation of Meritus Hotels and Resorts and related hotel management companies of the group:

The "Meritus" brand first originated in 1997 as a way to link certain subsidiary companies under a recognisable brand name, beginning first with "Meritus Hotels and Resorts Ltd."

The origin of "Singapore Mandarin International Hotels Private Limited" company, the hotel managing company of Mandarin Orchard Singapore as declared in 2013, can be traced back to the original "Mandarin (Singapore) International Hotels Private Limited" which was first incorporated on 14 December 1978.[1]

Brief Timeline:

- 1970: Annual report of 1970 states that the subsidiary "Mandarin Hotel (S) Private Limited", was first incorporated on 6 December 1965, the first company setup to oversee the "Mandarin Singapore" hotel.[2]
- 1978: It is then first stated in the 1978 annual report that "Mandarin (Singapore) International Hotels Private Limited" was incorporated on 14 December 1978.[3]
- 1990: The name of the company then changes in 1990 from "Mandarin (Singapore) International Hotels Private Limited" to "Singapore Mandarin International Hotels Private Limited."[4]
- 1997: The Meritus brand name is first developed to be gradually applied to various hotel management subsidiaries of the group over time. Two hotel management subsidiaries based in Malaysia and Singapore, as well as one hospitality marketing and promotion subsidiary based in Hong Kong have their company names changed to take on the "Meritus" name.[5]
- 2010: The name "Meritus International Private Limited" first appears in the 2010 annual report, listed as an investment holding company.[6]
- 2013: The name "Singapore Mandarin International Hotels Private Limited" is still in use as of the 2013 annual report.[7] The 2013 initial public offering prospectus for OUE Hospitality Trust states that "Singapore Mandarin International Hotels Private Limited" is the hotel manager of Mandarin Orchard Singapore and owned by "Meritus International Private Limited."[8] However, it is no longer listed within the subsidiary and associated companies section in the 2014 OUE Limited annual report notes, nor is it listed within the 2014 OUE Hospitality Trust annual report notes.[9]

List of Accolades for Mandarin Orchard Singapore and Meritus Hotels and Resorts:

<u>Accolades in 1994</u>

Meritus Mandarin Singapore:

- Top 10 Best Individual Hotels in the World — The Business Traveller

---

[1] See OUE Hospitality Trust (2013, p. 29).

[2] See Overseas Union Enterprise Limited (1971, p. 13).

[3] See Overseas Union Enterprise Limited (1979, p. 17).

[4] See Overseas Union Enterprise Limited (1991, p. 39).

[5] See Overseas Union Enterprise Limited (1998, pp. 7, 31).

[6] See Overseas Union Enterprise Limited (2011, p. 159).

[7] See OUE Limited (2014, p. 161).

[8] See OUE Hospitality Trust (2013, p. 29).

[9] See OUE Limited (2015) and OUE Hospitality Trust (2015).

Accolades in 2006

Meritus Mandarin Singapore:

- Conde Nast Traveller — Readers' Choice Gold List Hotels in Asia, Australia and Pacific Nations and Travel & Leisure — T&L500 Guide

Accolades in 2007

Meritus Hotels & Resorts:

- Best Sales Team — Travel Weekly Asia Industry Award 2007

Meritus Mandarin Singapore:

- Front Office Best Reception — Hospitality Asia Platinum Awards (Singapore Series) 2006/2007
- Most Promising Chef — Hospitality Asia Platinum Awards (Singapore Series) 2006/2007
- Excellent Service Awards — Spring Singapore 2007
- Singapore Tatler Best Restaurant Series 2007 — Top of the "M" Revolving Restaurant Pine Court Chinese Restaurant
- The Best of Singapore Local Food (Chicken Rice) — Singapore Tatler 2007

Accolades in 2008

Meritus Mandarin Singapore:

- Best Business Hotel: International Category Award — TravelWeekly China Awards 2008
- Hainanese Chicken Rice Heavenly King — LianHe WanBao and OMY 2008

Accolades in 2009

Meritus Hotels & Resorts:

- Top 3 Most Outstanding Performers — Chains — HotelClub Awards 2009

Mandarin Orchard Singapore:

- Best Practice in Online Distribution — Agoda Gold Circle Awards 2009
- Best Purchasing Team and Top 3 HAPA Best Front of the House — Hospitality Asia Platinum Awards 2009–2011 Singapore Series
- Meritus Mandarin 73.5 (Top 5) — SMU Customer Satisfaction Index of Singapore 2009
- Chicken Rice @ Chatterbox: Best Local Food Award — Singapore Tatler The Best of Singapore 2009
- Pine Court Chinese Restaurant and Chatterbox — Simply Dining Singapore's Top Restaurants 2009
- Pine Court Chinese Restaurant — Wine & Dine Singapore's Top Restaurant 2009
- Pine Court Chinese Restaurant: Top 5 Best Asian Cuisine Restaurant (Hotel) — Hospitality Asia Platinum Awards 2009–2011 Singapore Series

Accolades in 2010

Mandarin Orchard Singapore:

- Best City Hotel (Singapore) — 21st TG Travel Awards 2010

- Top 5: Mandarin Orchard Singapore (77.7 percent) — Customer Satisfaction Index Survey for Tourism, Hotels and Accommodation Services
- Hotel Security Award 2010 — Singapore Hotel Association (SHA) Excellence
- Triple Three: Buffet Lover's Dream — The Singapore Women's Weekly Gold Plate Awards 2010
- Mandarin Court Chinese Restaurant — Singapore Tatler's Regional Best Restaurant Series 2010
- Triple Three: Platinum Award and Best Buffet Restaurant — Simply Dining Restaurants Guide 2010
- Mandarin Court Chinese Restaurant: Gold Award — Simply Dining Restaurants Guide 2010
- Chatterbox — Simply Dining Restaurants Guide 2010

Accolades in 2011
Meritus Hotels & Resorts:

- Heritage Brand and Most Popular Heritage Brand — Singapore Brand Prestige Award 2011 by ASME and Lianhe Zao Bao
- Lifetime Achievement Award: Michael Sengol — Asian Gastronomic Awards of Excellence 2011 (in conjunction with the World Gourmet Summit)
- Leading CEO Award: Michael Sengol — The Singapore HR Awards 2011 by Singapore Human Resources Institute
- Most Admired Enterprise: Corporate Social Responsibility — 2011 ASEAN Most Admired Enterprises by ASEAN Business Awards
- Lifetime Achievement Award: Michael Sengol — Hospitality Asia Platinum Awards Regional Series 2011–2013 by World Asia Publishing

Mandarin Orchard Singapore:

- Champion, Hotel Category — "Our Productivity Story" 2011 Competition by Pacific Asia Travel Association (PATA)
- Hotel Security Excellence Award 2011 — Singapore Hotel Association
- Singapore Green Hotel Awards 2011 — Singapore Hotel Association
- Meritorious Defence Partner Awards 2011 — Ministry of Defence, Singapore
- Fire Safety Award 2011 — Singapore Hotel Association
- Anne Wong (Recipient): Employee of the Year Award 2011 — Singapore Hotel Association
- Mandarin Court Chinese Restaurant and Triple Three — Singapore Tatler Best Restaurant Series 2011
- Triple Three — Singapore Top Restaurants 2010/2011 by Wine & Dine
- Top 4 in Hotel Industry Category: Mandarin Orchard Singapore (79.8 percent) — The Customer Satisfaction Index of Singapore (CSISG) 2011 by the Institute of Service Excellence at Singapore Management University
- Executive Sous Chef Liew Tien Heong: Gold Winner, HAPA Master Chef (Asian Cuisine) and Executive Chef Shigeru Akashi: Platinum Winner HAPA Chef of the Year — Hospitality Asia Platinum Awards (HAPA) Regional Series 2011–2013 by World Asia Publishing

- 264 Individual Silver, Gold and Platinum Recipients — Excellent Service Award (EXSA) 2011 by Spring Singapore

Accolades in 2012
Meritus Hotels & Resorts:

- Global Winner: Luxury Brand — 2012 World Luxury Hotel Awards
- Meritus Hotels & Resorts: Heritage Brand — Singapore Brand Prestige Award 2012
- Most Admired ASEAN Enterprise for the category of "Growth" — 2012 ASEAN Business Awards
- Most Admired ASEAN Enterprise for the category of "Innovation" — 2012 ASEAN Business Awards

Mandarin Orchard Singapore:

- ASEAN Green Hotel Recognition Award 2012
- Best Hotel for Singapore — International Hotel Awards 2012 (Asia Pacific)
- Country Winner (Singapore): Luxury Hotel — 2012 World Luxury Hotel Awards
- Chatterbox: Heritage Brand — Singapore Brand Prestige Award 2012
- Hotel Security Excellence Award 2012 — Singapore Hotel Association
- Meritorious Defence Partner Award — Ministry of Defence (Singapore)
- Singapore Service Class — SPRING
- Mandarin Court, Triple Three and Chatterbox — Wine and Dine Singapore's Top Restaurants 2011/2012
- Mandarin Court and Triple Three — Singapore Tatler Best Restaurant Series 2012

Accolades in 2013–2014
Mandarin Orchard Singapore:

- Best Hotel (Singapore) and Best Hotel (Asia Pacific) — Asia Pacific Hotel Awards 2013–2014
- Best City Hotel (Singapore) — 24th Annual TTG Travel Awards 2013

Accolades in 2015
Mandarin Orchard Singapore:

- Chatterbox: Heritage Brand — Singapore Prestige Brand Award 2015
- Best City Hotel (Singapore) — 26th Annual TTG Travel Awards 2015
- Excellent Service Award 2015
- Singapore Green Hotel Award 2015

APPENDIX 3

DIVESTMENT OF OUE LIMITED AND A NON-EXHAUSTIVE LIST OF OUE LIMITED PROPERTIES AND COMMERCIAL TRANSFORMATION PROJECTS

Regulatory changes requiring Singapore banks to divest non-financial businesses were first introduced in the bill for the Banking (Amendment) Act 2001. This bill was announced by then Deputy Prime Minister Lee Hsien Loong and passed by Parliament on 16 May 2001, giving the amendment legislative effect with a grace period of three years for banks to comply, as detailed in Section 34 of the amended Banking Act.[10]

On 22 August 2003, the MAS announced it would extend the grace period for Singapore banks to divest to 17 July 2006 upon application for extension due to difficult market conditions.[11] The revised framework for the enforcement and implementation of the Act via the amendments to the Banking Regulations were subsequently announced on 5 May 2004.[12]

Figure A1 Timeline of OUE Limited Divestment

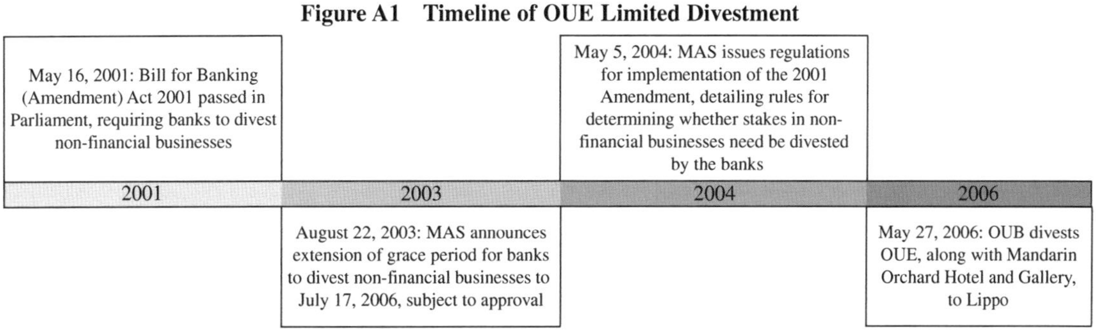

Source: Monetary Authority of Singapore; United Overseas Bank

The financial adviser to United Overseas Bank for the divestment of "Overseas Union Enterprise Limited" was Credit-Suisse, and the deal structure involved two parts: the divestment of "Overseas Union Enterprise Limited" by United Overseas Bank and its affiliated entities for S$989.9 million and a put option granted by Lippo Property Investment Private Limited to United Overseas Bank and Overseas Union Facilities worth S$68.2 million for the divestment of 16.67 percent of the issued shares in OUB Centre to Lippo Property.[13] In this announcement, it was stated that the rationale for the divestment was "undertaken with a view towards compliance

[10] See Monetary Authority of Singapore (2001).

[11] See Monetary Authority of Singapore (2003).

[12] See Monetary Authority of Singapore (2004).

[13] See United Overseas Bank (2006).

with the pronouncements of the Monetary Authority of Singapore", specifically, the aforementioned regulations on the "segregation of financial and non-financial businesses".[14]

The relevant portions of the United Overseas Bank announcement of the rationale for divesting has been extracted for illustration:

Figure A2 Rationale for OUE Limited Divestment

> 1.3 Rationale. Both the OUE Divestment and the OUB Centre Divestment have been undertaken with a view towards compliance with the pronouncements of the Monetary Authority of Singapore ("**MAS**") and the relevant provisions of the Banking Act, Chapter 10 of Singapore (the "**Banking Act**") and the Banking Regulations 2001, as amended or modified from time to time (the "**Banking Regulations**") on the segregation of financial and non-financial businesses. Singapore incorporated banks are required to divest their interests in non-financial businesses to reduce the aggregate interests held by them and their affiliated entities (as defined in the Banking Regulations) ("**Affiliated Entities**") to not more than 10% or such other percentage as MAS may specify (the "**Banking Act Requirement**"). UOB has obtained the approval of the MAS to comply with the Banking Act Requirement by 17 July 2006.

Source: Adapted from United Overseas Bank (2006)

At the time of acquisition of OUE Limited, the company held a portfolio of more than 10 properties, spanning the hospitality, retail, commercial, industrial and residential sectors, to name a few (Table A2).

The following brief non-exhaustive list illustrates OUE Limited's strategy of asset enhancement and value creation for other commercial transformation projects.

(i) Crowne Plaza Changi Airport Hotel

OUE Limited acquired the hotel, which was officially opened in 2008, for a property value of S$293 million in 2011.[15] Dr Riady was keen to purchase the hotel due to the heightened demand for tourism and limited hotels for sale in the Singapore market, as he shared during an interview with the case study report team in 2015, that "a lot of hotels are owned by family groups, and a lot of time they don't put their hotels up for sale on the market".[16] Therefore, when the opportunity arose to purchase the hotel in 2011, OUE Limited was quick to seize it.

A hotel surrounded by palm trees and bougainvillea, it was named World's Best Airport Hotel and Best Airport Hotel in Asia by London-based Skytrax, a global source of airline ratings and reviews in 2015.[17] The 320-room hotel has embarked on a 10-storey extension to add additional

[14] See United Overseas Bank (2006, p. 1).

[15] See Overseas Union Enterprise Limited (2011).

[16] Asia Competitiveness Institute interviews of senior management staff of OUE Limited (2015).

[17] See Vasko (2015).

Table A2 List of Properties with OUE Limited at Time of Acquisition in 2006

Property name	Property description	Property type	Country
Overseas Union Building (Hotel: Meritus Mandarin Singapore, Shopping arcade: Mandarin Gallery)	A 39-storey main tower with a 37-storey South Wing extension known as the "Meritus Mandarin Singapore" with 1,051 rooms and shopping arcade at 333 Orchard Road	Hospitality and Retail	Singapore
Marina Mandarin Singapore	A 640-room hotel, operations first began in January 1987	Hospitality	Singapore
Change Alley Aerial Plaza	Comprising a shopping ramp of 47 shop units and a tower building erected on two adjoining sites at Collyer Quay	Retail	Singapore
Overseas Union House	An eight-storey office and carpark building with 720 car park facilities at Collyer Quay	Commercial	Singapore
The Parisian	A residential property development located at 21 Angullia Park	Residential	Singapore
Asiawide Industrial Building	Two factory/office units at 5 Pereira Road	Industrial	Singapore
Cavenagh House	Freehold property located at 100 Clemenceau Avenue North, unit number #13-107	Classified as property, plant and equipment	Singapore
Meritus Mandarin Haikou	A 23-storey hotel with 318 rooms at Wenhua Road, Longhua District, Central Haikou City	Hospitality	The People's Republic of China
Meritus Shantou	A 21-storey hotel with 318 rooms at Jin Sha East Road, Shantou, Guangdong Province	Hospitality	The People's Republic of China
Shanghai JC Mandarin	515-room hotel located on Nanjing Road	Hospitality	The People's Republic of China
Meritus Pelangi Beach Resort and Spa Langkawi	350-room resort in Langkawi	Hospitality	Malaysia

Source: OUE Limited

capacity to the hotel. The extension is slated to cost S$82 million and will be completed in June 2016.[18]

(ii) OUE Bayfront, OUE Tower and OUE Link

OUE Bayfront used to be the historic Overseas Union House. As reported in the 2006 OUE Limited annual report, it consisted of an old carpark building with 720 carpark facilities and a restaurant.[19] Its ancillary properties, OUE Tower and OUE Link, were formerly known respectively as Change Alley Aerial plaza and Change Alley Link Bridge, with asset enhancement works completed in 2011.[20]

OUE Limited purchased it in 2010 and rebuilt it as a commercial complex housing OUE Limited's corporate head office and other corporate offices. The renovation involved

[18] See Heng (2016).

[19] See Overseas Union Enterprise Limited (2007, p. 30).

[20] See OUE Limited (2015, p. 8).

demolishing the earlier building and rebuilding, as shared by Dr Riady during interviews with the case study report team in 2015, that he was clear that "we are a premium developer; this is a corporate office. Everybody that walks into this place must have that wow-factor and believe in us, that we can add value."[21]

The refurbishment was completed in 2011, showcasing an 18-storey office tower with panoramic views of Singapore's scenic Marina Bay.[22] The building also offers state-of-the-art amenities, waterfront views and features a restaurant "Me @OUE" on floor 19.

(iii) One Raffles Place

One Raffles Place was one of the original assets of OUE Limited, formerly known as the OUB Centre Limited. Also located in the central business district, the property was built by OUB banker Dr Lien Ying Chow and launched in 1988.[23]

After the acquisition by Lippo group, the property was transformed from an office tower to a one-stop hub for quality dining, indulgent lifestyle services and convenient daily necessities. The development comprises three parts. Tower One is a 62-storey commercial building, offering Singapore's tallest observation point. The retail section is a five-storey retail podium with one level of basement shopping. Tower Two, a 38-storey commercial building, was officially opened on 18 September 2012.[24]

(iv) OUE Downtown

In line with the company's strategy to enhance assets based in strategic locations, both DBS Towers One and Two, located near the Maria Bay area at 6 Shenton Way, were acquired by OUE Limited in 2010 for S$870.5 million.[25] Both DBS Towers One and Two were commercial buildings located at the heart of Singapore's central business district. DBS Tower One was a 49-storey building constructed in 1975, while Tower Two was a 37-storey building completed some 20 years later in 1994.[26] Both towers have been transformed into a mixed-use development and the enhancement work at OUE Downtown is targeted for completion by end 2016.[27]

(v) U.S. Bank Tower

In 2013, OUE Limited acquired a 72-storey office space located in downtown Los Angeles for US$367.5 million.[28] The company also plans to invest US$50 million in refurbishments to transform the tower to include an outdoor bar, two upscale restaurants and an open-air observation deck.[29]

---

21 Asia Competitiveness Institute interviews of senior management staff of OUE Limited (2015).

22 See Overseas Union Enterprise Limited (2012, p. 12).

23 See Chua (2011).

24 See One Raffles Place (2014).

25 See Overseas Union Enterprise Limited (2010).

26 See Teo (2010).

27 See OUE Limited (2015, p. 52).

28 See Vincent (2013).

29 See Vincent (2015).

The purchase of the U.S. bank tower was also an opportunity for OUE Limited to step foot in the U.S. market and raise the corporate profile of the company. The valuation of the asset based upon the OUE Limited 2014 annual report was US$487 million.[30] The asset enhancement works are expected to be completed by 2016.[31]

As of 2014, the portfolio of properties of OUE Limited has increased to at least 15 notable assets (Table A3).

Table A3 Shortlist of OUE Limited Property Portfolio in 2014

Property name	Property description	Property type	Country
Mandarin Orchard Singapore	A 39-storey main tower with a 37-storey South Wing extension, with 1,077 rooms at 333 Orchard Road	Hospitality	Singapore
Mandarin Gallery	Four-storey retail property with a 152 metre frontage along Orchard Road	Retail	Singapore
OUE Downtown	Mixed-use hub, comprising two tower blocks OUE Downtown 1 and OUE Downtown 2, as well as a retail mall named "Downtown Gallery" with a 262 metre frontage, completion expected in 2016	Commercial, Residential and Retail	Singapore
OUE Bayfront	Asset enhancement of Overseas Union House completed in 2011, into an 18-storey premium Grade-A office building	Commercial	Singapore
OUE Tower	Formerly the Change Alley Aerial Plaza Tower, an ancillary property to OUE Bayfront located at 60 Collyer Quay	Retail	Singapore
OUE Link	Formerly the Change Alley Link Bridge, an ancillary property to OUE Bayfront located at 62 Collyer Quay	Retail	Singapore
OUE Twin Peaks	A residential project, 99 year leasehold development comprising two identical 35-storey towers	Residential	Singapore
One Raffles Place	Revitalisation of shopping mall, opened May 2014, and redevelopment of One Raffles Place Tower 2 into a 38-storey office building from a low-rise building completed in August 2012	Commercial and Retail	Singapore
Crowne Plaza Changi Airport	320-room business hotel, with an additional 243 rooms being built in an adjacent site	Hospitality	Singapore
Marina Mandarin Singapore	A 575-room hotel, operations first began in January 1987	Hospitality	Singapore
Cavenagh House	Freehold property located at 100 Clemenceau Avenue North, unit number #13-107	Classified as property, plant and equipment	Singapore

(Continued)

[30] See OUE Limited (2015, p. 14).

[31] *Ibid* (p. 39).

Table A3 (*Continued*)

Property name	Property description	Property type	Country
Roche Building	Freehold property located at 30 Shaw Road, units number #03-03 and #03-04	(Undeclared)	Singapore
U.S. Bank Tower	Acquired in June 2013, one of the world's 100 tallest buildings located in southern California to undergo asset enhancement	Commercial and Retail	United States of America
Lippo Plaza	36-storey Grade-A commercial building located in central Shanghai	Commercial	The People's Republic of China
Meritus Pelangi Beach Resort and Spa Langkawi	350-room resort in Langkawi	Hospitality	Malaysia

Source: OUE Limited (2015)

APPENDIX 4
FORMULAS HIGHLIGHTED IN THE CASE STUDY

DISCOUNTED CASH FLOW METHOD: FORMULA

The discounted cash flow method as it applies to real estate is detailed as follows:

$$V = \frac{NOI_1}{(1+r_1)} + \frac{NOI_2}{(1+r_2)^2} + \cdots + \frac{NOI_T}{(1+r_T)^T} + \frac{P_T}{(1+r_T)^T}$$

where V is the value of the real estate asset, r_n is the discount rate at period n, NOI_n is the net operating income less debt obligations and capital expenditures at period n and P_T is the terminal value of the real estate asset.

COMPUTING LEASE TERM, VACANCY BETWEEN LEASES, PROBABILITY OF RENEWAL AND VACANCY RATE IN ESTIMATING CASH INFLOWS

To compute the lease term T,

$$T = f(L, V, P) = \frac{L(1-P)}{V} - L(1-P)$$

To compute the vacancy between leases L,

$$L = f(T, V, P) = \frac{-VT}{P + V - PV - 1}$$

To compute the probability of renewal P,

$$P = f(L, V, T) = \frac{VT}{LV - L} + 1$$

As such, vacancy rate V,

$$V = \frac{L(1-P)}{T + L(1-P)}$$

ESTIMATING CASH INFLOWS

The estimation of cash inflows can be done with the following three methods:

- Method 1 assumes that value increases at the expected inflation rate. *I* represents the average expected inflation rate, while *n* represents the number of years till the end of the investment horizon. This is expressed as follows:

$$\text{Terminal Value} = \text{Current Value}^{\,I * n}$$

- Method 2 assumes that cash flows in the terminal year will continue to grow constantly in perpetuity. Here, this is expressed by the discount rate *r*, the growth rate *g*, and cash flow at period *n* + 1, as shown by CF_{n+1},

$$\text{Terminal Value of Equity/Asset}_n = \frac{\text{Expected CF}_{n+1}}{r-g}$$

- Method 3 divides operating income by the capitalisation rate,

$$\text{Property value} = \frac{\text{Operating income after taxes}}{\text{Capitalisation rate}}$$

AVERAGE LABOUR PRODUCTIVITY FORMULA

Average labour productivity is *ALP*, value added is *VA*, operational revenue is *OR* and *L* is total employment.

(1) *ALP* is calculated as a fraction, *VA* over *L*,

$$ALP = \frac{VA}{L}$$

Multiplying both the numerator and denominator of (1) with *OR* yields the following:

$$ALP = \frac{VA}{L} = \frac{VA}{OR} \times \frac{OR}{L}$$

APPENDIX 5

DATA TABLES FOR FIGURES AND CHARTS IN THE REPORT

Table A4 Mandarin Orchard Singapore Data Values and Indicators

Year	Valuation (S$ m)	Gross operating revenue (S$'000s)	Operating expenses (S$'000s)	Gross operating profit (S$'000s)	Gross operating profit margin (%)	Number of hotel rooms	Average room rate/ average daily rate ($)	Average occupancy rate (%)	Revenue per available room ($)	Total hotel employees (persons)	Value added per employee ($)	Occupied rooms per employeed full-time equivalent	Gross floor area (sq ft)
2000	449.2	84,717	58,865	25,852	30.50	—	140.25	73.26	102.74	1,051	35,198	—	—
2001	404.75	76,919	54,767	22,152	28.80	1,200	156.56	61.57	96.40	994	45,934	—	—
2002	310.00	71,056	50,947	20,109	28.30	—	139.79	64.94	90.78	1,022	41,481	—	—
2003	276.00	65,475	47,598	17,877	27.30	1,200	120.90	61.65	74.53	974	39,131	—	—
2004	281.00	80,788	54,556	26,232	32.50	1,068	142.28	75.63	107.61	1,011	47,880	—	—
2005	375.00	89,752	55,377	34,375	38.30	1,064	168.88	76.85	129.79	1,044	52,602	—	1,170,242
2006	482.00	102,225	58,597	43,627	42.70	1,051	201.54	78.17	157.55	1,075	57,498	282.00	1,170,242
2007	813.00	121,664	57,304	64,360	52.90	1,200	240.00	85.06	204.13	992	83,793	329.00	1,170,251
2008	780.00	122,819	58,637	64,132	52.30	1,051	285.46	72.92	208.16	910	93,911	308.00	995,748
2009	800.00	95,081	51,343	43,738	46.00	1,051	207.56	74.52	154.66	848	78,575	337.00	990,286
2010	1,135.08	133,130	60,201	72,929	54.80	1,051	254.26	84.62	215.14	858	109,180	378.00	990,286
2011	1,180.00	151,096	64,184	86,912	57.50	1,051	277.34	85.76	237.86	816	129,230	403.00	990,286
2012	1,230.00	154,410	66,758	87,652	56.80	1,051	281.47	86.45	243.34	788	135,489	422.00	990,286
2013	1,220.00	156,580	72,550	84,030	53.70	1,077	274.36	92.25	253.11	824	88,513	432.00	990,277
2014	1,220.00	161,680	74,094	87,535	54.20	1,077	273.49	91.06	249.04	836	41,330	428.00	990,277

Table A5 Hospitality Indicators by Tiers and Industry Averages

	Average room rate/average daily rate ($)					Average occupancy rate (%)					Revenue per available room ($)				
	Industry average	Economy	Mid-tier	Upscale	Luxury	Industry average	Economy	Mid-tier	Upscale	Luxury	Industry average	Economy	Mid-tier	Upscale	Luxury
2005	$137.00	—	—	—	—	84.00%	—	—	—	—	$114.80	—	—	—	—
2006	$164.40	—	—	—	—	85.00%	—	—	—	—	$140.10	—	—	—	—
2007	$201.70	—	—	—	—	87.00%	—	—	—	—	$175.50	—	—	—	—
2008	$245.90	—	—	—	—	81.00%	—	—	—	—	$199.20	—	—	—	—
2009	$189.60	—	—	—	—	76.00%	—	—	—	—	$143.70	—	—	—	—
2010	$217.90	—	—	—	—	85.00%	—	—	—	—	$185.70	—	—	—	—
2011	$247.10	$110.30	$188.50	$279.30	$399.10	86.00%	85.30%	87.50%	87.30%	80.40%	$213.50	$94.30	$164.60	$243.90	$320.40
2012	$261.30	$110.70	$197.10	$301.40	$431.40	87.00%	84.90%	86.70%	87.80%	81.70%	$226.00	$94.00	$170.80	$264.70	$351.80
2013	$258.10	$100.40	$190.60	$268.50	$435.90	86.30%	84.20%	86.50%	85.90%	88.10%	$222.80	$84.60	$165.00	$230.70	$384.00
2014	$258.00	$109.80	$185.20	$266.80	$461.80	85.50%	80.10%	85.00%	87.20%	87.60%	$220.50	$87.80	$157.30	$232.50	$404.30

Table A6 Mandarin Gallery Data Values and Indicator

Year	Valuation (S$ million)	Gross revenue (S$'000s)	Property operating expenses (S$'000)	Gross operating profit (S$'000s)	Gross operating profit margin (%)	Occupancy rate (committed) (%)	Gross floor area (sq ft)	Net lettable area (sq ft)	Effective monthly gross retail rent per square feet ($)
2002	61.50	—	—	—	—	—	—	—	—
2003	60.00	—	—	—	—	—	—	—	—
2004	66.00	—	—	—	—	—	—	—	—
2005	68.00	7,193	1,739	5,454	75.83	99.20		66,457	8.76
2006	71.00	7,673	1,905	5,768	75.17	95.30		68,240	9.54
2007	135.00	9,158	1,876	7,282	79.52	96.80	183,881	69,287	11.75
2008	225.00	631	593	38	6.04	n.a.	188,207	n.a.	n.a.
2009	418.00	1,362	1,309	53	3.89	98.40	196,336	125,281	15.79
2010	520.00	32,068	12,041	20,027	62.45	100.00	196,337	125,280	20.45
2011	520.00	33,913	23,734	23,734	69.98	100.00	196,337	125,280	21.32
2012	540.00	32,731	24,894	24,894	76.06	98.90	196,337	125,282	21.52
2013	536.00	35,697	27,471	27,471	76.96	100.00	196,336	125,293	23.69
2014	536.00	37,243	28,261	28,261	75.88	98.20	196,336	125,293	23.6

Table A7 Monthly Wage Rates for the Hospitality Industry in Singapore

As of June 2005 Occupation name (2006)	Median basic (S$)	Median gross (S$)	As of June 2014 Occupation name (2015)	Median basic (S$)	Median gross (S$)
Hotel services manager	$3,000	$3,200	Hotel operations/Lodging services manager	$3,378	$3,552
Bellboy/Hotel porter	$880	$997	Bellboy/Hotel porter	$1,280	$1,370
Cleaner (Industrial establishment)	$650	$750	Cleaner and helper in hotels and related establishments	$1,224	$1,381
Housekeeper (Hotels and other establishments)	$1,800	$1,936	Housekeeper and related worker	$2,000	$2,346
Hotel receptionists	$1,330	$1,507	Receptionist and information clerk	$1,700	$1,863

APPENDIX 6

BEFORE AND AFTER — DESIGN AND FLOOR PLANS FOR MANDARIN ORCHARD SINGAPORE AND MANDARIN GALLERY

Table A8 Design Artwork and Concepts for Revamping Mandarin Gallery

Description	Picture
Artwork for façade of revamped Mandarin Gallery	
Design concept for frontage of Mandarin Gallery	
Concept for first floor of Mandarin Gallery	

(*Continued*)

Table A8 (*Continued*)

Description	Picture
Concept for second floor of Mandarin Gallery	
Concept for third floor of Mandarin Gallery	

Source: OUE Limited

The following "before and after" floor plans illustrate the development outline for Mandarin Orchard Singapore and Mandarin Gallery

Figure A3 Basement One (Before)

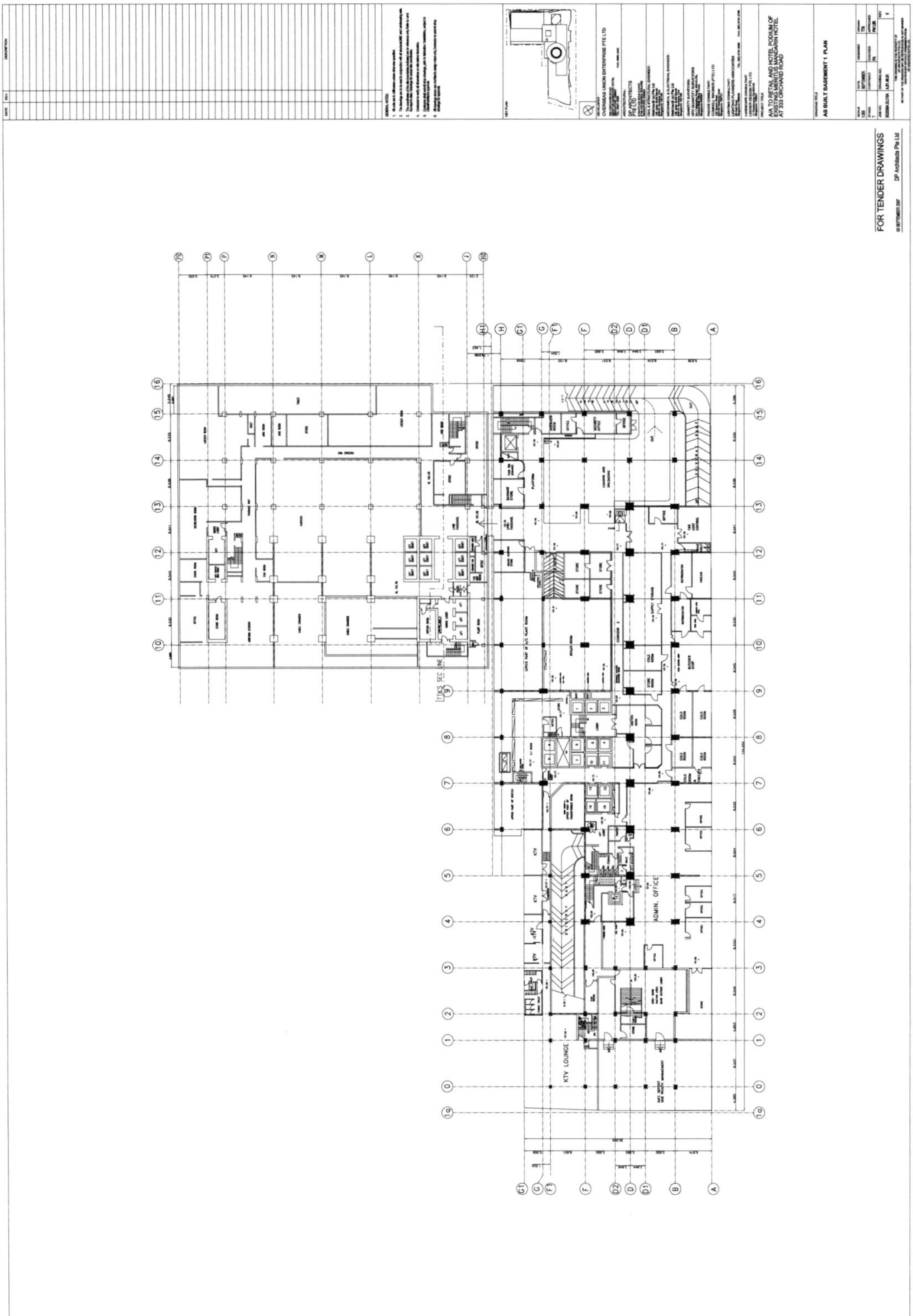

Source: OUE Limited

Figure A4 First Floor (Before)

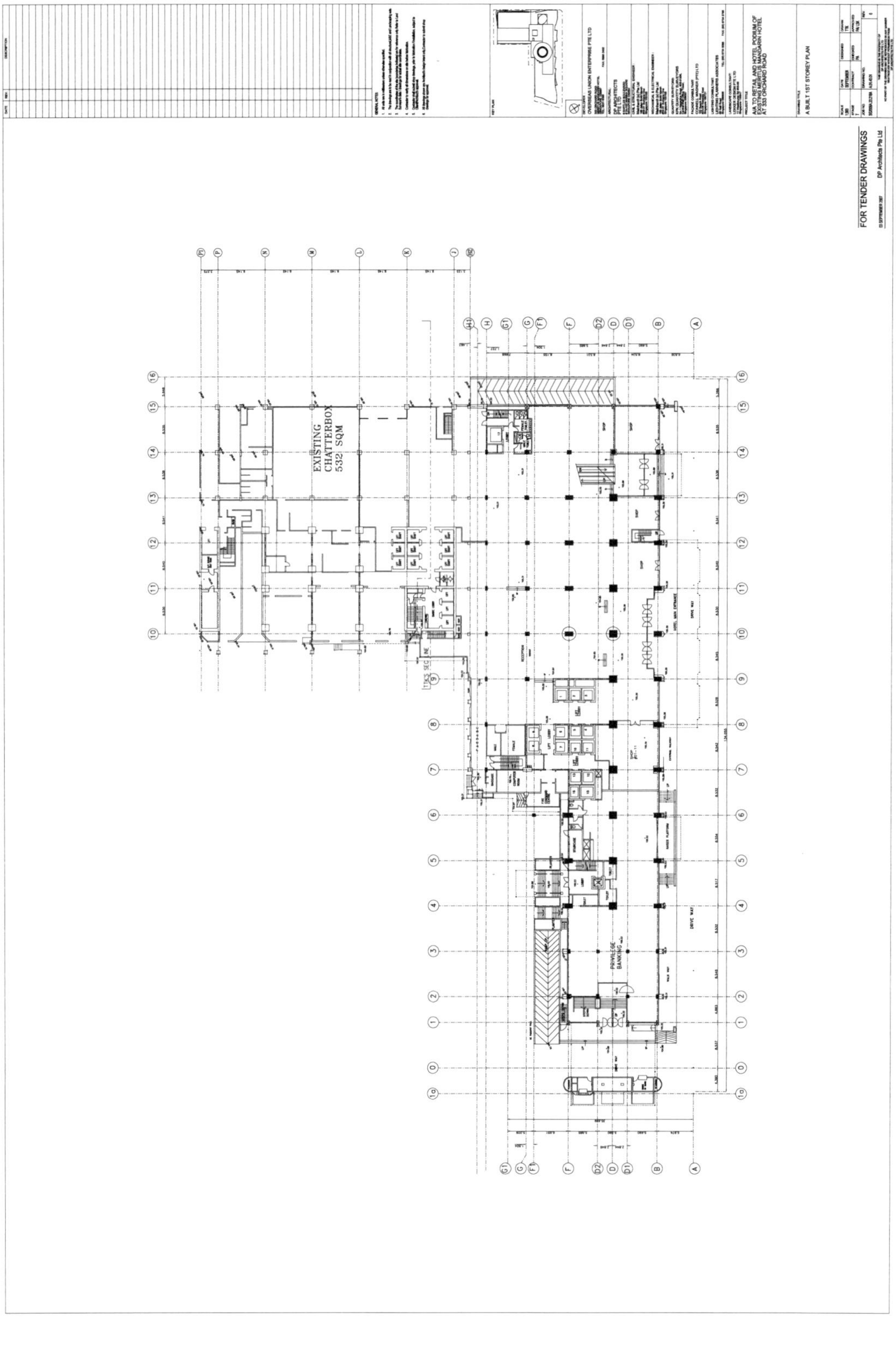

Source: OUE Limited

Figure A5 Second Floor (Before)

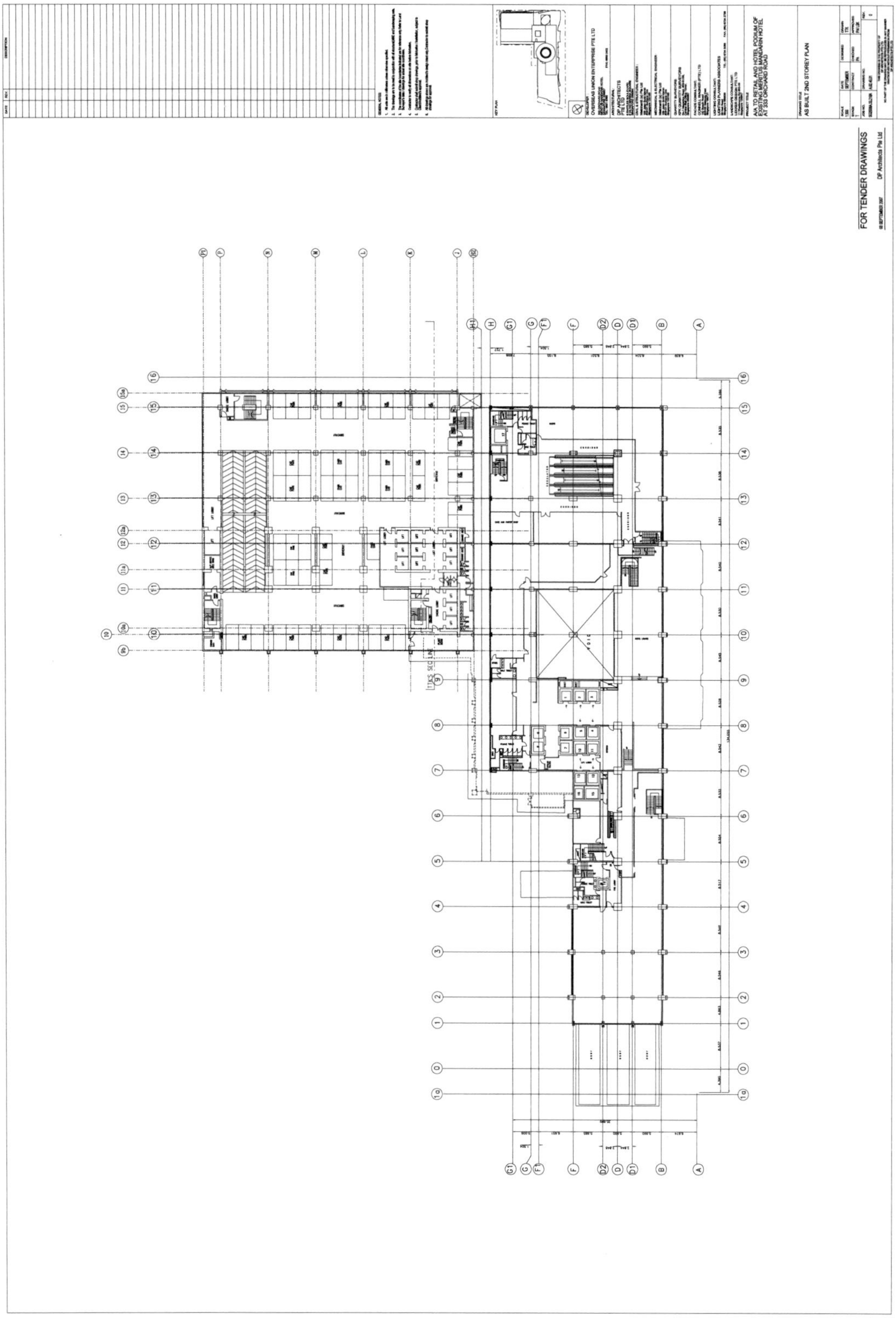

Source: OUE Limited

Figure A6 Third Floor (Before)

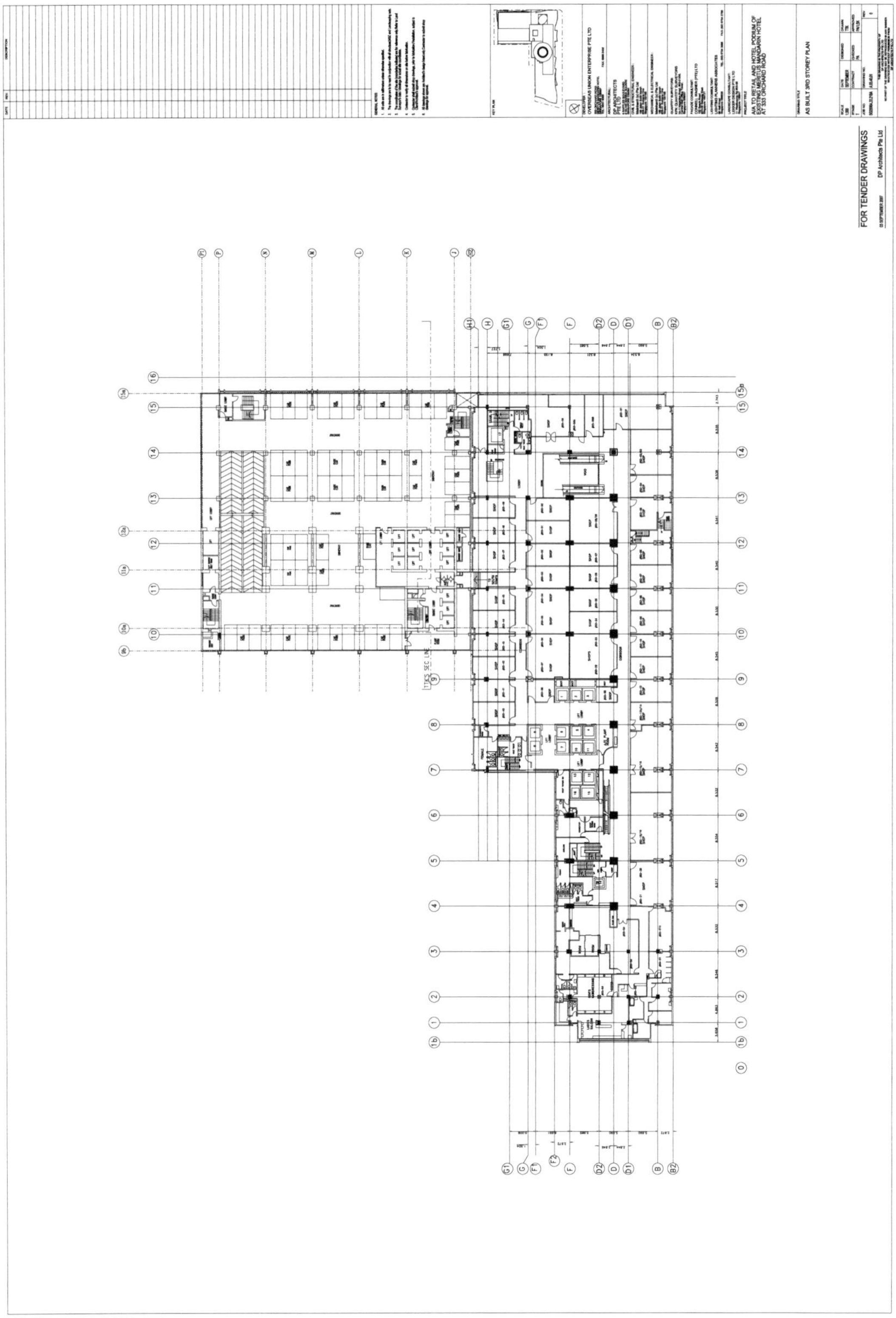

Source: OUE Limited

Figure A7 Fourth Floor (Before)

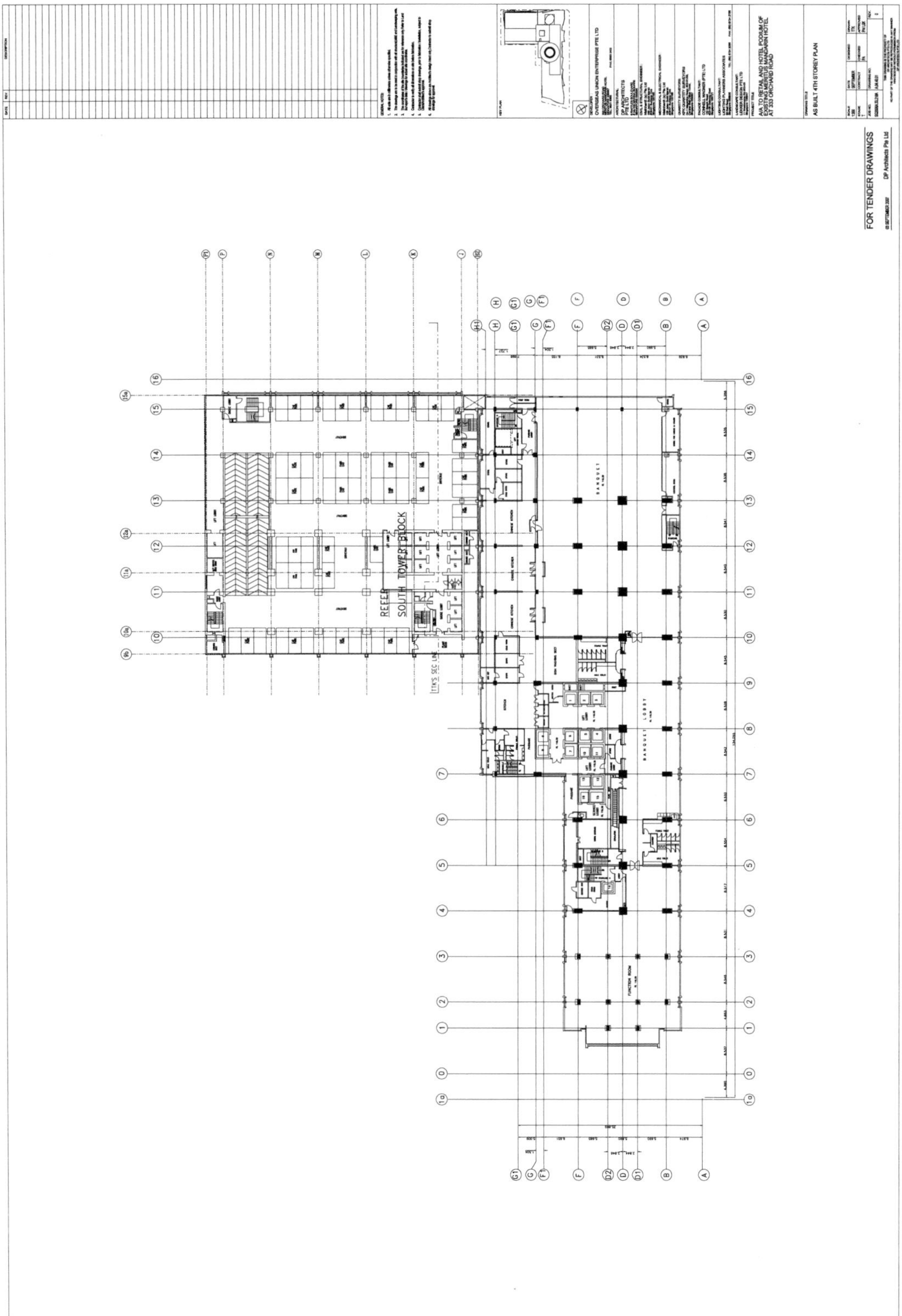

Source: OUE Limited

Figure A8 Fifth Floor (Before)

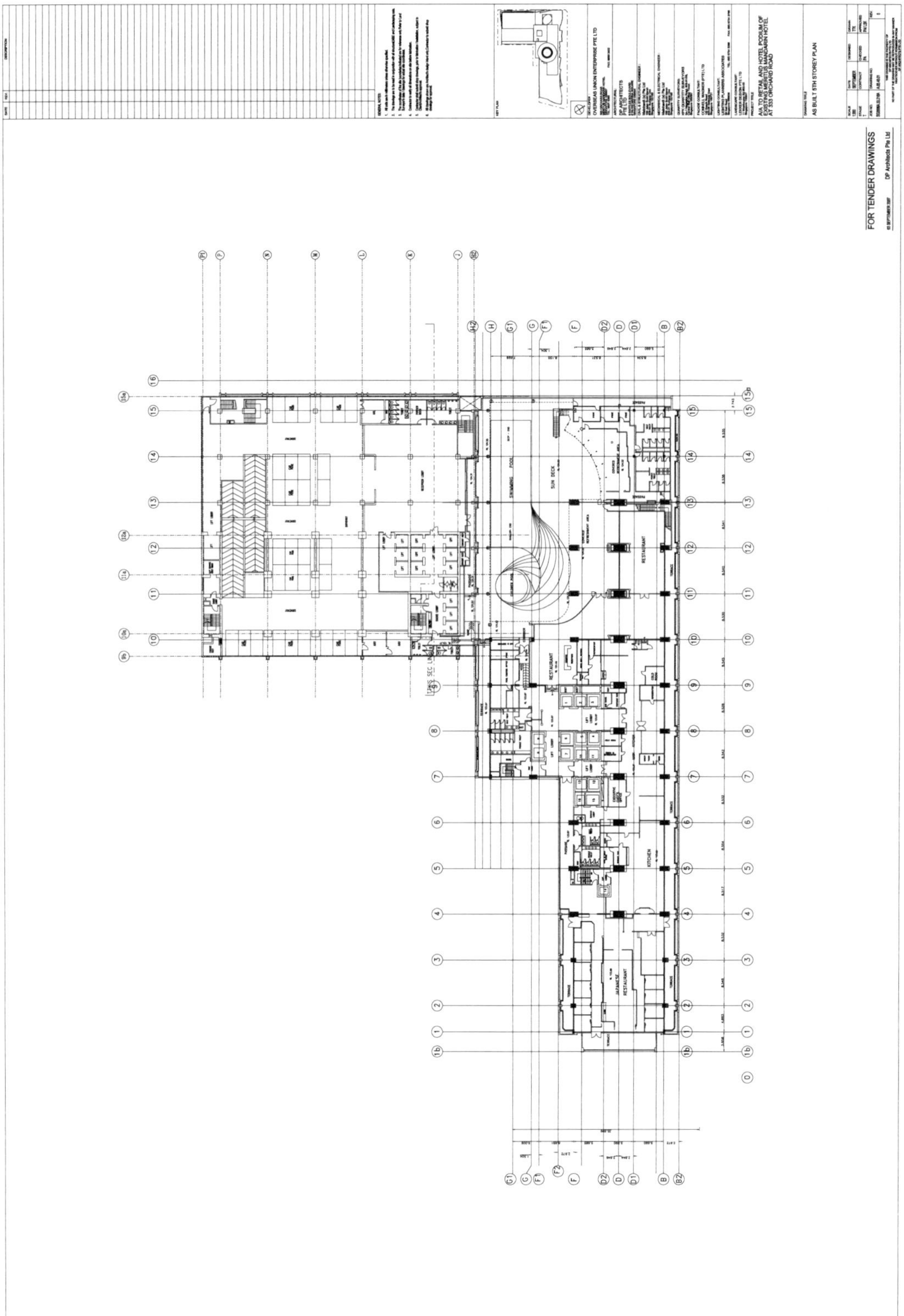

Source: OUE Limited

Figure A9 Basement One (After)

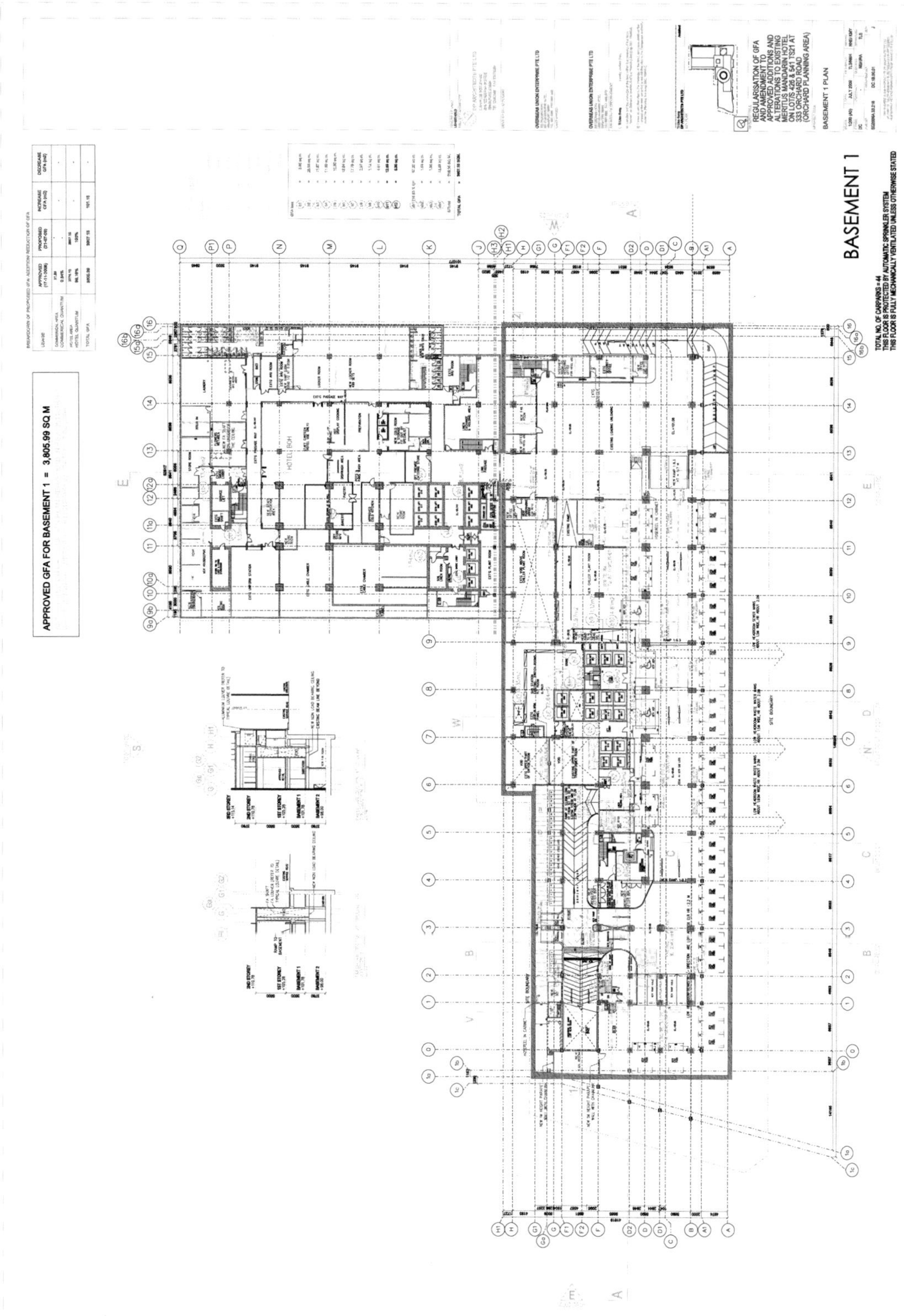

Source: OUE Limited

Figure A10 First Floor (After)

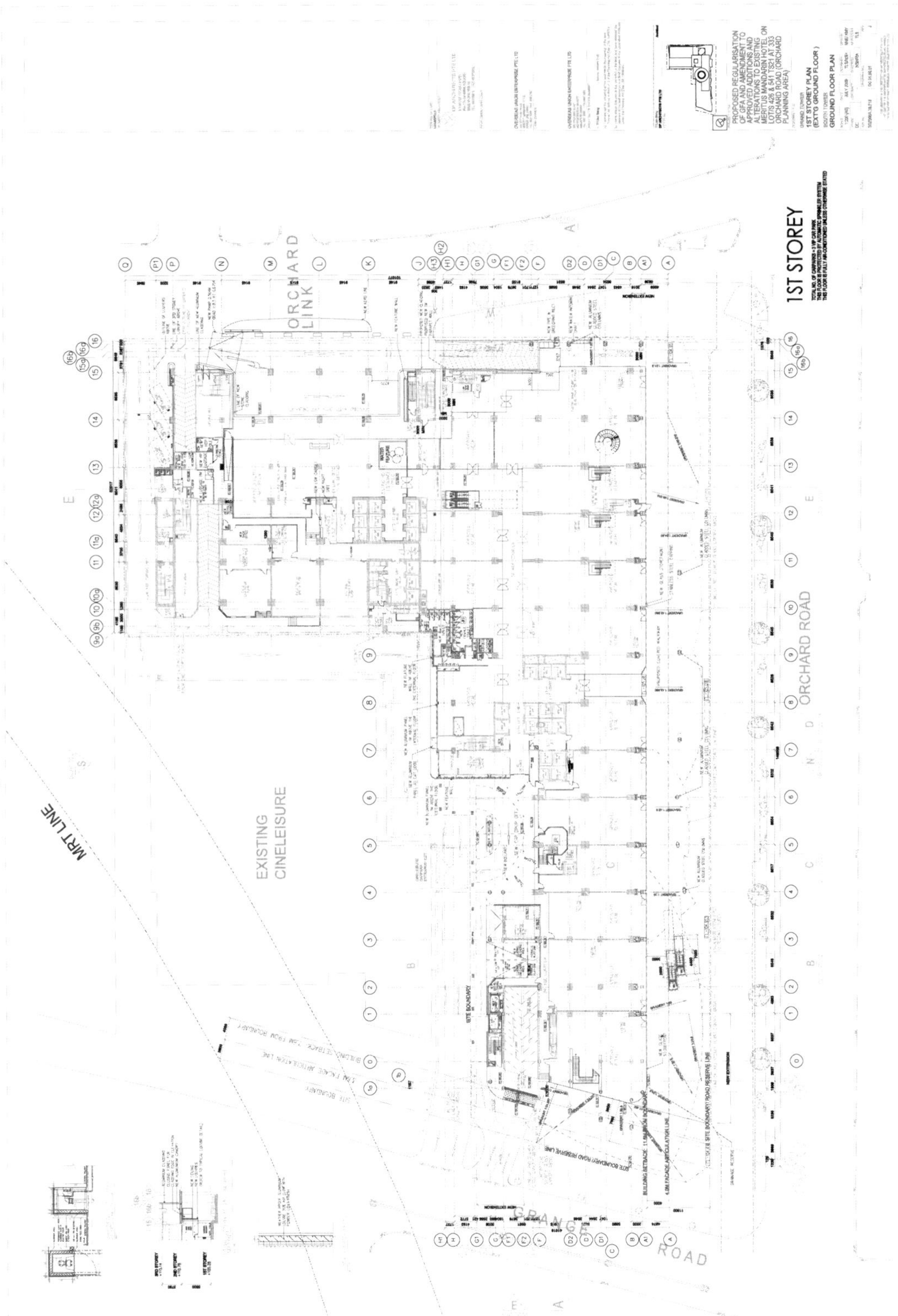

Source: OUE Limited

Figure A11 Second Floor (After)

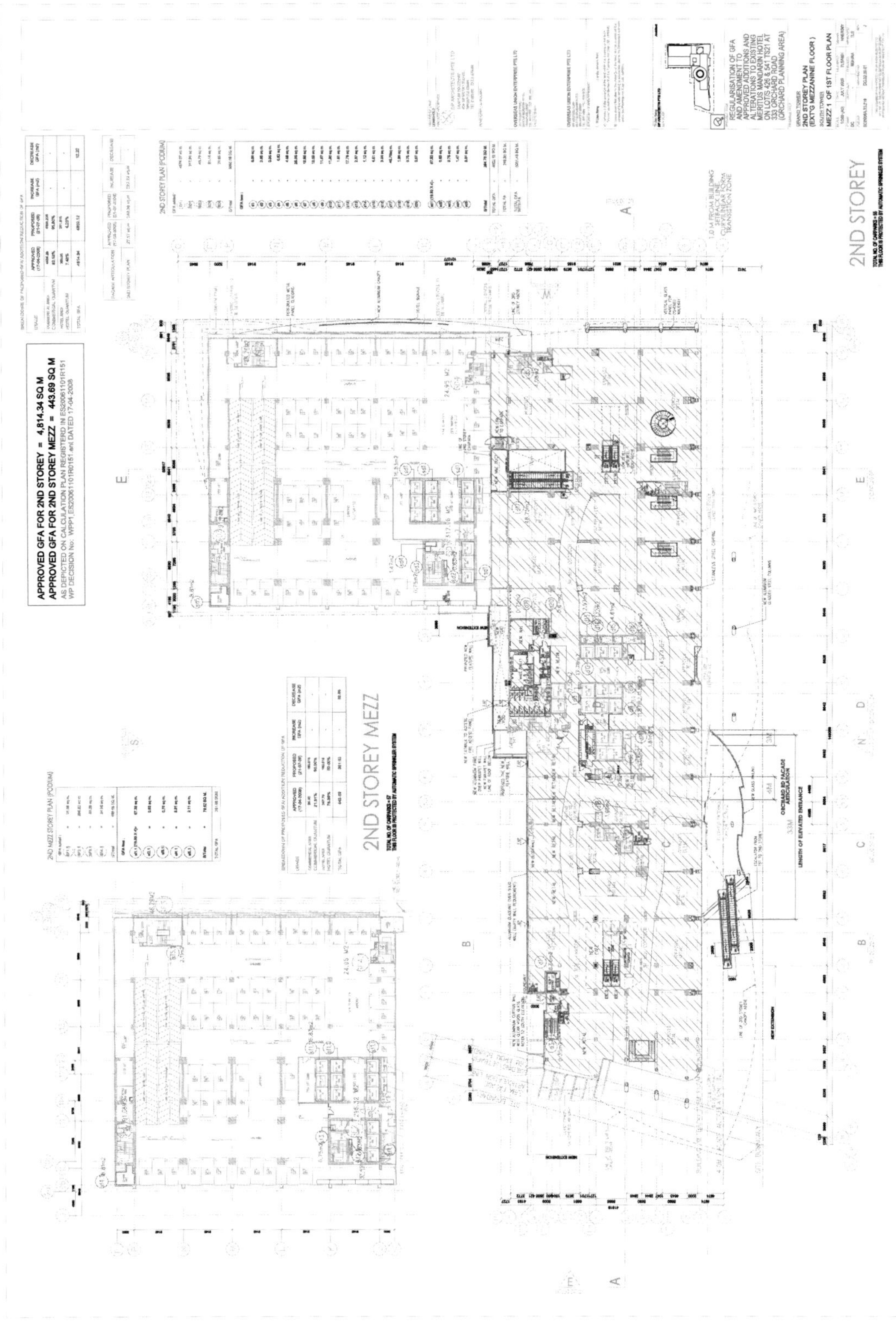

Source: OUE Limited

Figure A12 Third Floor (After)

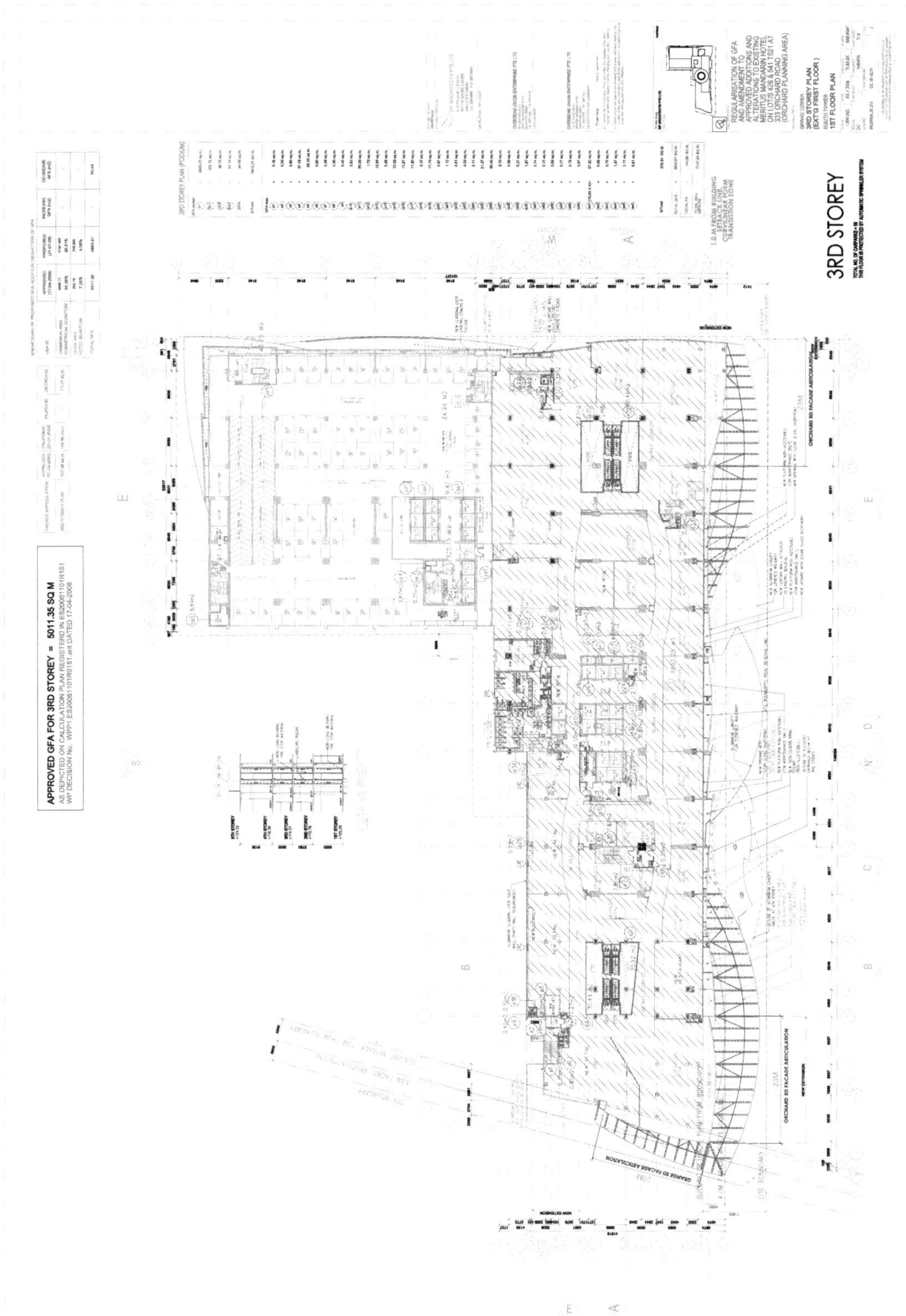

Source: OUE Limited

Figure A13 Fourth Floor (After)

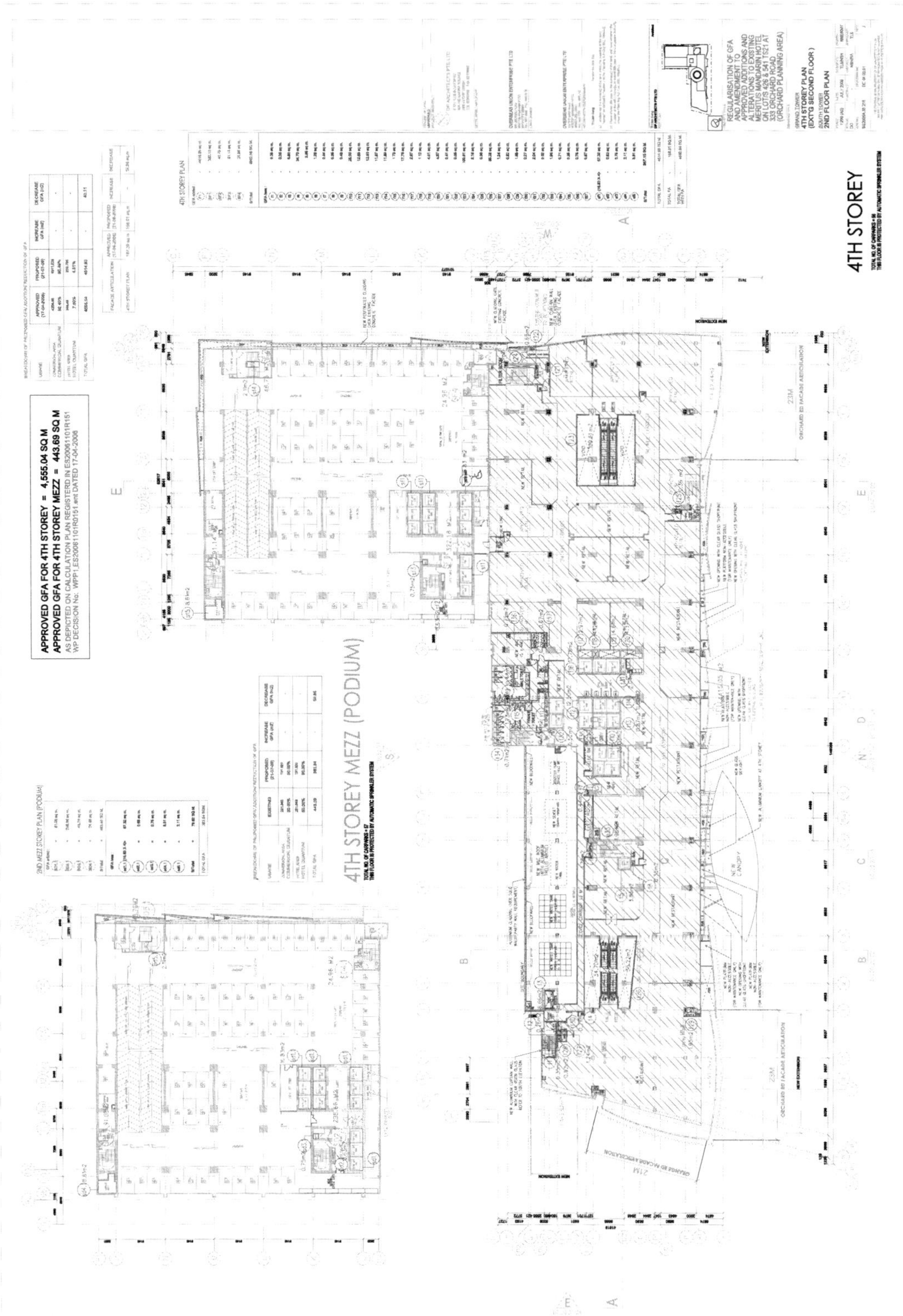

Source: OUE Limited

Figure A14 Fifth Floor (After)

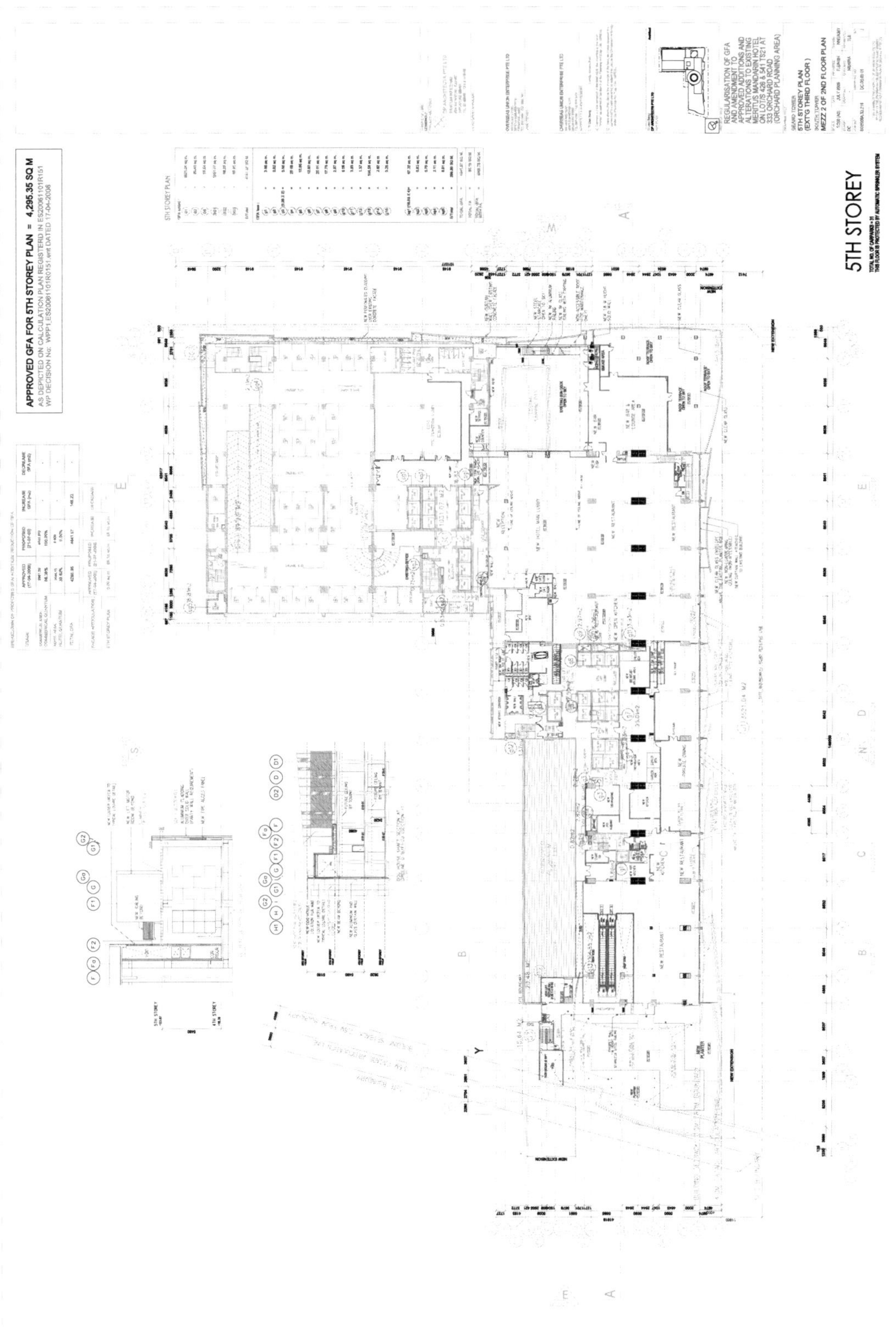

Source: OUE Limited